RUNAWAYS

DEAD WRONG

WRITER: **TERRY MOORE**

PENCILS: **HUMBERTO RAMOS**

INKS: **DAVE MEIKIS**

COLORS: **CHRISTINA STRAIN**

LETTERS: **VC'S JOE CARAMAGNA**
WITH **CORY PETIT**

ASSISTANT EDITOR: **DANIEL KETCHUM**

EDITOR: **NICK LOWE**

RUNAWAYS CREATED BY **BRIAN K. VAUGHAN** &
ADRIAN ALPHONA

COLLECTION EDITOR: **JENNIFER GRÜNWALD**

EDITORIAL ASSISTANT: **ALEX STARBUCK**

ASSISTANT EDITORS: **CORY LEVINE** & **JOHN DENNING**

EDITOR, SPECIAL PROJECTS: **MARK D. BEAZLEY**

SENIOR EDITOR, SPECIAL PROJECTS: **JEFF YOUNGQUIST**

SENIOR VICE PRESIDENT OF SALES: **DAVID GABRIEL**

BOOK DESIGNER: **RODOLFO MURAGUCHI**

EDITOR IN CHIEF: **JOE QUESADA**

PUBLISHER: **DAN BUCKLEY**

RUNAWAYS: DEAD WRONG. Contains material originally published in magazine form as RUNAWAYS VOL. 3 1-6. First printing 2009. ISBN# 978-0-7851-2939-4. Published by MARVEL PUBLISHING, INC., a subsidiary of MARVEL ENTERTAINMENT, INC. OFFICE OF PUBLICATION: 417 5th Avenue, New York, NY 10016. Copyright © 2008 and 2009 Marvel Characters, Inc. All rights reserved. $19.99 per copy in the U.S. (GST #R127032852); Canadian Agreement #40668537. All characters featured in this issue and the distinctive names and likenesses thereof, and all related indicia are trademarks of Marvel Characters, Inc. No similarity between any of the names, characters, persons, and/or institutions in this magazine with those of any living or dead person or institution is intended, and any such similarity which may exist is purely coincidental. **Printed in the U.S.A.** ALAN FINE, CEO Marvel Toys & Publishing Divisions and CMO Marvel Characters, Inc.; JIM SOKOLOWSKI, Chief Operating Officer; DAVID GABRIEL, SVP of Publishing Sales & Circulation; DAVID BOGART, SVP of Business Affairs & Talent Management; MICHAEL PASCIULLO, VP Merchandising & Communications; JIM O'KEEFE, VP of Operations & Logistics; DAN CARR, Executive Director of Publishing Technology; JUSTIN F. GABRIE, Director of Publishing & Editorial Operations; SUSAN CRESPI, Editorial Operations Manager; ALEX MORALES, Publishing Operations Manager; STAN LEE, Chairman Emeritus. For information regarding advertising in Marvel Comics or on Marvel.com, please contact Mitch Dane, Advertising Director, at mdane@marvel.com. For Marvel subscription inquiries, please call 800-217-9158.

10 9 8 7 6 5 4 3 2 1

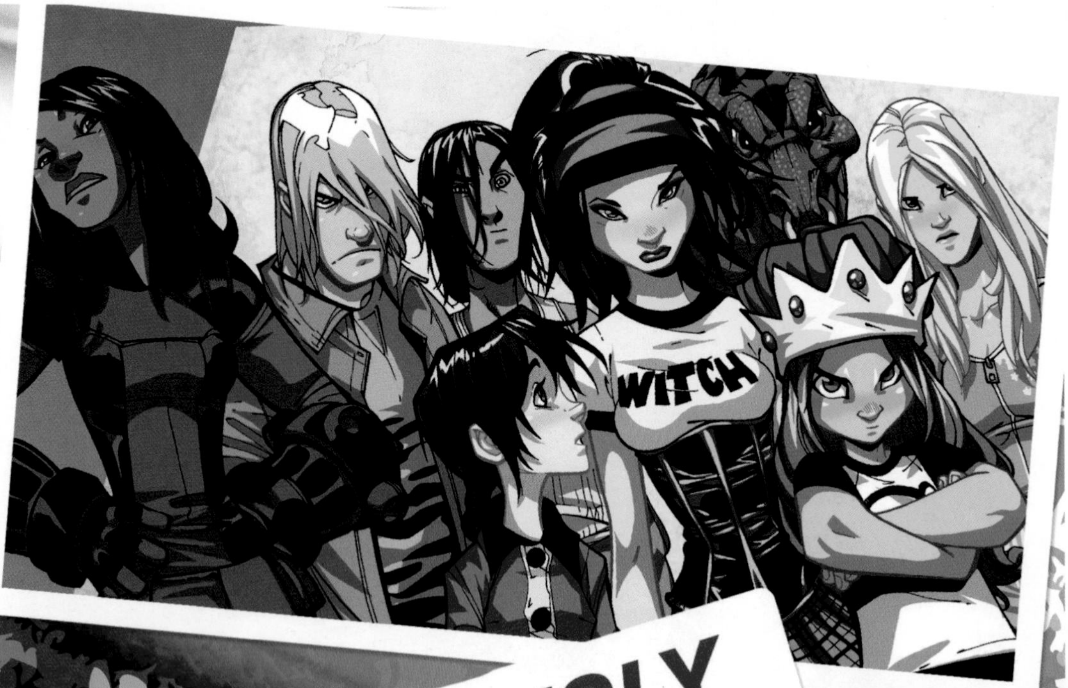
WITCH

PREVIOUSLY

AT SOME POINT IN THEIR LIVES, ALL KIDS THINK THAT THEIR PARENTS ARE EVIL. FOR MOLLY HAYES AND HER FRIENDS, THIS IS ESPECIALLY TRUE.

ONE NIGHT, MOLLY AND HER FRIENDS DISCOVERED THAT THEIR PARENTS WERE A GROUP OF SUPER-POWERED CRIME BOSSES WHO CALLED THEMSELVES "THE PRIDE." USING TECHNOLOGY AND RESOURCES STOLEN FROM THEIR PARENTS, THE TEENAGERS WERE ABLE TO STOP THE PRIDE AND BREAK THEIR CRIMINAL HOLD ON LOS ANGELES. BUT THEY'VE BEEN ON THE RUN ON EVER SINCE.

NOW, AFTER A FEW PERILOUS ADVENTURES IN NEW YORK CITY, NICO MINORU, CHASE STEIN, KAROLINA DEAN, MOLLY HAYES, VICTOR MANCHA, XAVIN AND KLARA ARE RETURNING TO THE CITY THEY KNOW BEST...

1

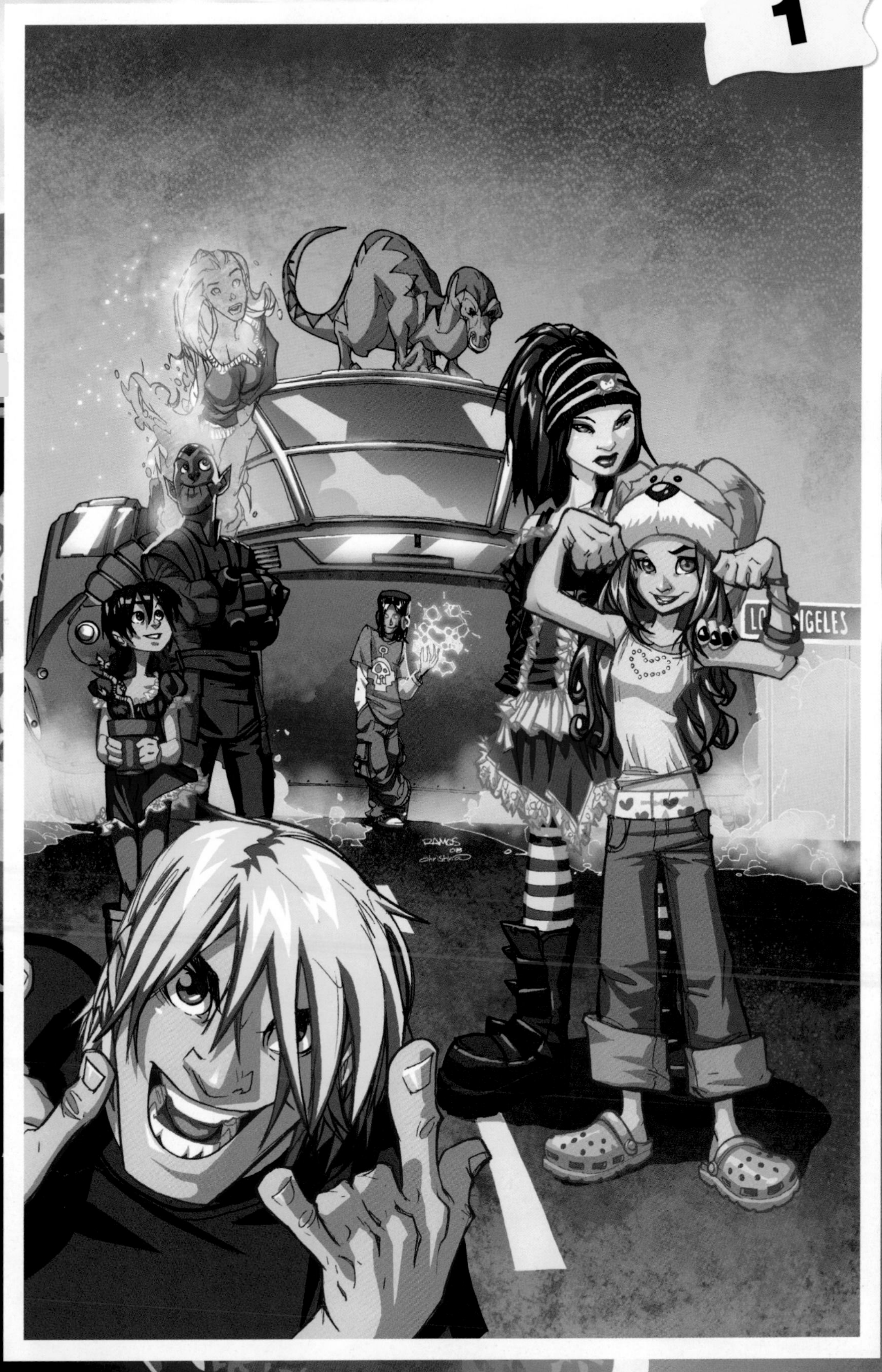
RAMOS
08
christina

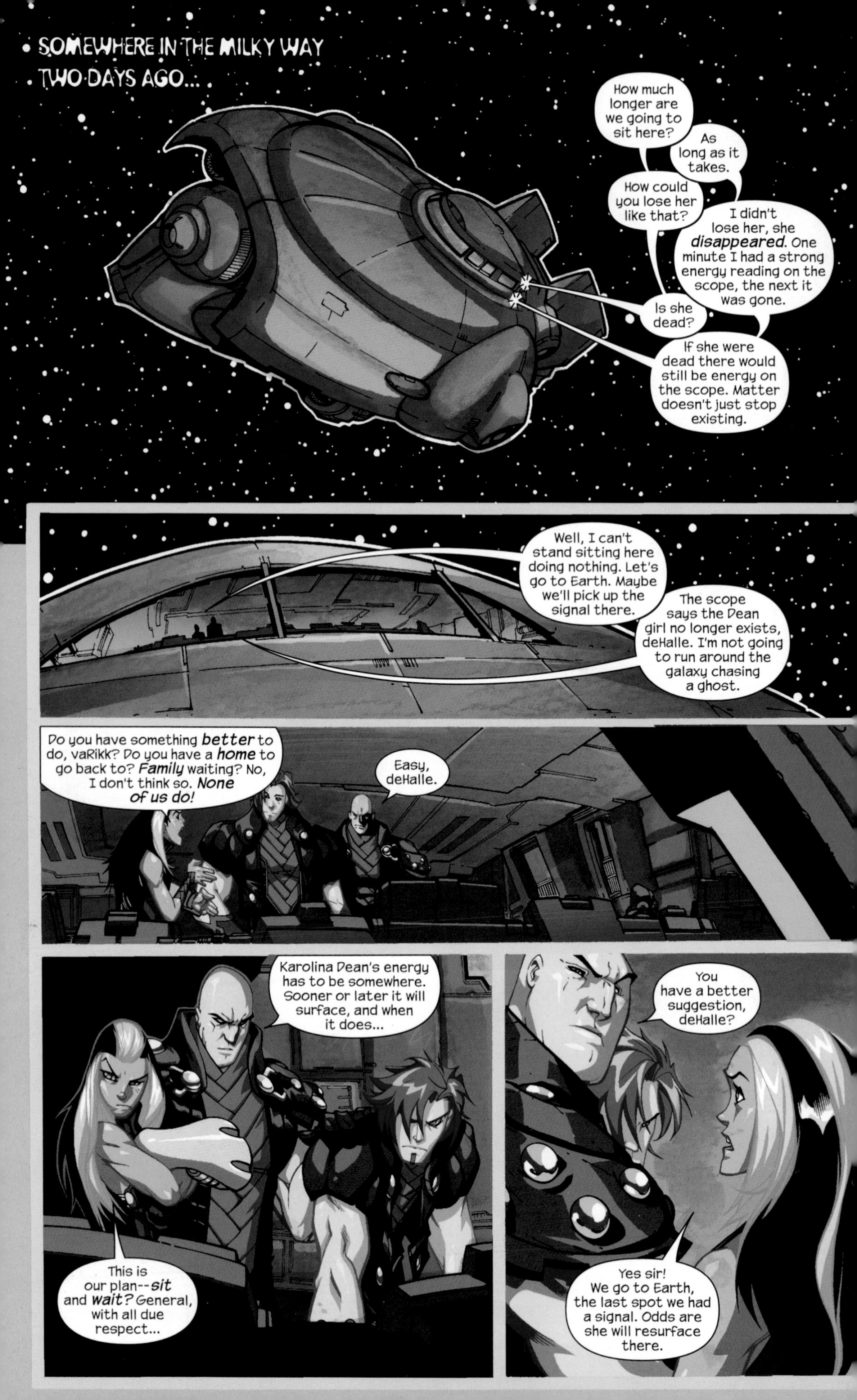
SOMEWHERE IN THE MILKY WAY
TWO DAYS AGO...
How much longer are we going to sit here?
As long as it takes.
How could you lose her like that?
I didn't lose her, she *disappeared*. One minute I had a strong energy reading on the scope, the next it was gone.
Is she dead?
If she were dead there would still be energy on the scope. Matter doesn't just stop existing.
Well, I can't stand sitting here doing nothing. Let's go to Earth. Maybe we'll pick up the signal there.
The scope says the Dean girl no longer exists, deHalle. I'm not going to run around the galaxy chasing a ghost.
Do you have something *better* to do, vaRikk? Do you have a *home* to go back to? *Family* waiting? No, I don't think so. *None of us do!*
Easy, deHalle.
Karolina Dean's energy has to be somewhere. Sooner or later it will surface, and when it does...
This is our plan--*sit* and *wait?* General, with all due respect...
You have a better suggestion, deHalle?
Yes sir! We go to Earth, the last spot we had a signal. Odds are she will resurface there.

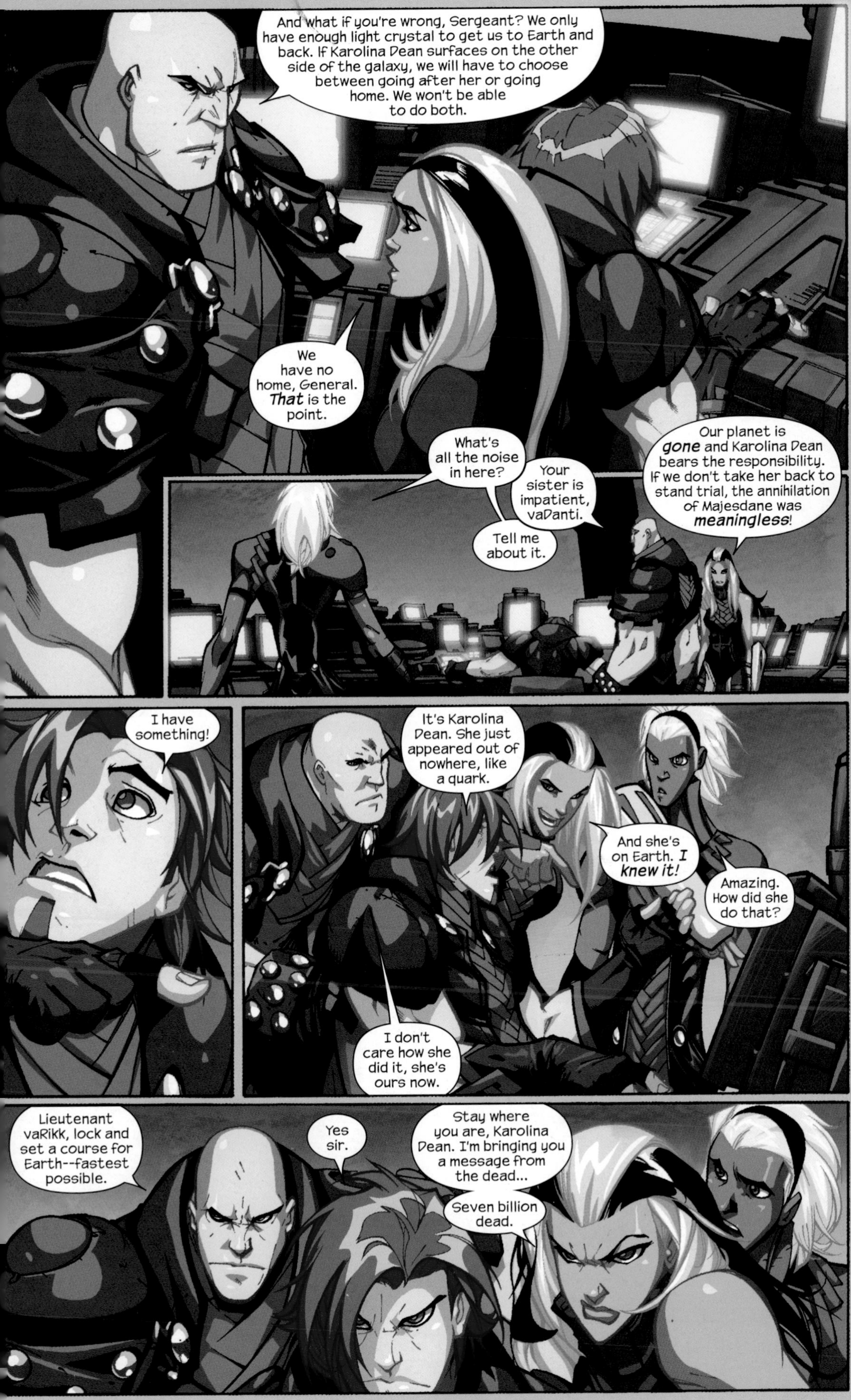

And what if you're wrong, Sergeant? We only have enough light crystal to get us to Earth and back. If Karolina Dean surfaces on the other side of the galaxy, we will have to choose between going after her or going home. We won't be able to do both.
We have no home, General. *That* is the point.
What's all the noise in here?
Your sister is impatient, vaDanti.
Tell me about it.
Our planet is *gone* and Karolina Dean bears the responsibility. If we don't take her back to stand trial, the annihilation of Majesdane was *meaningless*!
I have something!
It's Karolina Dean. She just appeared out of nowhere, like a quark.
And she's on Earth. *I knew it!*
Amazing. How did she do that?
I don't care how she did it, she's ours now.
Lieutenant vaRikk, lock and set a course for Earth--fastest possible.
Yes sir.
Stay where you are, Karolina Dean. I'm bringing you a message from the dead...
Seven billion dead.

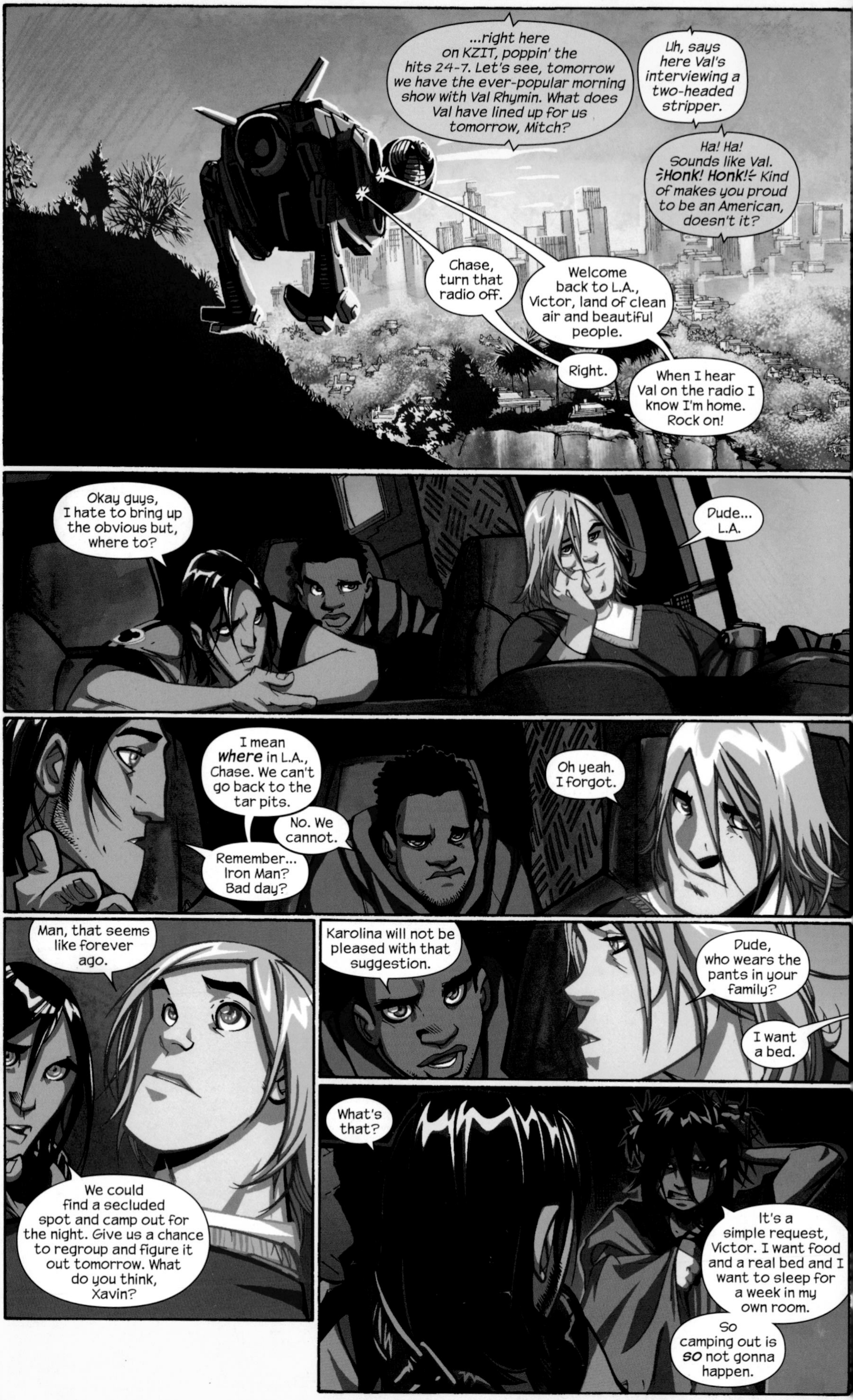

...right here on KZIT, poppin' the hits 24-7. Let's see, tomorrow we have the ever-popular morning show with Val Rhymin. What does Val have lined up for us tomorrow, Mitch?
Uh, says here Val's interviewing a two-headed stripper.
Ha! Ha! Sounds like Val. HONK! HONK! Kind of makes you proud to be an American, doesn't it?
Chase, turn that radio off.
Welcome back to L.A., Victor, land of clean air and beautiful people.
Right.
When I hear Val on the radio I know I'm home. Rock on!
Okay guys, I hate to bring up the obvious but, where to?
Dude... L.A.
I mean where in L.A., Chase. We can't go back to the tar pits.
Remember... Iron Man? Bad day?
No. We cannot.
Oh yeah. I forgot.
Man, that seems like forever ago.
We could find a secluded spot and camp out for the night. Give us a chance to regroup and figure it out tomorrow. What do you think, Xavin?
Karolina will not be pleased with that suggestion.
Dude, who wears the pants in your family?
I want a bed.
What's that?
It's a simple request, Victor. I want food and a real bed and I want to sleep for a week in my own room.
So camping out is SO not gonna happen.

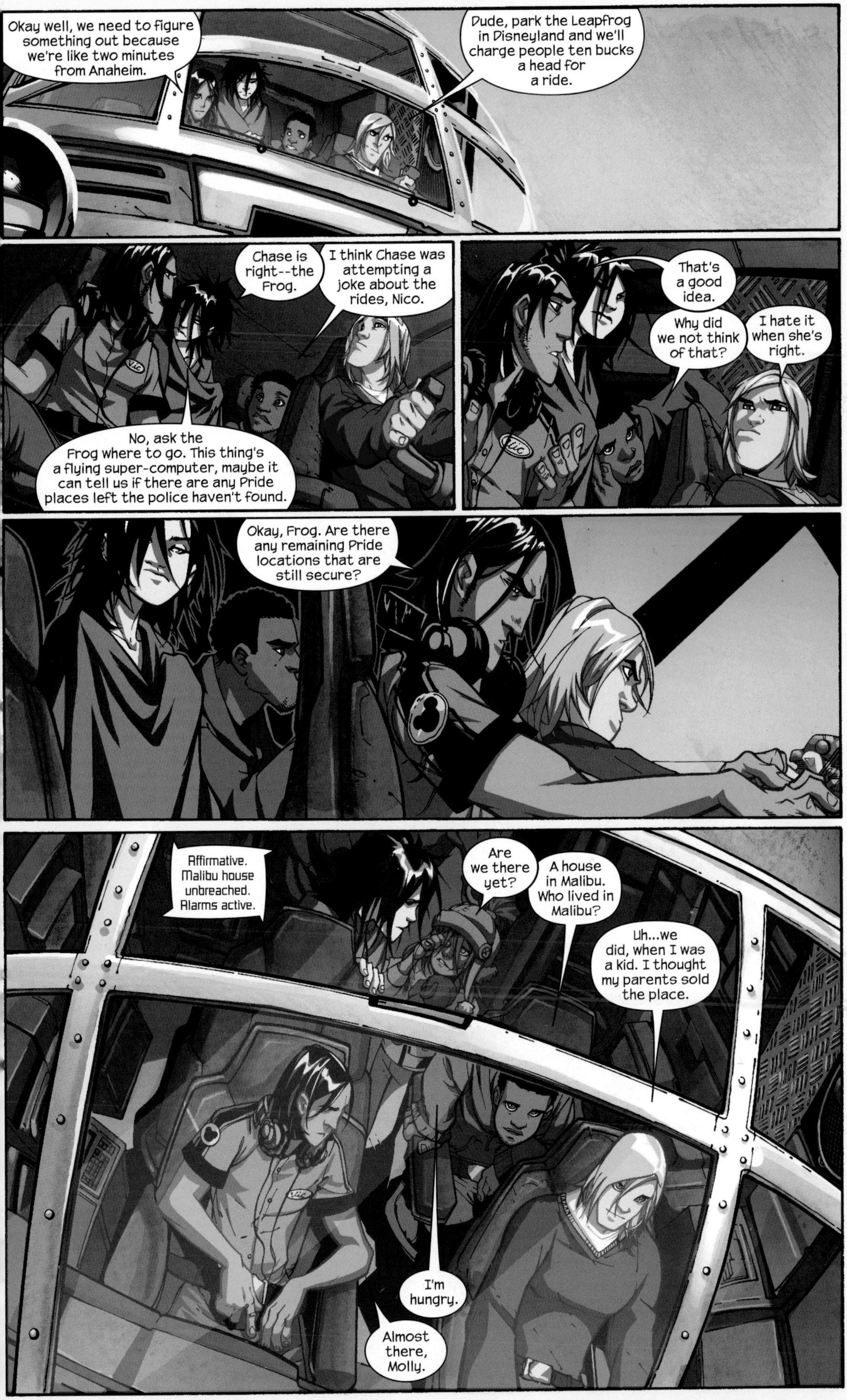
Okay well, we need to figure something out because we're like two minutes from Anaheim.
Dude, park the Leapfrog in Disneyland and we'll charge people ten bucks a head for a ride.
Chase is right--the Frog.
I think Chase was attempting a joke about the rides, Nico.
No, ask the Frog where to go. This thing's a flying super-computer, maybe it can tell us if there are any Pride places left the police haven't found.
That's a good idea.
Why did we not think of that?
I hate it when she's right.
Okay, Frog. Are there any remaining Pride locations that are still secure?
Affirmative. Malibu house unbreached. Alarms active.
Are we there yet?
A house in Malibu. Who lived in Malibu?
Uh...we did, when I was a kid. I thought my parents sold the place.
I'm hungry.
Almost there, Molly.

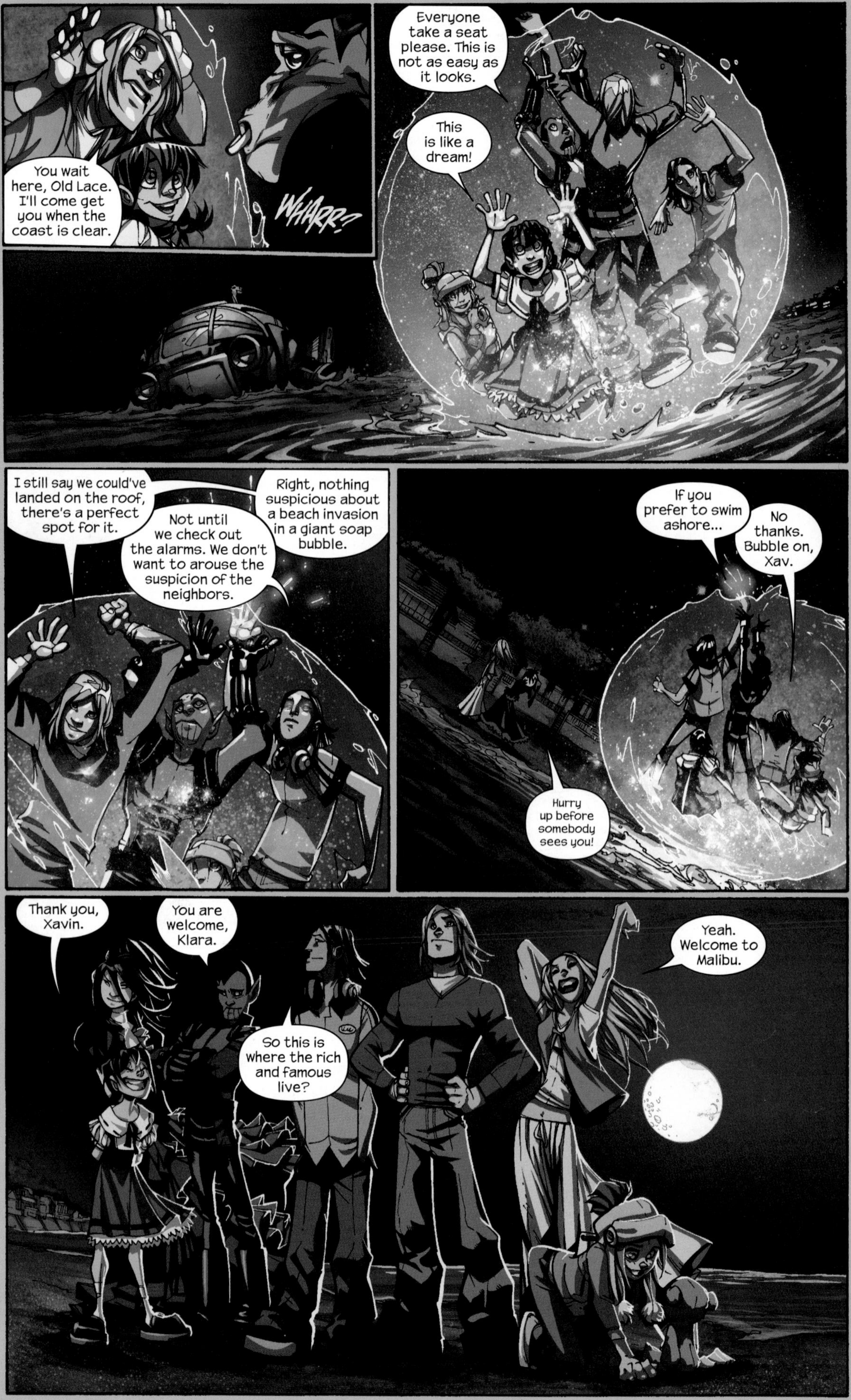
You wait here, Old Lace. I'll come get you when the coast is clear.
WHARR?
Everyone take a seat please. This is not as easy as it looks.
This is like a dream!
I still say we could've landed on the roof, there's a perfect spot for it.
Right, nothing suspicious about a beach invasion in a giant soap bubble.
Not until we check out the alarms. We don't want to arouse the suspicion of the neighbors.
If you prefer to swim ashore...
No thanks. Bubble on, Xav.
Hurry up before somebody sees you!
Thank you, Xavin.
You are welcome, Klara.
So this is where the rich and famous live?
Yeah. Welcome to Malibu.

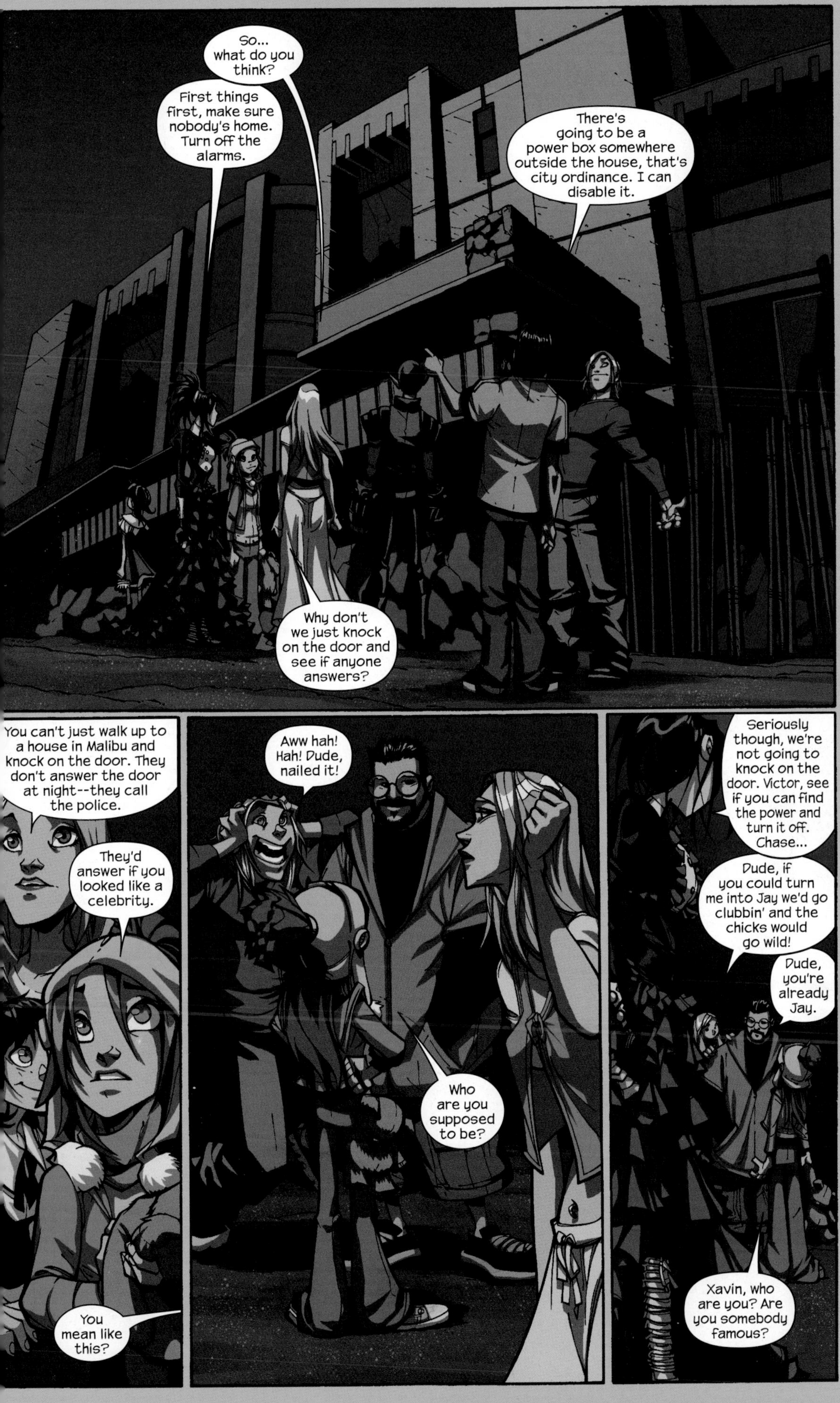

So... what do you think?
First things first, make sure nobody's home. Turn off the alarms.
There's going to be a power box somewhere outside the house, that's city ordinance. I can disable it.
Why don't we just knock on the door and see if anyone answers?
You can't just walk up to a house in Malibu and knock on the door. They don't answer the door at night--they call the police.
They'd answer if you looked like a celebrity.
You mean like this?
Aww hah! Hah! Dude, nailed it!
Who are you supposed to be?
Seriously though, we're not going to knock on the door. Victor, see if you can find the power and turn it off. Chase...
Dude, if you could turn me into Jay we'd go clubbin' and the chicks would go wild!
Dude, you're already Jay.
Xavin, who are you? Are you somebody famous?

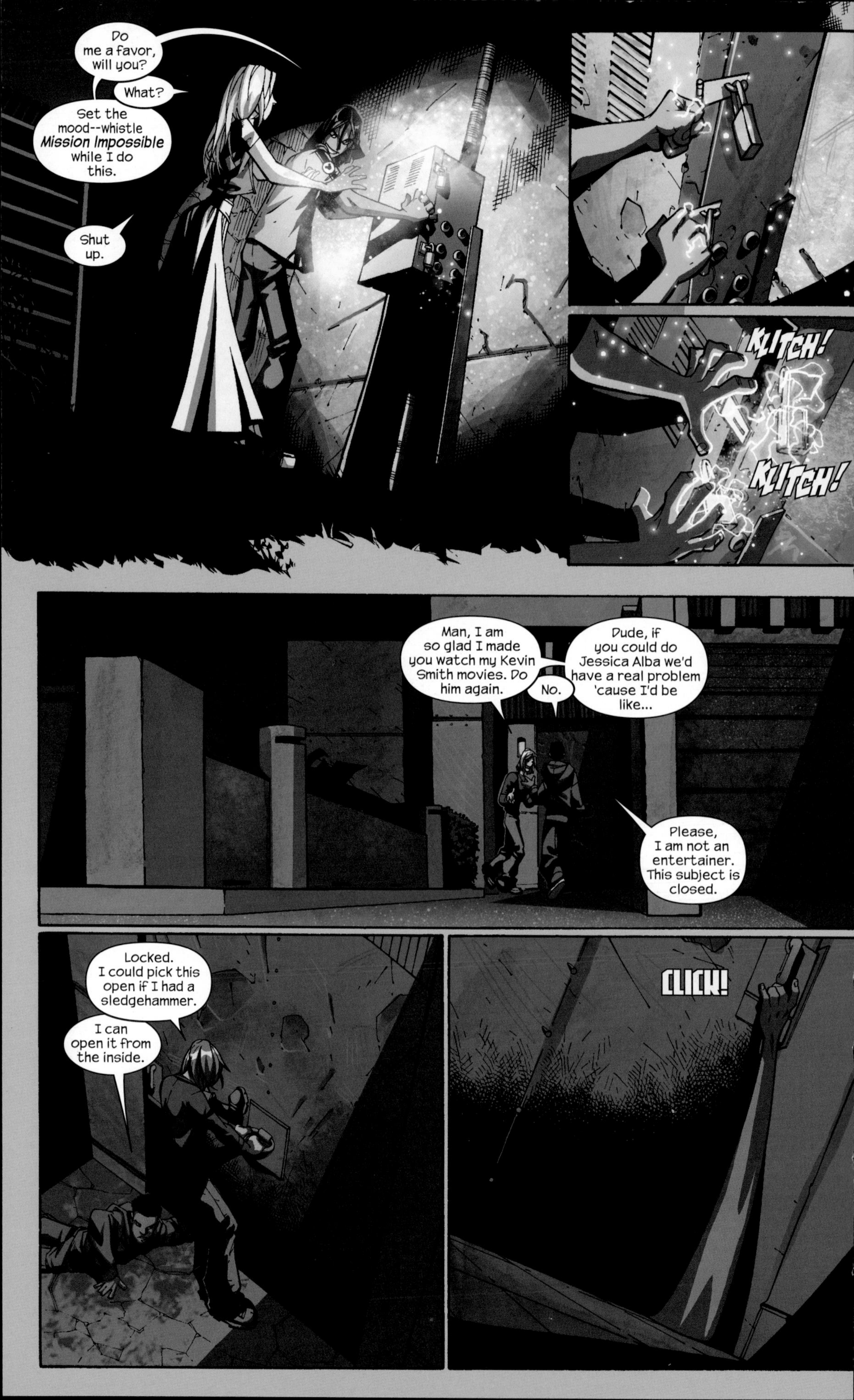
Do me a favor, will you?
What?
Set the mood--whistle *Mission Impossible* while I do this.
Shut up.
KLITCH!
KLITCH!
Man, I am so glad I made you watch my Kevin Smith movies. Do him again.
No.
Dude, if you could do Jessica Alba we'd have a real problem 'cause I'd be like...
Please, I am not an entertainer. This subject is closed.
Locked. I could pick this open if I had a sledgehammer.
I can open it from the inside.
CLICK!

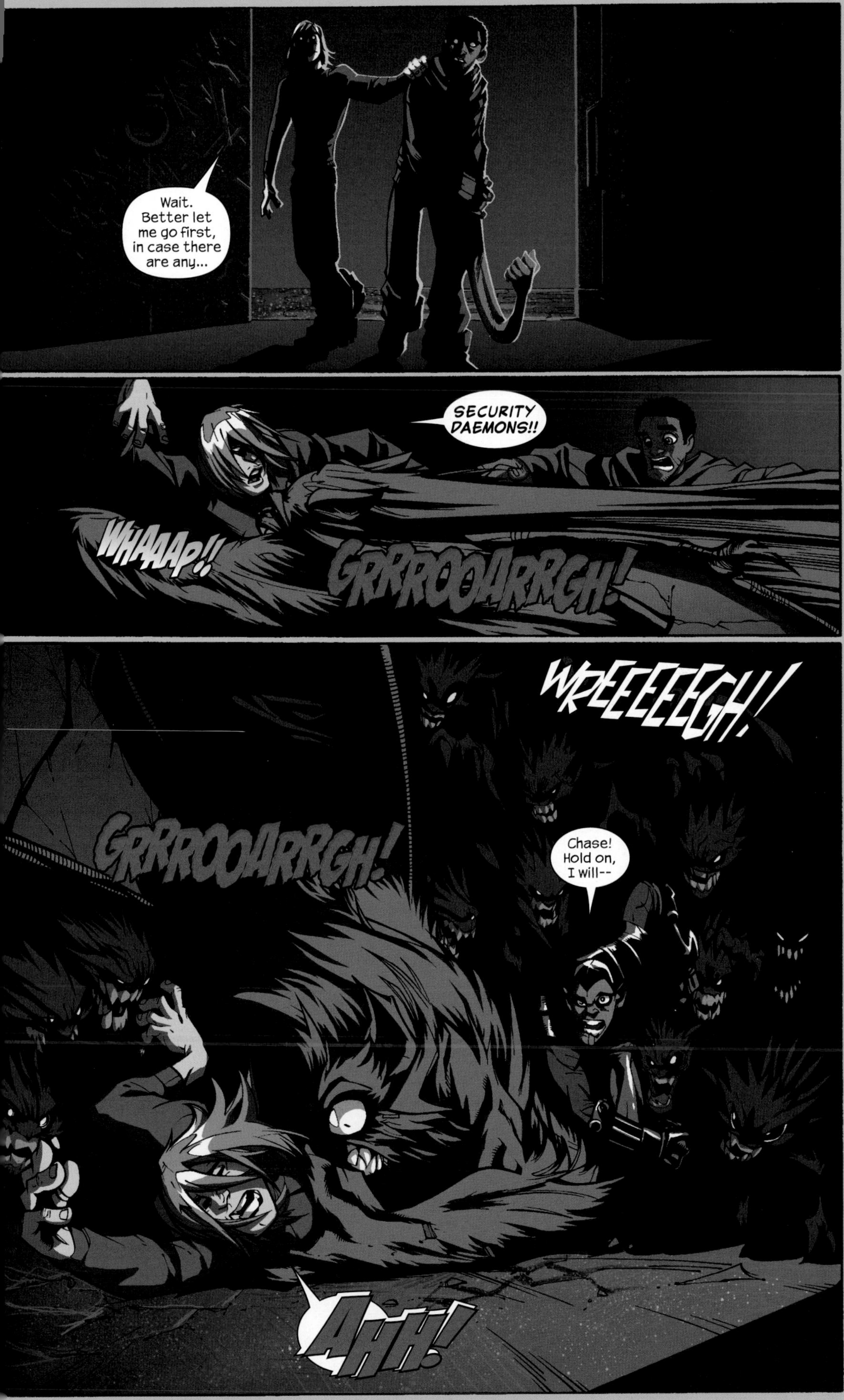
Wait. Better let me go first, in case there are any...
SECURITY DAEMONS!!
WHAAAP!!
GRRROOARRGH!
WREEEEEEGH!
GRRROOARRGH!
Chase! Hold on, I will--
AHH!

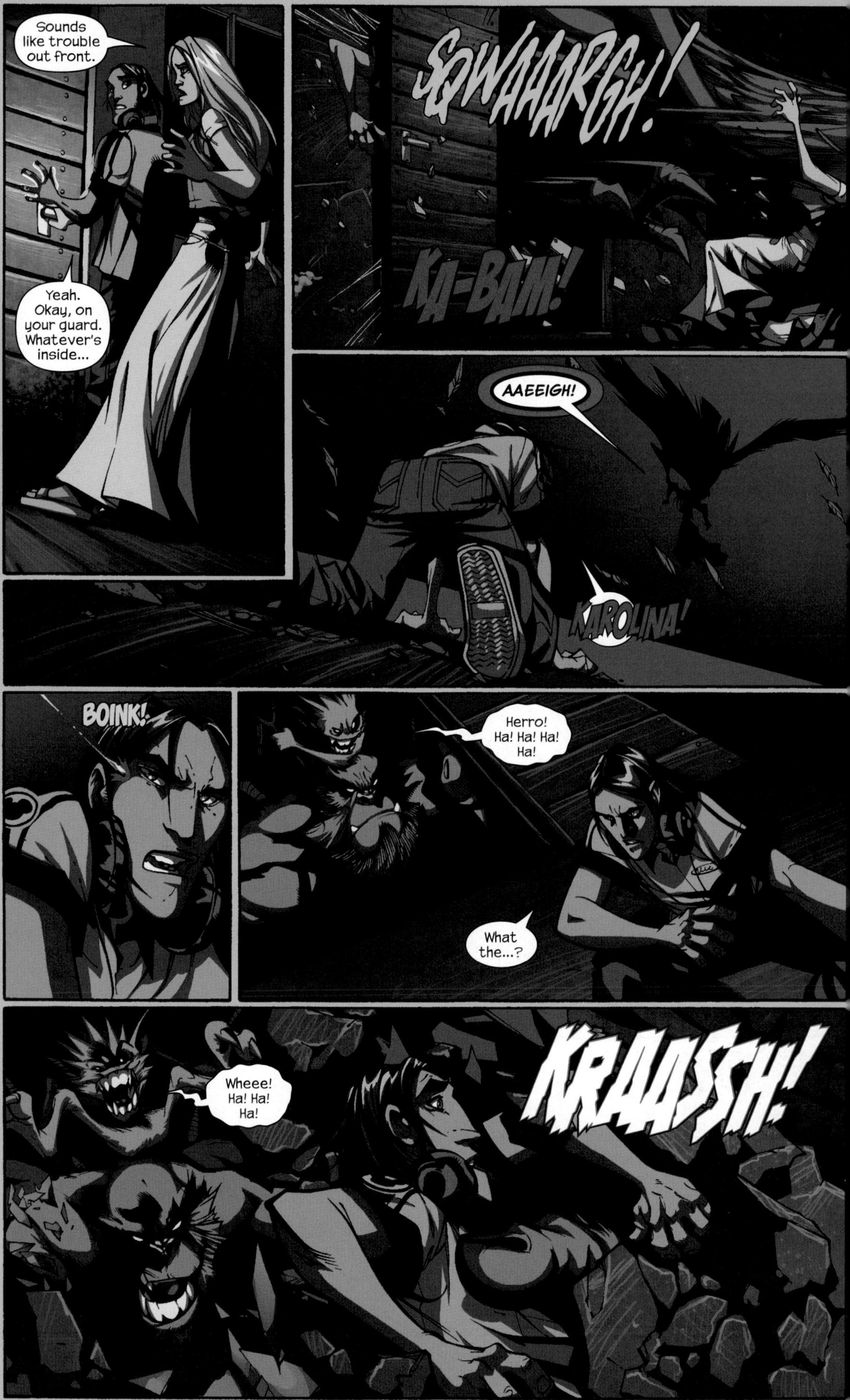
Sounds like trouble out front.
Yeah. Okay, on your guard. Whatever's inside...
SQWAAARGH!
KA-BAM!
AAEEIGH!
KAROLINA!
BOINK!
Herro! Ha! Ha! Ha! Ha!
What the...?
KRAASSH!
Wheee! Ha! Ha! Ha!

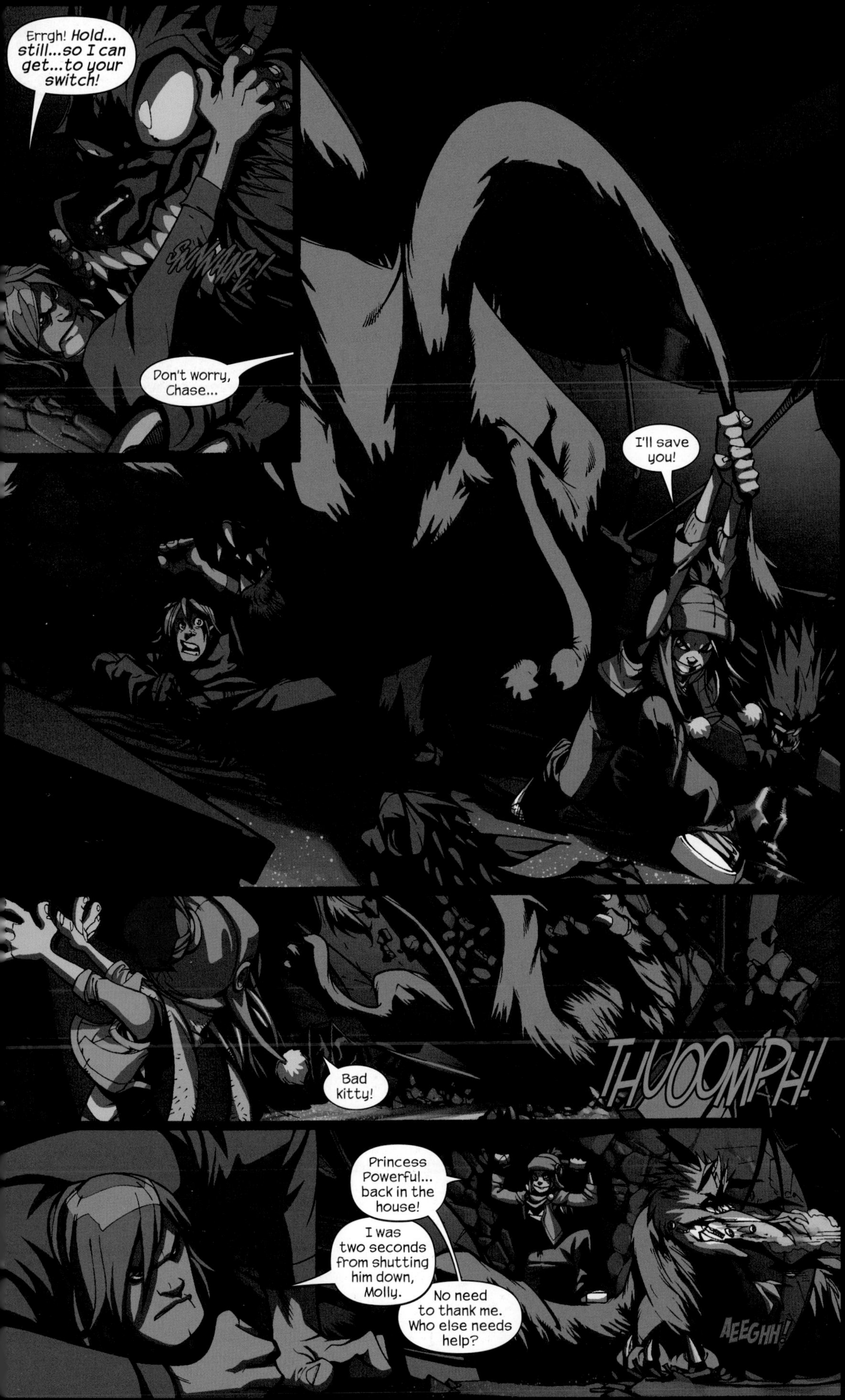

Errgh! Hold... still...so I can get...to your switch!
SKWAARL!
Don't worry, Chase...
I'll save you!
Bad kitty!
THUOOMPH!
Princess Powerful... back in the house!
I was two seconds from shutting him down, Molly.
No need to thank me. Who else needs help?
AEEGHH!

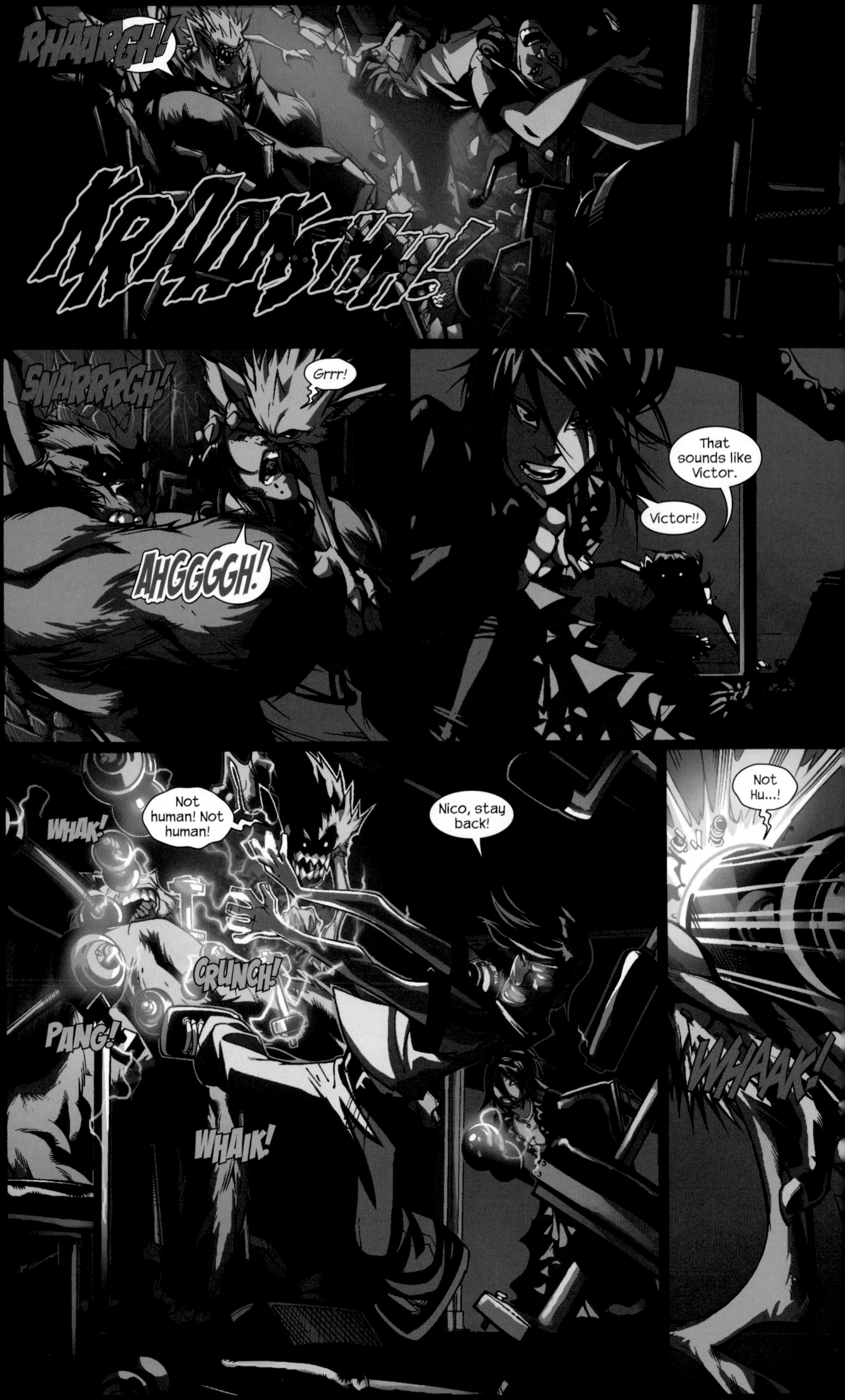

RHAARGH!
SNARRRGH!
Grrr!
AHGGGGH!
That sounds like Victor.
Victor!!
WHAK!
Not human! Not human!
Nico, stay back!
CRUNCH!
PANG!
WHAIK!
Not Hu...!
WHAAK!

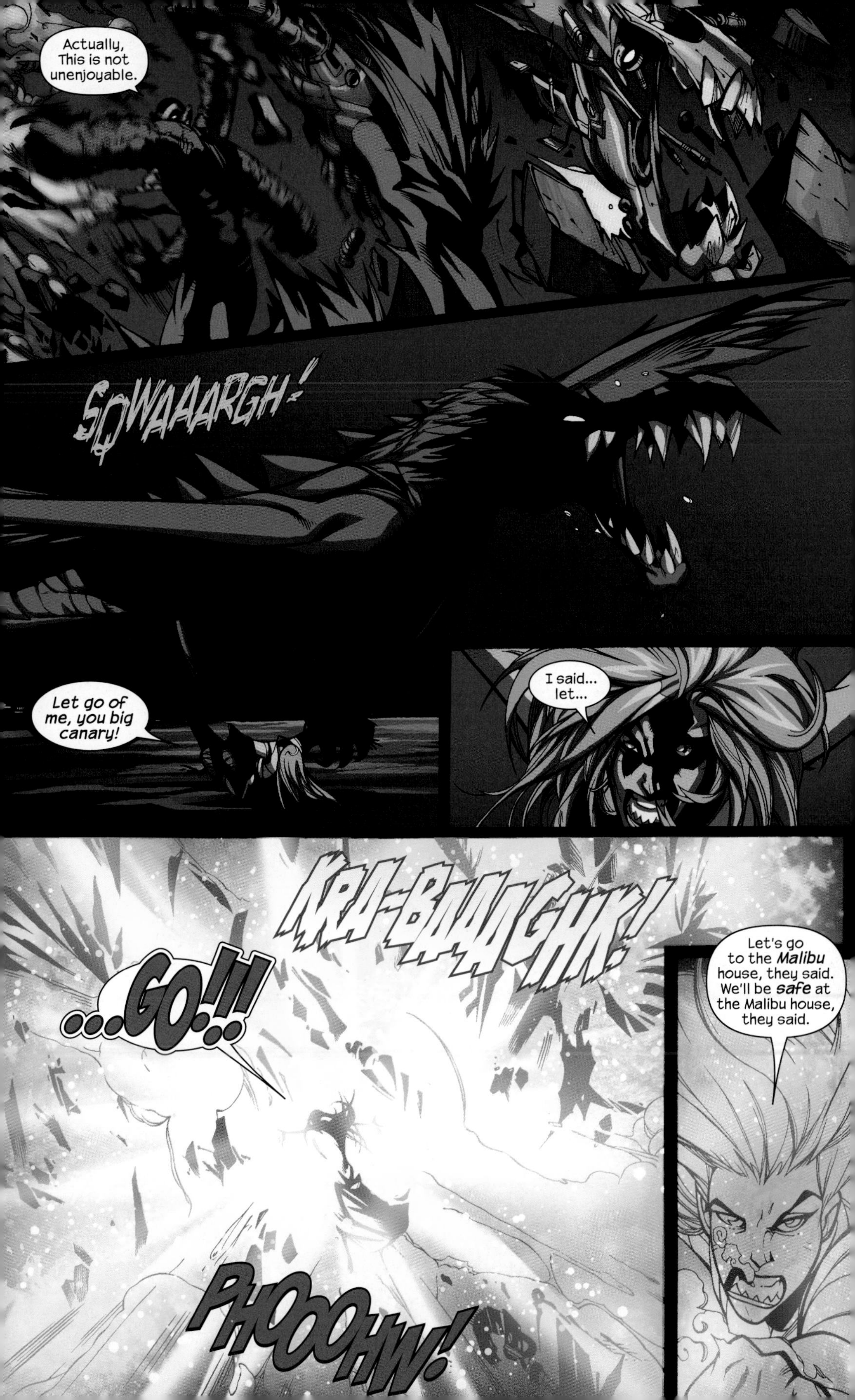
Actually, This is not unenjoyable.
SQWAAARGH!
Let go of me, you big canary!
I said... let...
KRA-BAAAGHK!
...GO!!!
PHOOOHW!
Let's go to the *Malibu* house, they said. We'll be *safe* at the Malibu house, they said.

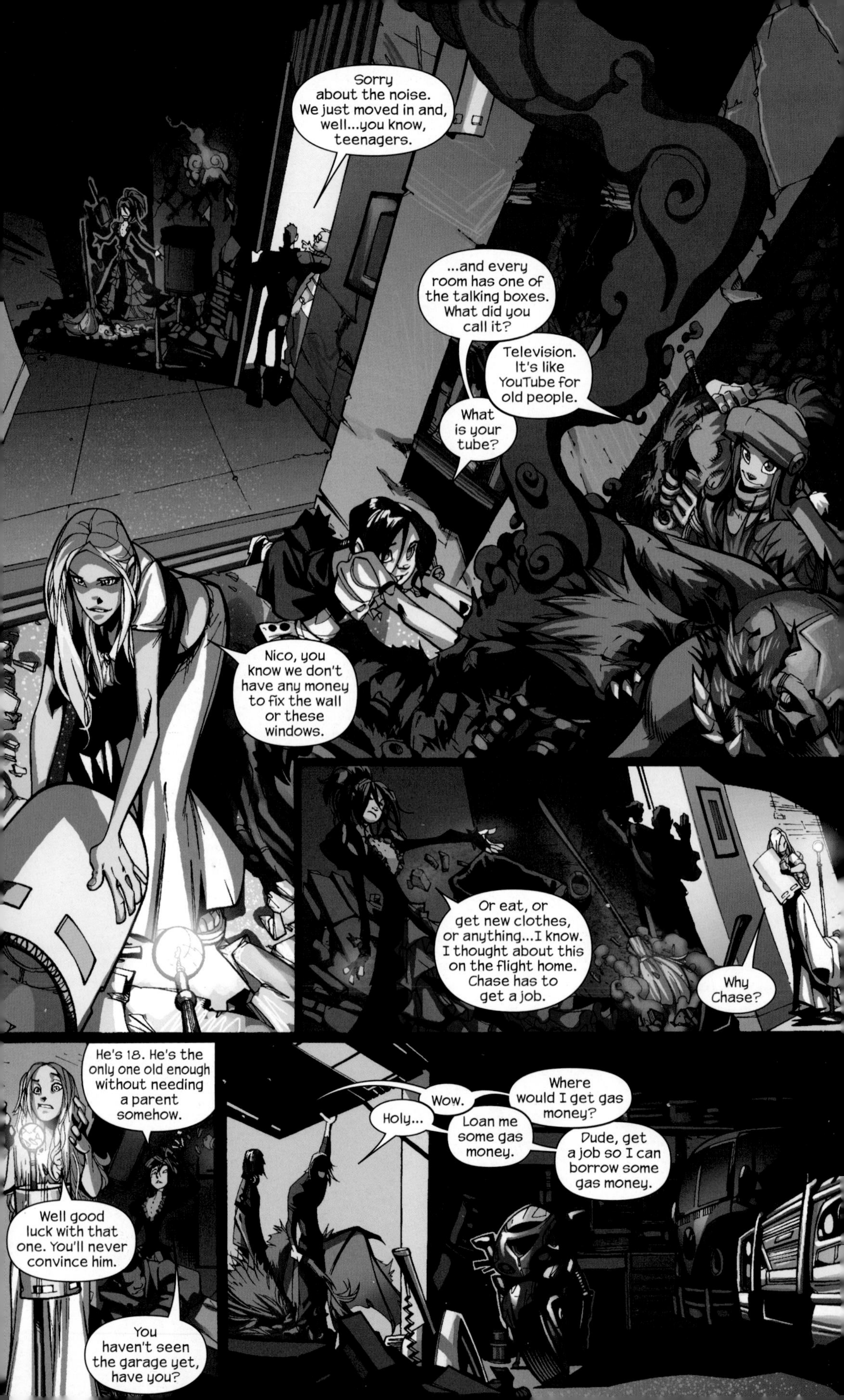
Sorry about the noise. We just moved in and, well...you know, teenagers.
...and every room has one of the talking boxes. What did you call it?
Television. It's like YouTube for old people.
What is your tube?
Nico, you know we don't have any money to fix the wall or these windows.
Or eat, or get new clothes, or anything...I know. I thought about this on the flight home. Chase has to get a job.
Why Chase?
He's 18. He's the only one old enough without needing a parent somehow.
Well good luck with that one. You'll never convince him.
You haven't seen the garage yet, have you?
Wow.
Holy...
Where would I get gas money?
Loan me some gas money.
Dude, get a job so I can borrow some gas money.

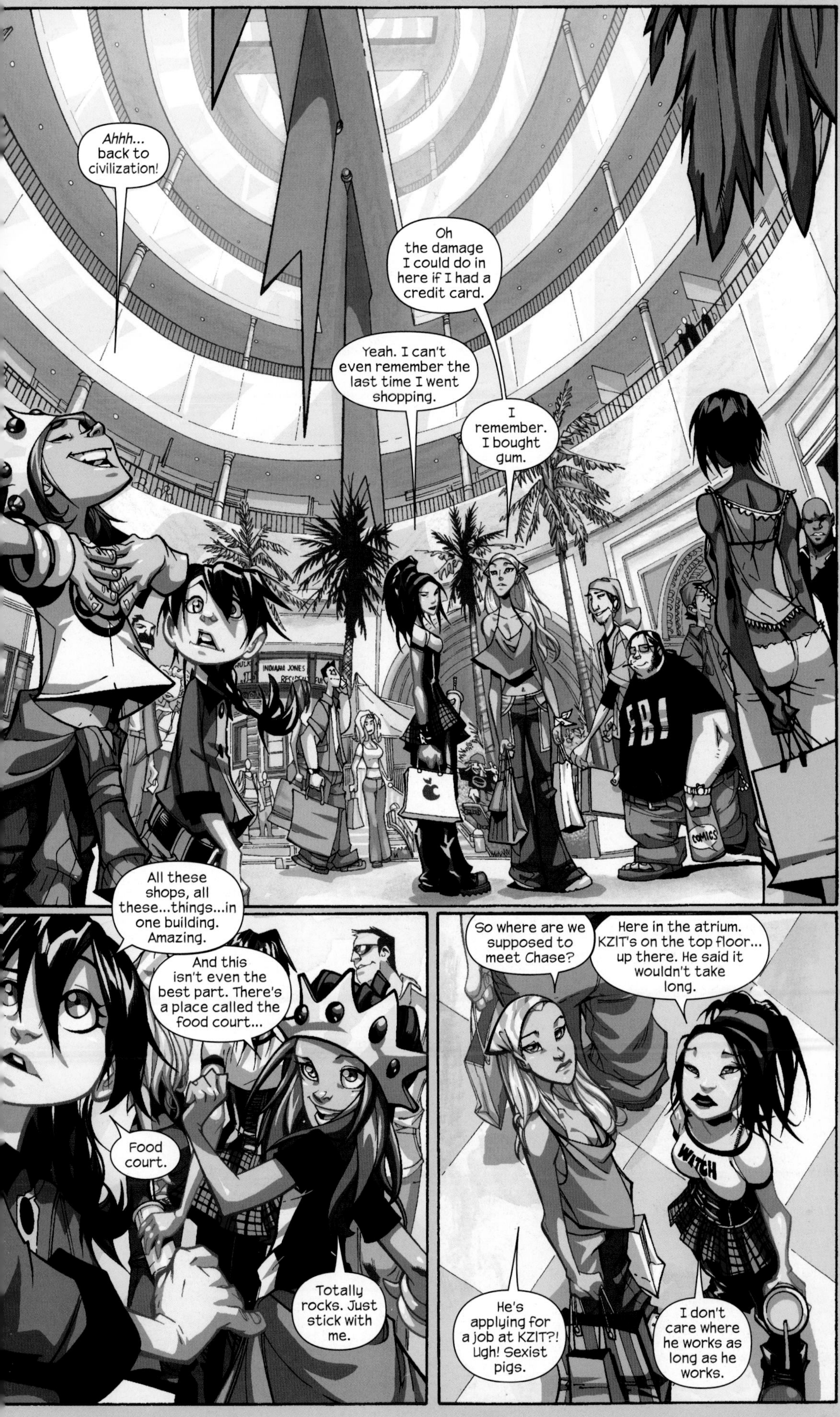

Ahhh... back to civilization!
Oh the damage I could do in here if I had a credit card.
Yeah. I can't even remember the last time I went shopping.
I remember. I bought gum.
INDIANA JONES
FBI
COMICS
All these shops, all these...things...in one building. Amazing.
And this isn't even the best part. There's a place called the food court...
Food court.
Totally rocks. Just stick with me.
So where are we supposed to meet Chase?
Here in the atrium. KZIT's on the top floor... up there. He said it wouldn't take long.
WITCH
He's applying for a job at KZIT?! Ugh! Sexist pigs.
I don't care where he works as long as he works.

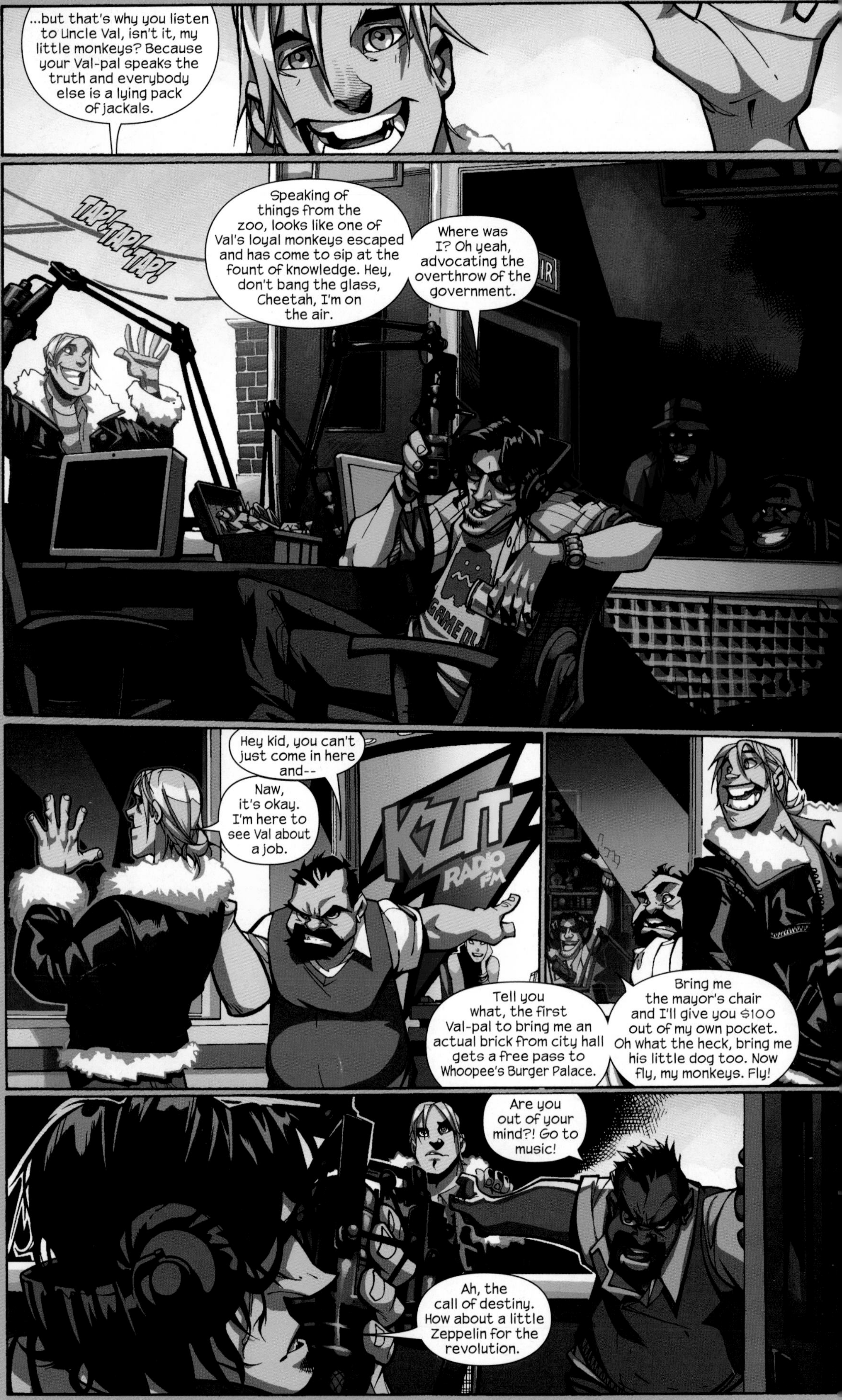
...but that's why you listen to Uncle Val, isn't it, my little monkeys? Because your Val-pal speaks the truth and everybody else is a lying pack of jackals.
TAP! TAP! TAP!
Speaking of things from the zoo, looks like one of Val's loyal monkeys escaped and has come to sip at the fount of knowledge. Hey, don't bang the glass, Cheetah, I'm on the air.
Where was I? Oh yeah, advocating the overthrow of the government.
Hey kid, you can't just come in here and--
Naw, it's okay. I'm here to see Val about a job.
KZIT RADIO FM
Tell you what, the first Val-pal to bring me an actual brick from city hall gets a free pass to Whoopee's Burger Palace.
Bring me the mayor's chair and I'll give you $100 out of my own pocket. Oh what the heck, bring me his little dog too. Now fly, my monkeys. Fly!
Are you out of your mind?! Go to music!
Ah, the call of destiny. How about a little Zeppelin for the revolution.

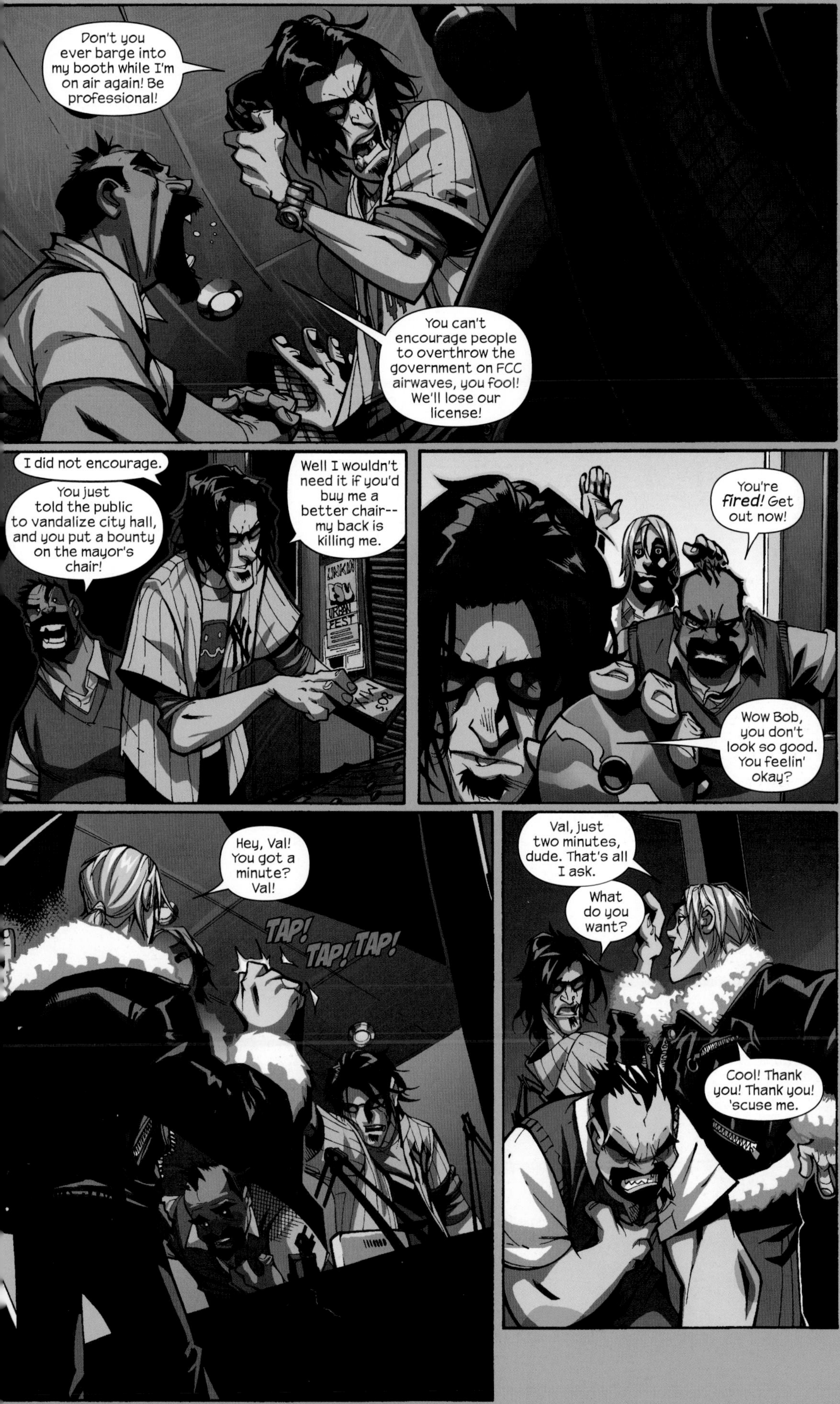
Don't you ever barge into my booth while I'm on air again! Be professional!
You can't encourage people to overthrow the government on FCC airwaves, you fool! We'll lose our license!
I did not encourage.
You just told the public to vandalize city hall, and you put a bounty on the mayor's chair!
Well I wouldn't need it if you'd buy me a better chair--my back is killing me.
URBAN FEST
You're fired! Get out now!
Wow Bob, you don't look so good. You feelin' okay?
Hey, Val! You got a minute? Val!
TAP! TAP! TAP!
Val, just two minutes, dude. That's all I ask.
What do you want?
Cool! Thank you! Thank you! 'scuse me.

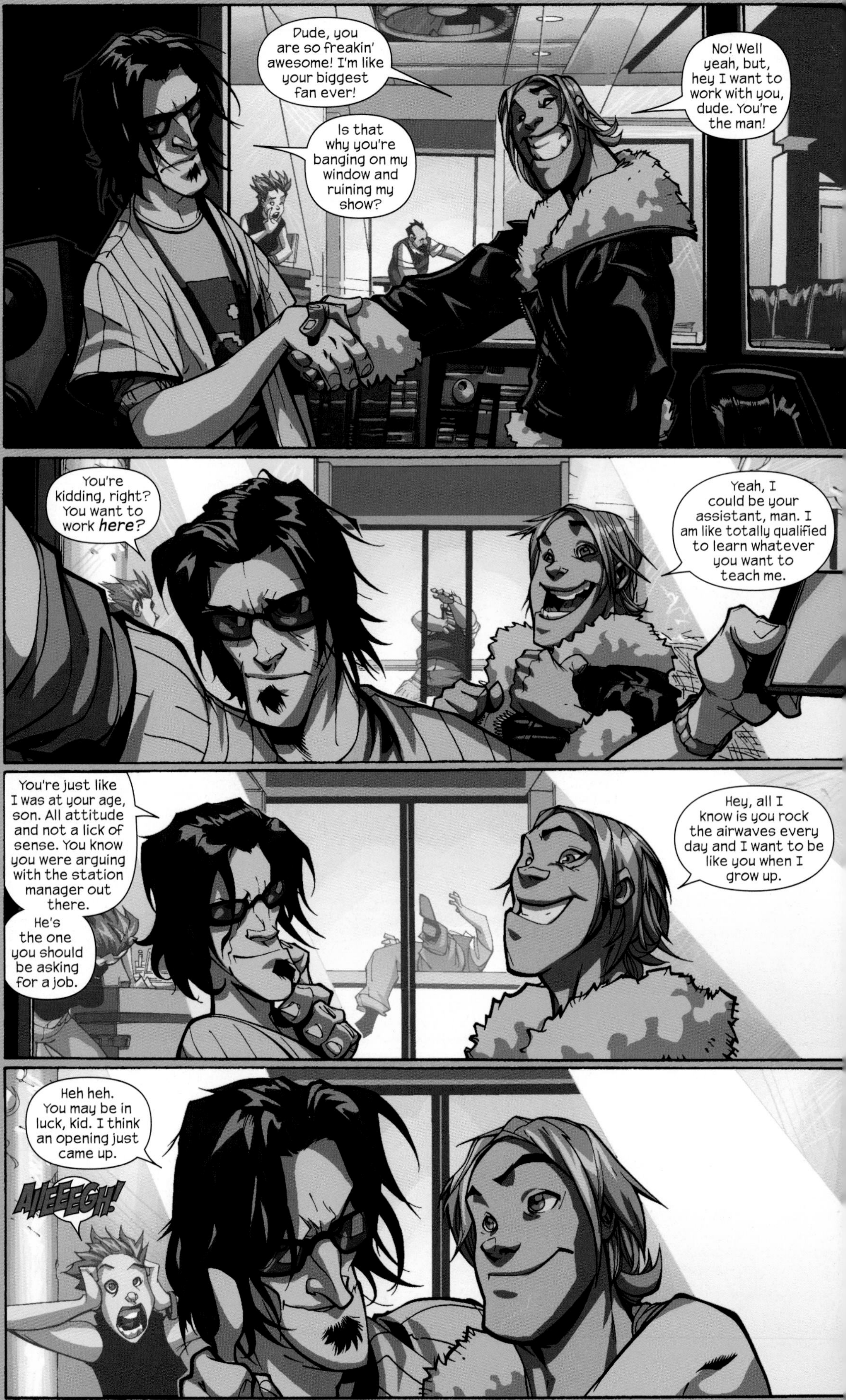
Dude, you are so freakin' awesome! I'm like your biggest fan ever!
Is that why you're banging on my window and ruining my show?
No! Well yeah, but, hey I want to work with you, dude. You're the man!
You're kidding, right? You want to work *here*?
Yeah, I could be your assistant, man. I am like totally qualified to learn whatever you want to teach me.
You're just like I was at your age, son. All attitude and not a lick of sense. You know you were arguing with the station manager out there.
He's the one you should be asking for a job.
Hey, all I know is you rock the airwaves every day and I want to be like you when I grow up.
Heh heh. You may be in luck, kid. I think an opening just came up.
AIEEEGH!

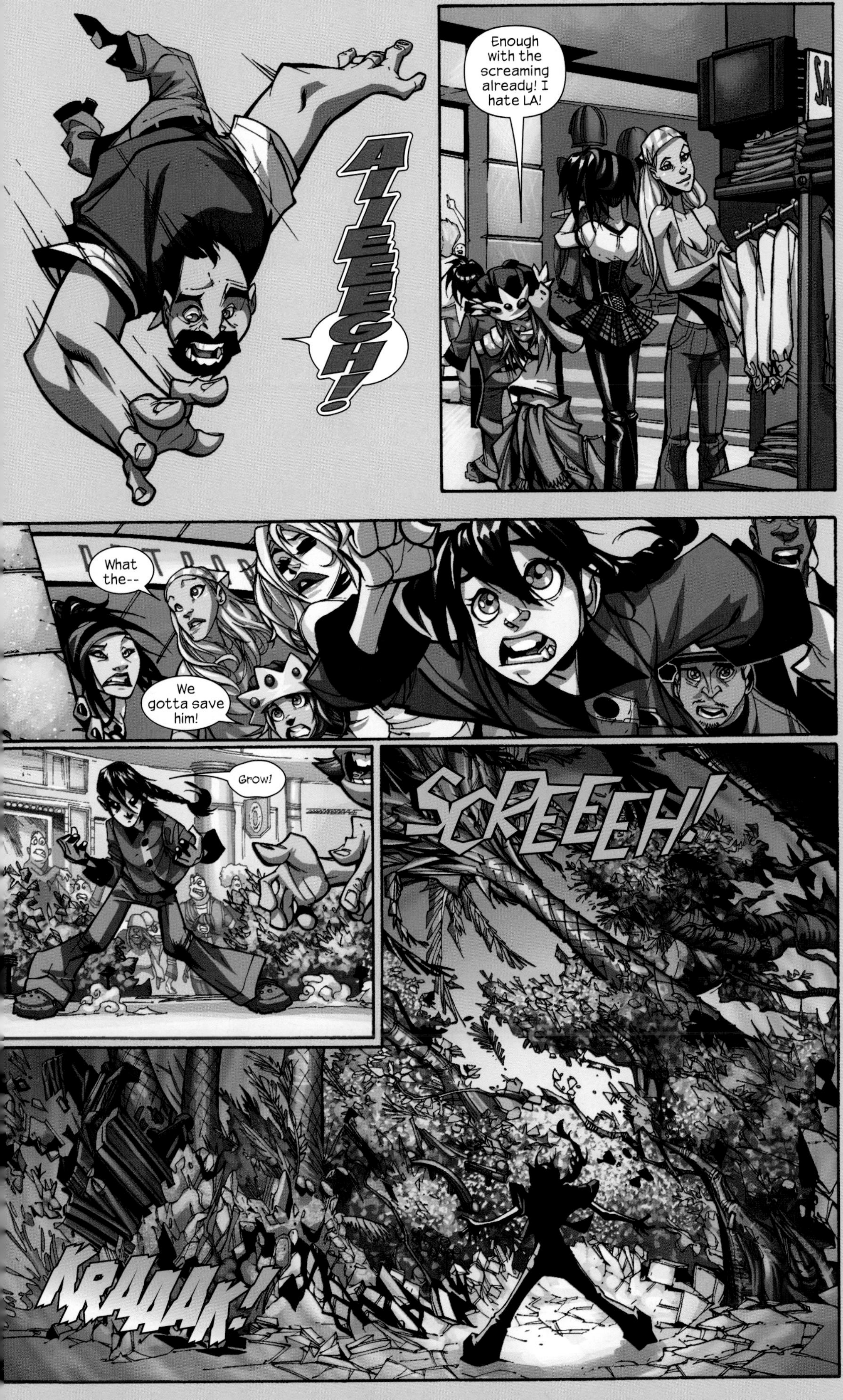
AIIEEEGH!
Enough with the screaming already! I hate LA!
What the--
We gotta save him!
Grow!
SCREEEH!
KRAAAK!

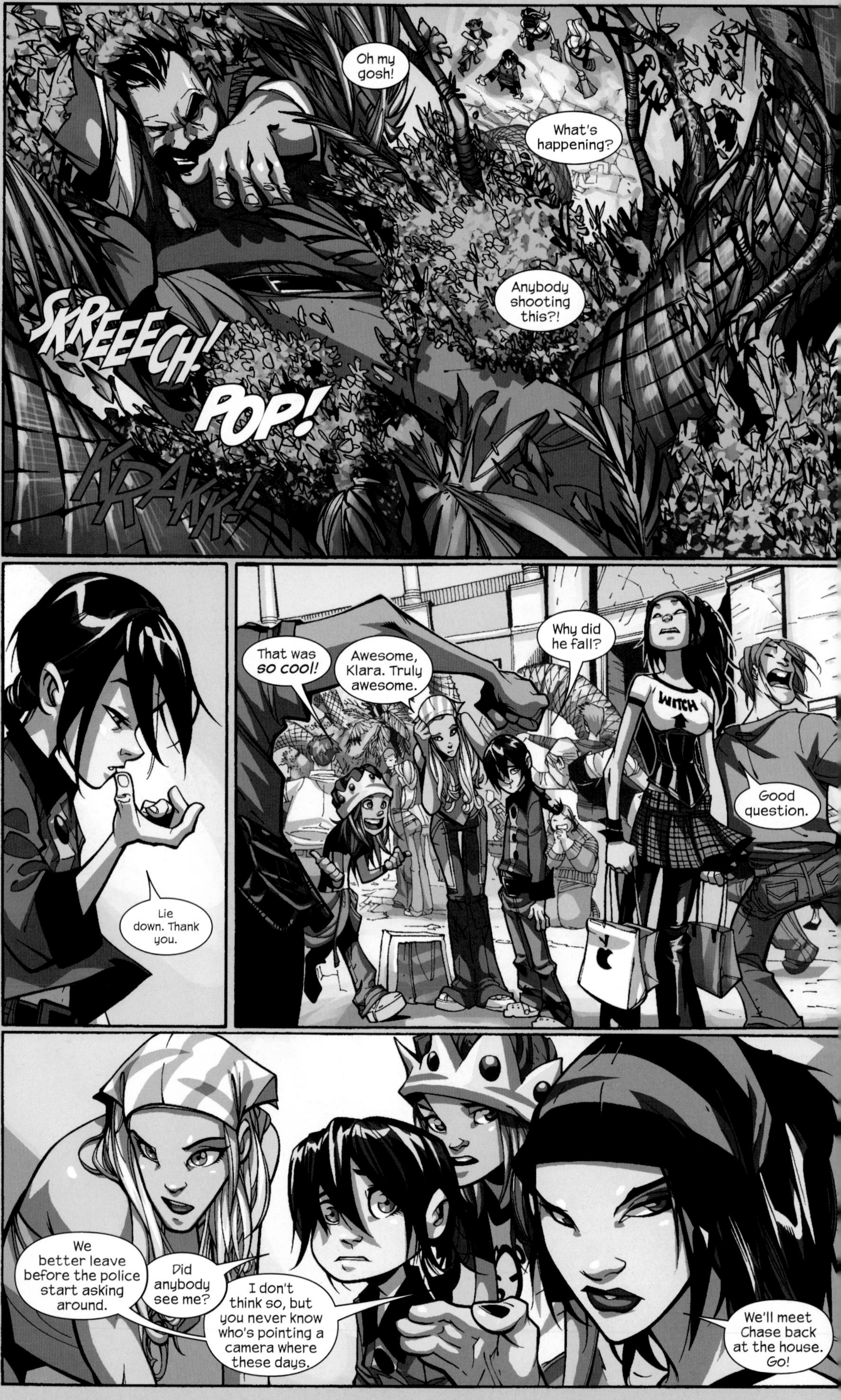
Oh my gosh!
What's happening?
Anybody shooting this?!
SKREEECH!
POP!
KRAKK!
Lie down. Thank you.
That was *so cool!*
Awesome, Klara. Truly awesome.
Why did he fall?
WITCH
Good question.
We better leave before the police start asking around.
Did anybody see me?
I don't think so, but you never know who's pointing a camera where these days.
We'll meet Chase back at the house. Go!

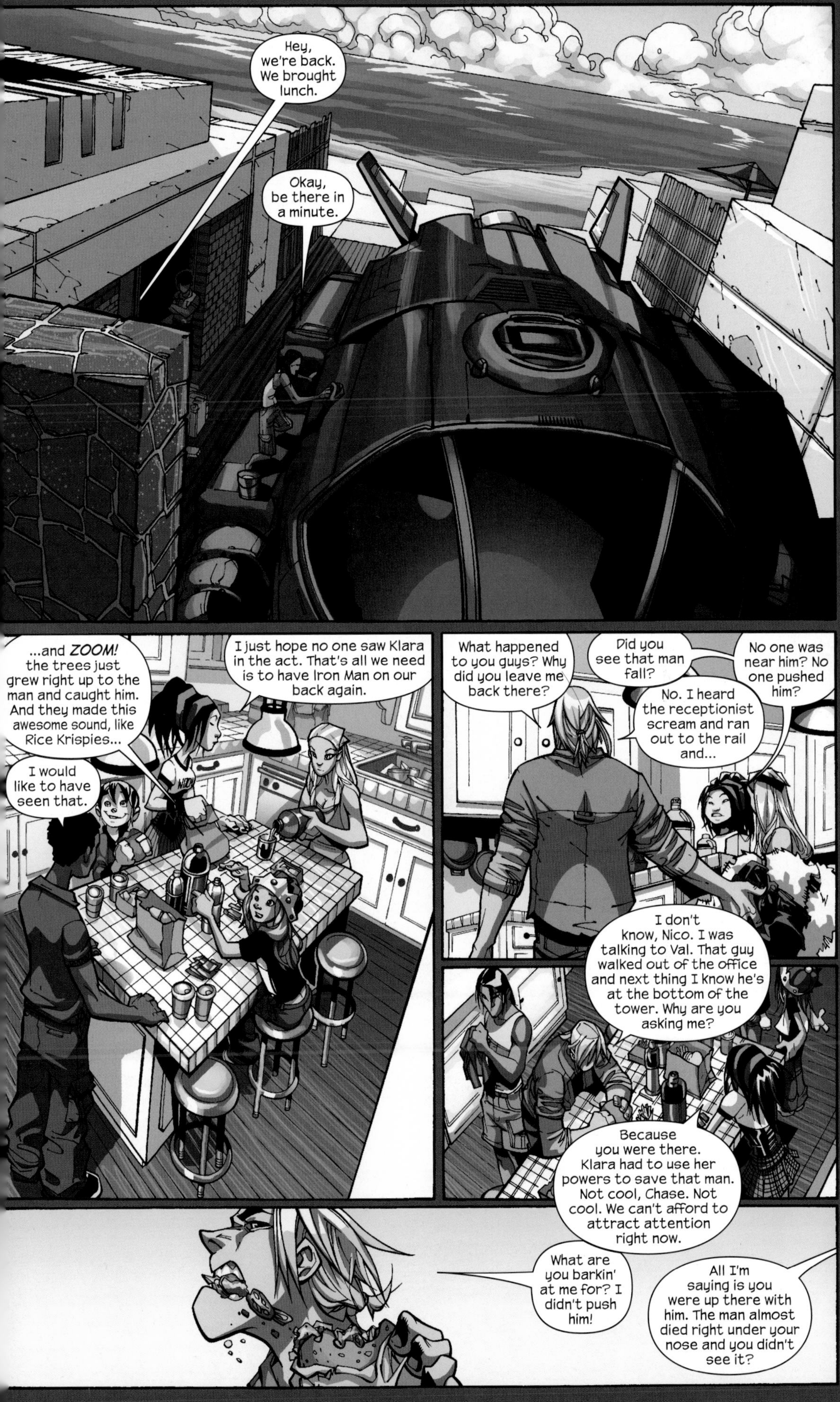
Hey, we're back. We brought lunch.
Okay, be there in a minute.
...and ZOOM! the trees just grew right up to the man and caught him. And they made this awesome sound, like Rice Krispies...
I just hope no one saw Klara in the act. That's all we need is to have Iron Man on our back again.
I would like to have seen that.
What happened to you guys? Why did you leave me back there?
Did you see that man fall?
No one was near him? No one pushed him?
No. I heard the receptionist scream and ran out to the rail and...
I don't know, Nico. I was talking to Val. That guy walked out of the office and next thing I know he's at the bottom of the tower. Why are you asking me?
Because you were there. Klara had to use her powers to save that man. Not cool, Chase. Not cool. We can't afford to attract attention right now.
What are you barkin' at me for? I didn't push him!
All I'm saying is you were up there with him. The man almost died right under your nose and you didn't see it?

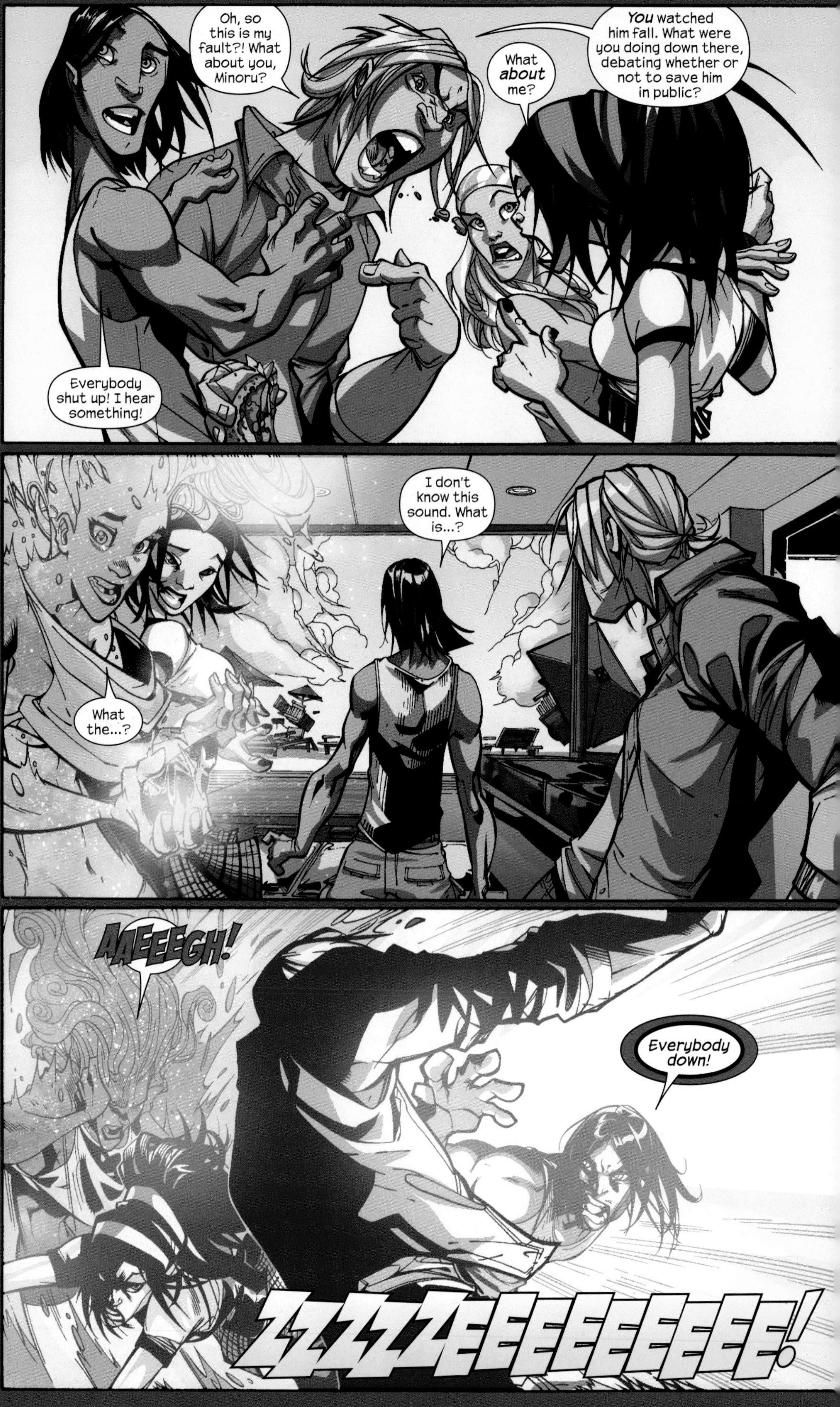
Oh, so this is my fault?! What about you, Minoru?
What about me?
You watched him fall. What were you doing down there, debating whether or not to save him in public?
Everybody shut up! I hear something!
I don't know this sound. What is...?
What the...?
AAEEEGH!
Everybody down!
ZZZZZEEEEEEEEEEE!

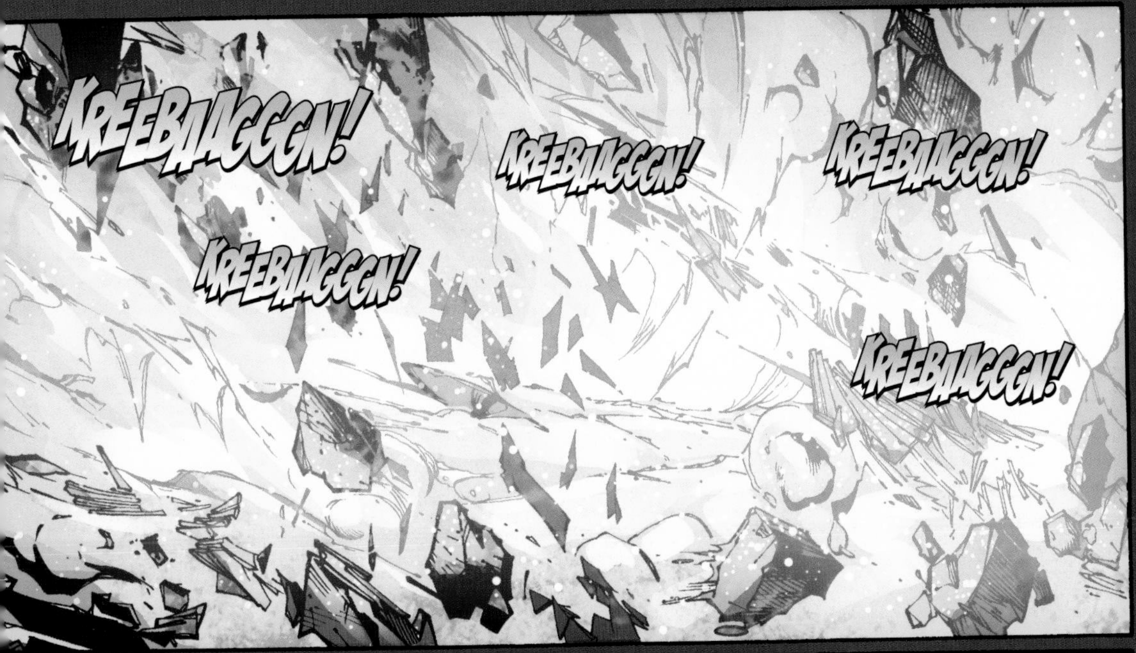
KREEBAAGGGN!
KREEBAAGGGN!
KREEBAAGGGN!
KREEBAAGGGN!
KREEBAAGGGN!

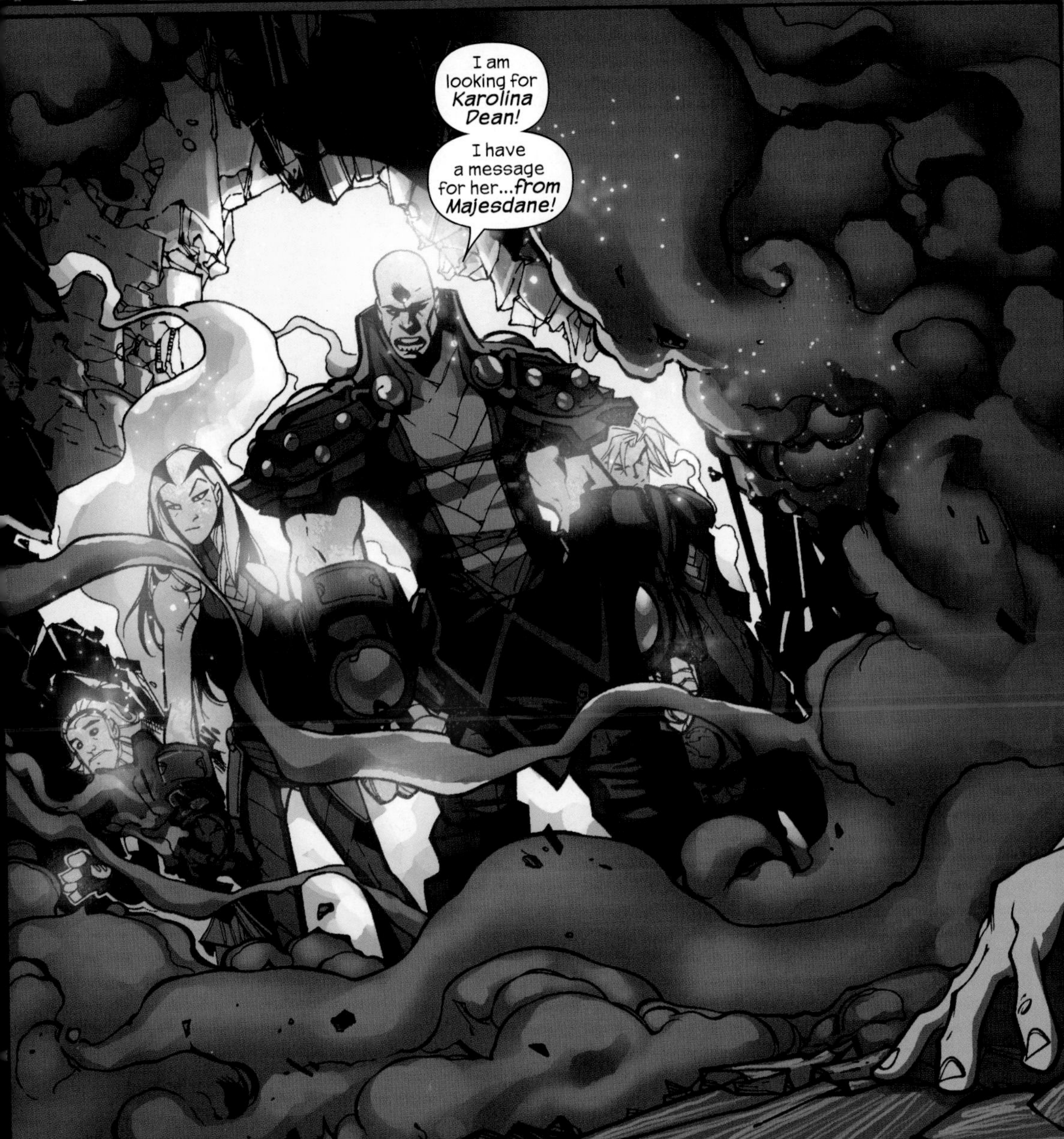
I am looking for *Karolina Dean!*
I have a message for her...*from Majesdane!*

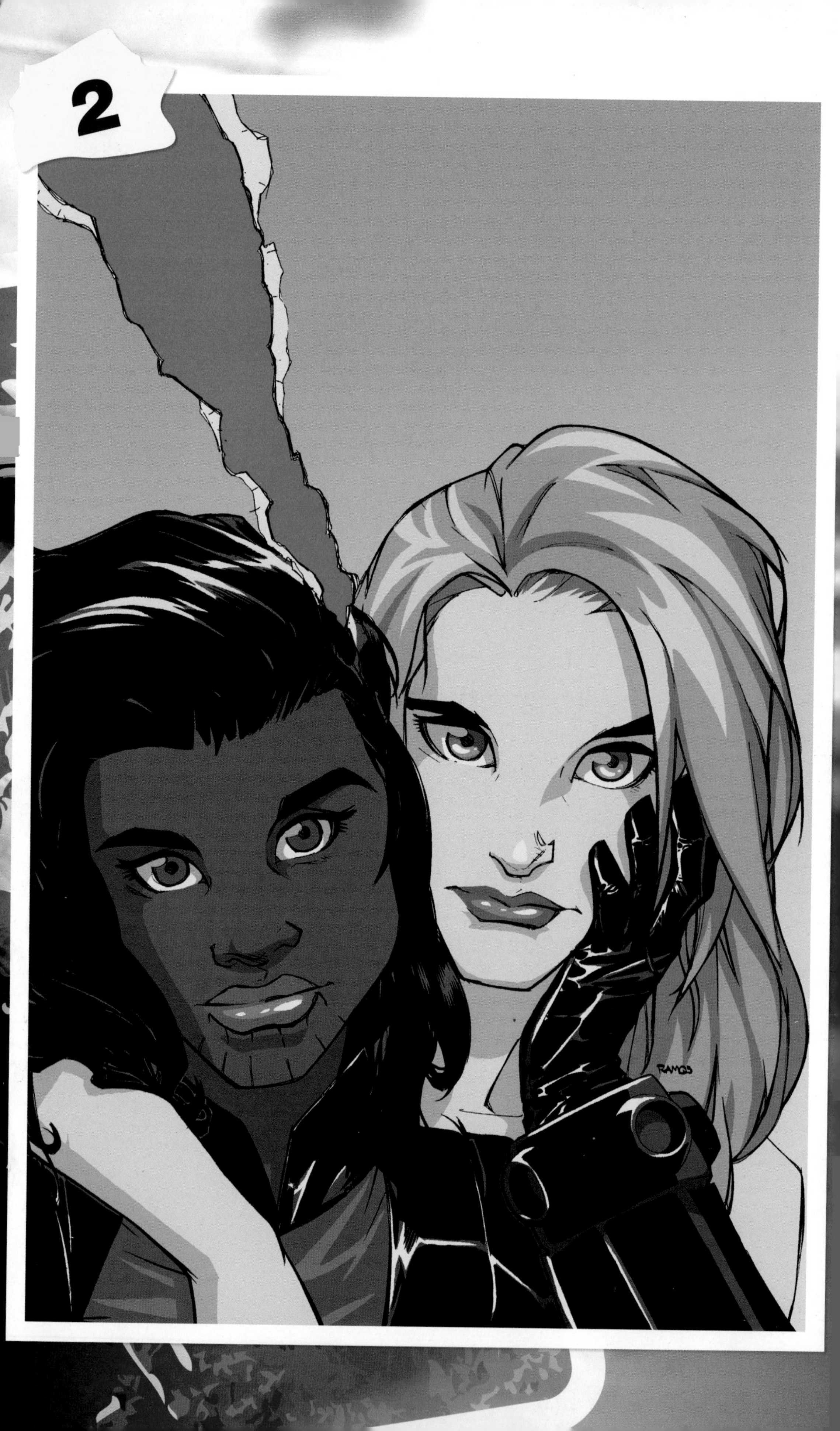
2
RAMOS

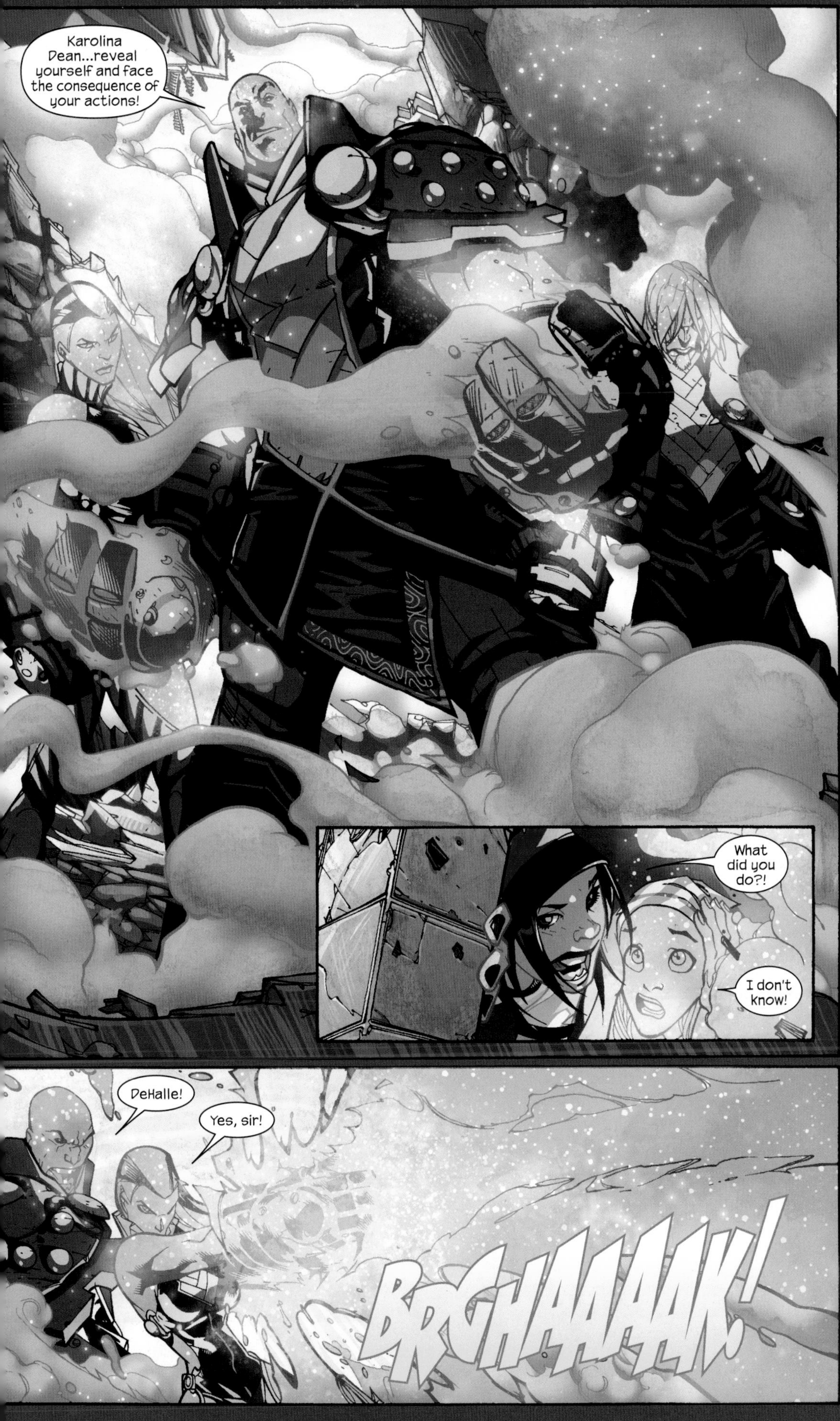

Karolina Dean...reveal yourself and face the consequence of your actions!
What did you do?!
I don't know!
DeHalle!
Yes, sir!
BRCHAAAAK!

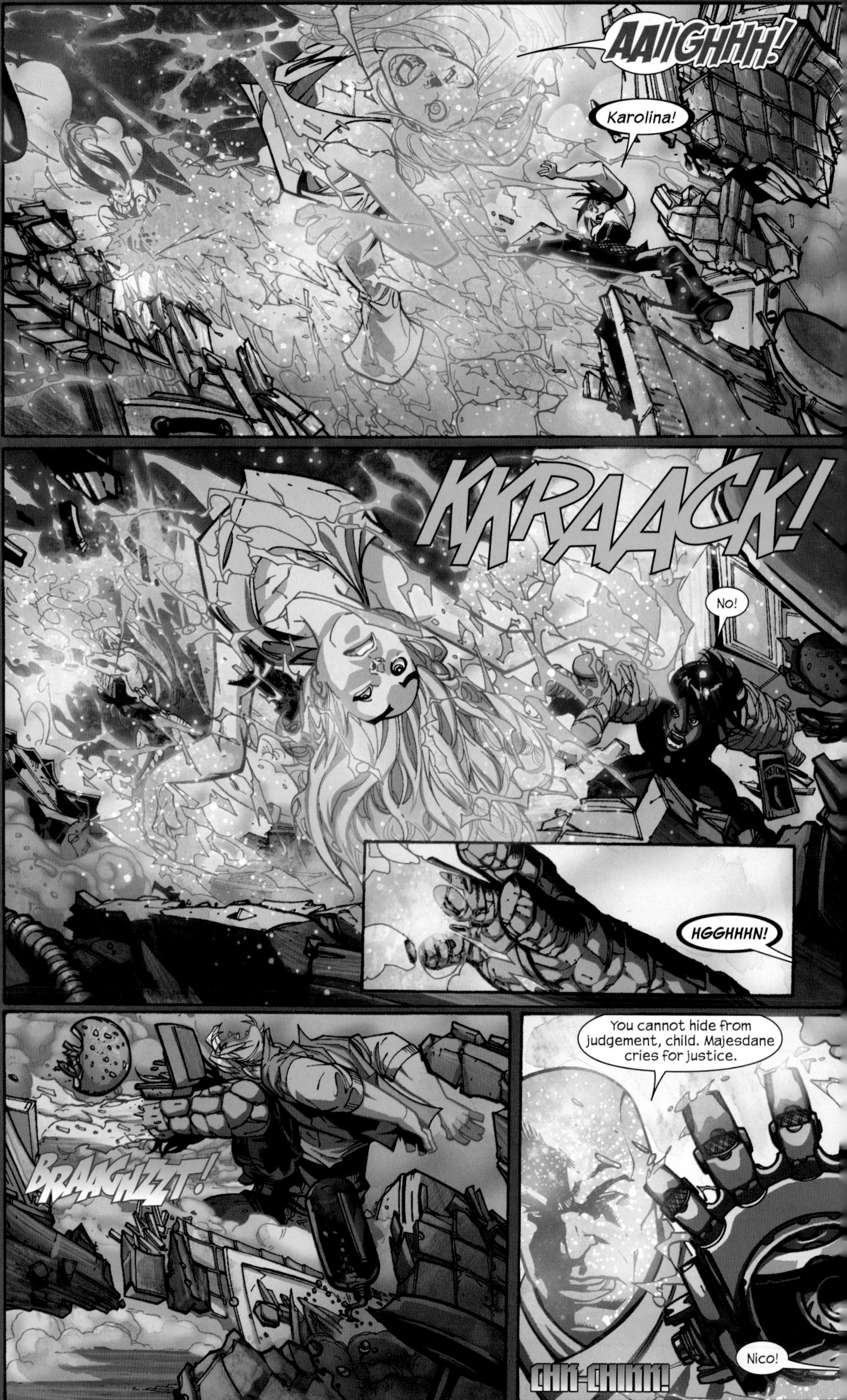
AAIIGHHH!
Karolina!
KKRAACK!
No!
HGGHHHN!
BRAAGHZZT!
You cannot hide from judgement, child. Majesdane cries for justice.
Nico!
CHK-CHIKK!

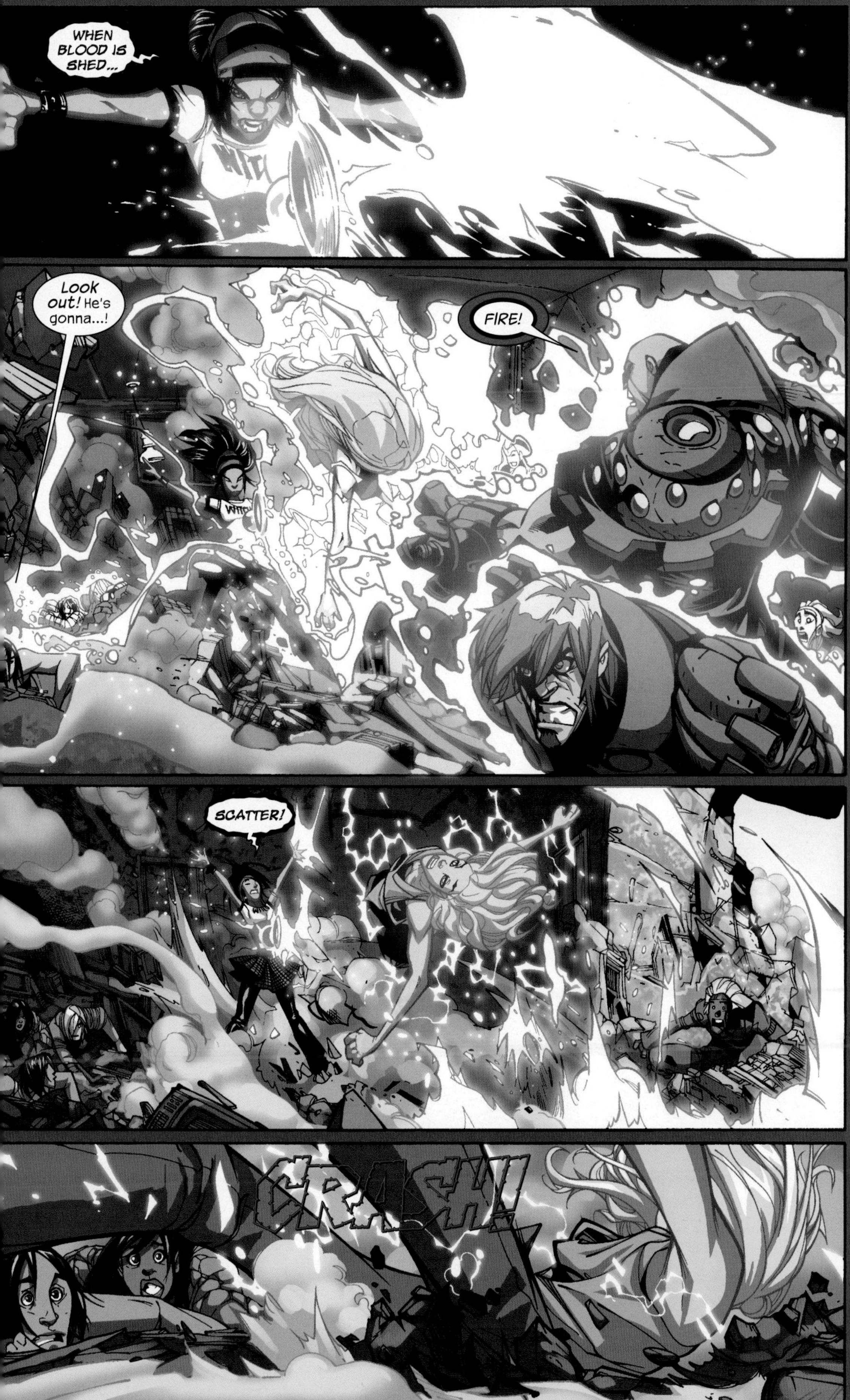
WHEN BLOOD IS SHED...
Look out! He's gonna...!
FIRE!
SCATTER!
CRASH!

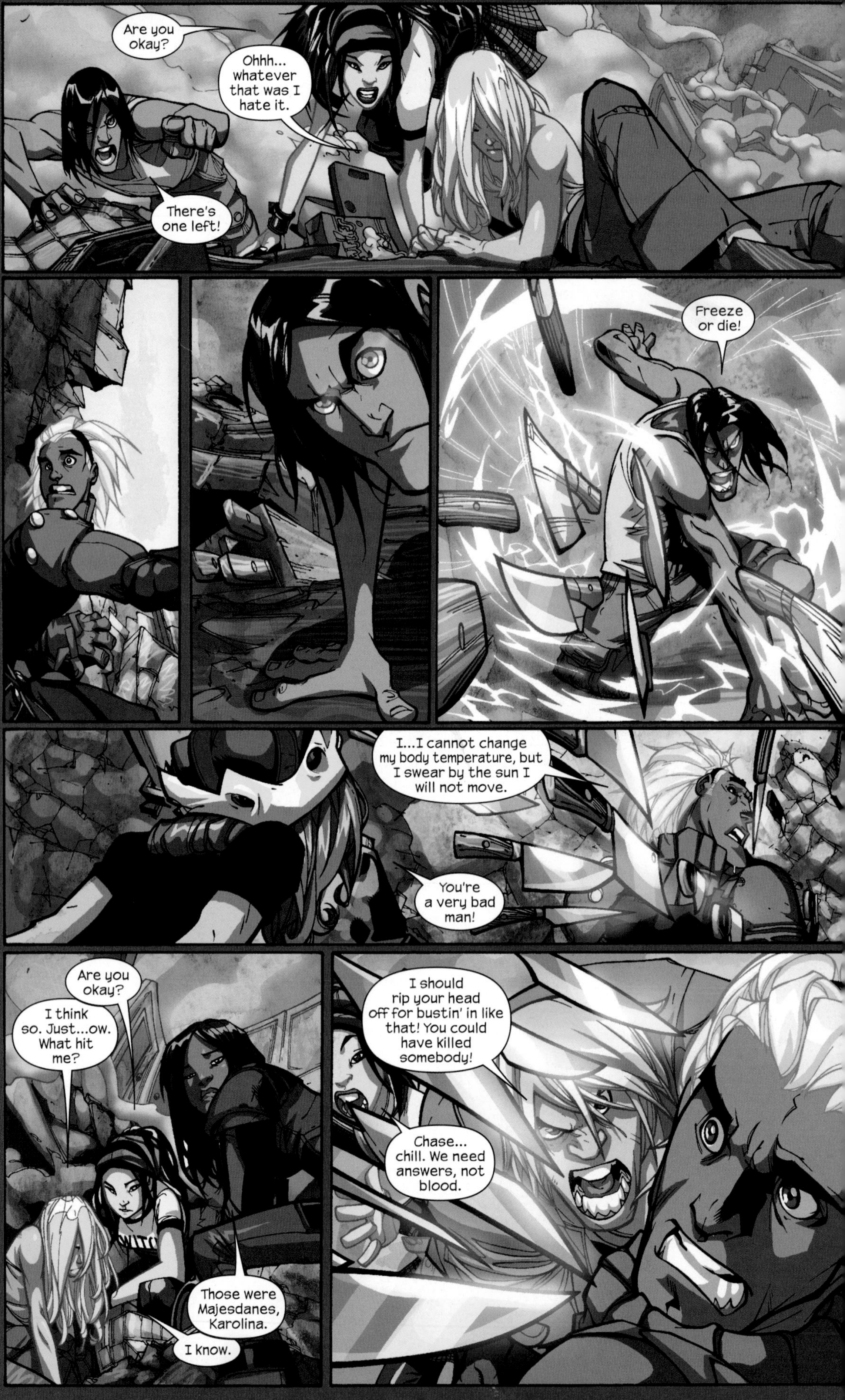
Are you okay?
Ohhh... whatever that was I hate it.
There's one left!
Freeze or die!
I...I cannot change my body temperature, but I swear by the sun I will not move.
You're a very bad man!
Are you okay?
I think so. Just...ow. What hit me?
Those were Majesdanes, Karolina.
I know.
I should rip your head off for bustin' in like that! You could have killed somebody!
Chase... chill. We need answers, not blood.

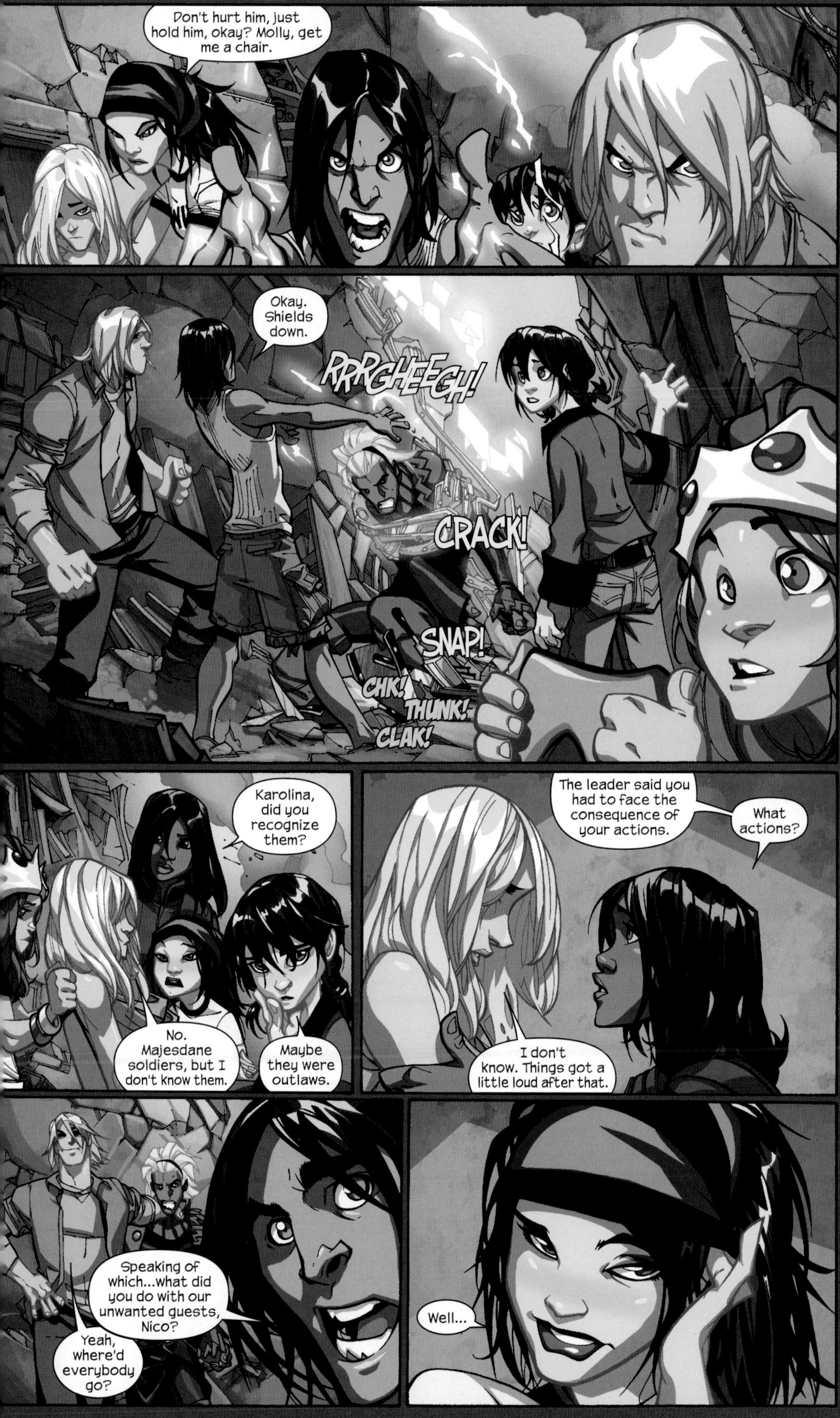

Don't hurt him, just hold him, okay? Molly, get me a chair.
Okay. Shields down.
RRRGHEEGH!
CRACK!
SNAP!
CHK!
THUNK!
CLAK!
Karolina, did you recognize them?
No. Majesdane soldiers, but I don't know them.
Maybe they were outlaws.
The leader said you had to face the consequence of your actions.
What actions?
I don't know. Things got a little loud after that.
Speaking of which...what did you do with our unwanted guests, Nico?
Yeah, where'd everybody go?
Well...

This is for my--

KRVFFFFT!

SQUEEEEE!

What the sun?!

RRROOOOWRRR!

AWK! SQUAWK! SQU
AWK! SQUAWK! SQU
AWK! SQUAWK! SQU
AWK! SQUAWK! SQU
AWK! SQU WK! SQU

Cursed planet! This is not...Where is Los Angeles?

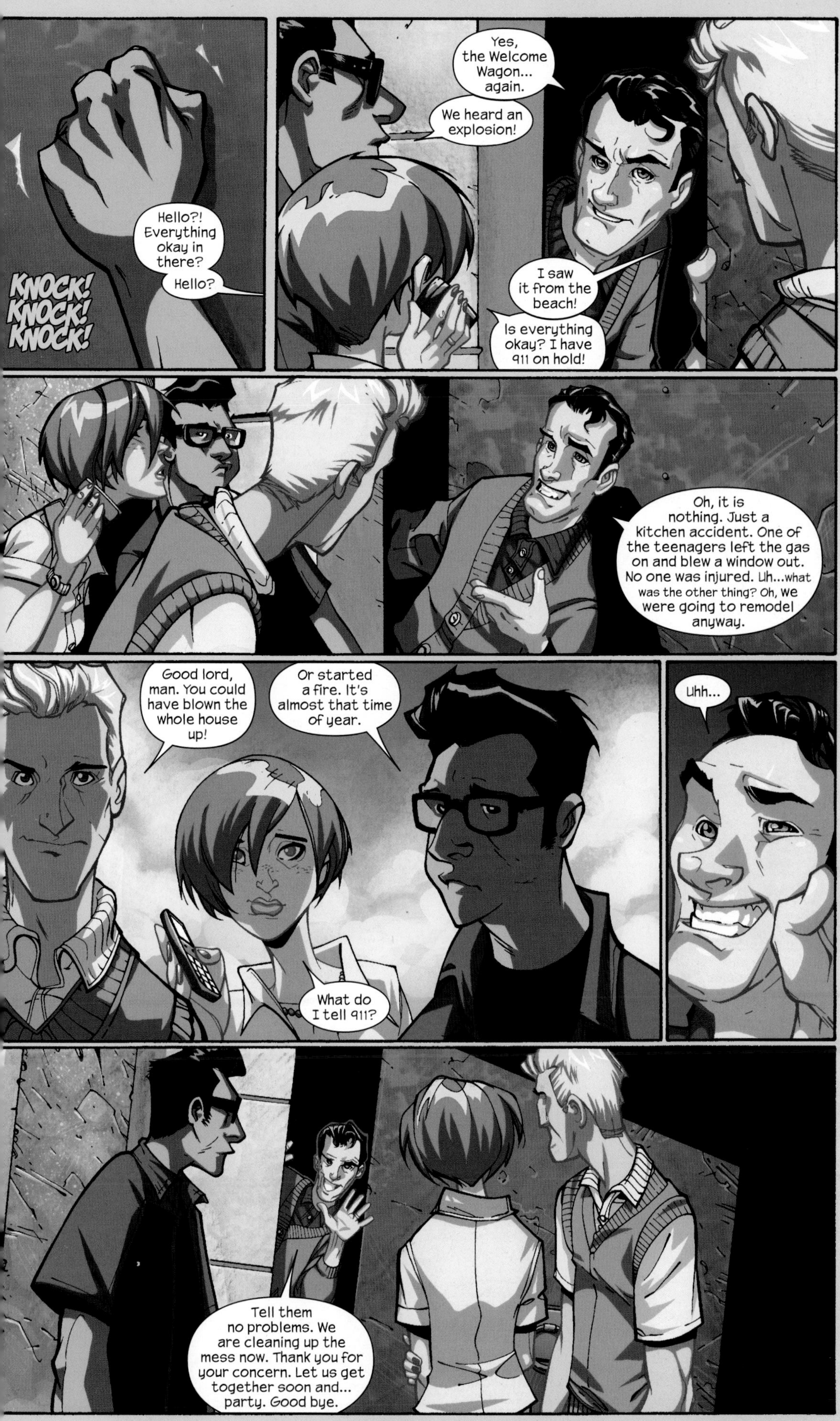

Hello?! Everything okay in there?
Hello?
KNOCK! KNOCK! KNOCK!
Yes, the Welcome Wagon... again.
We heard an explosion!
I saw it from the beach!
Is everything okay? I have 911 on hold!
Oh, it is nothing. Just a kitchen accident. One of the teenagers left the gas on and blew a window out. No one was injured. Uh...what was the other thing? Oh, we were going to remodel anyway.
Good lord, man. You could have blown the whole house up!
Or started a fire. It's almost that time of year.
What do I tell 911?
Uhh...
Tell them no problems. We are cleaning up the mess now. Thank you for your concern. Let us get together soon and... party. Good bye.

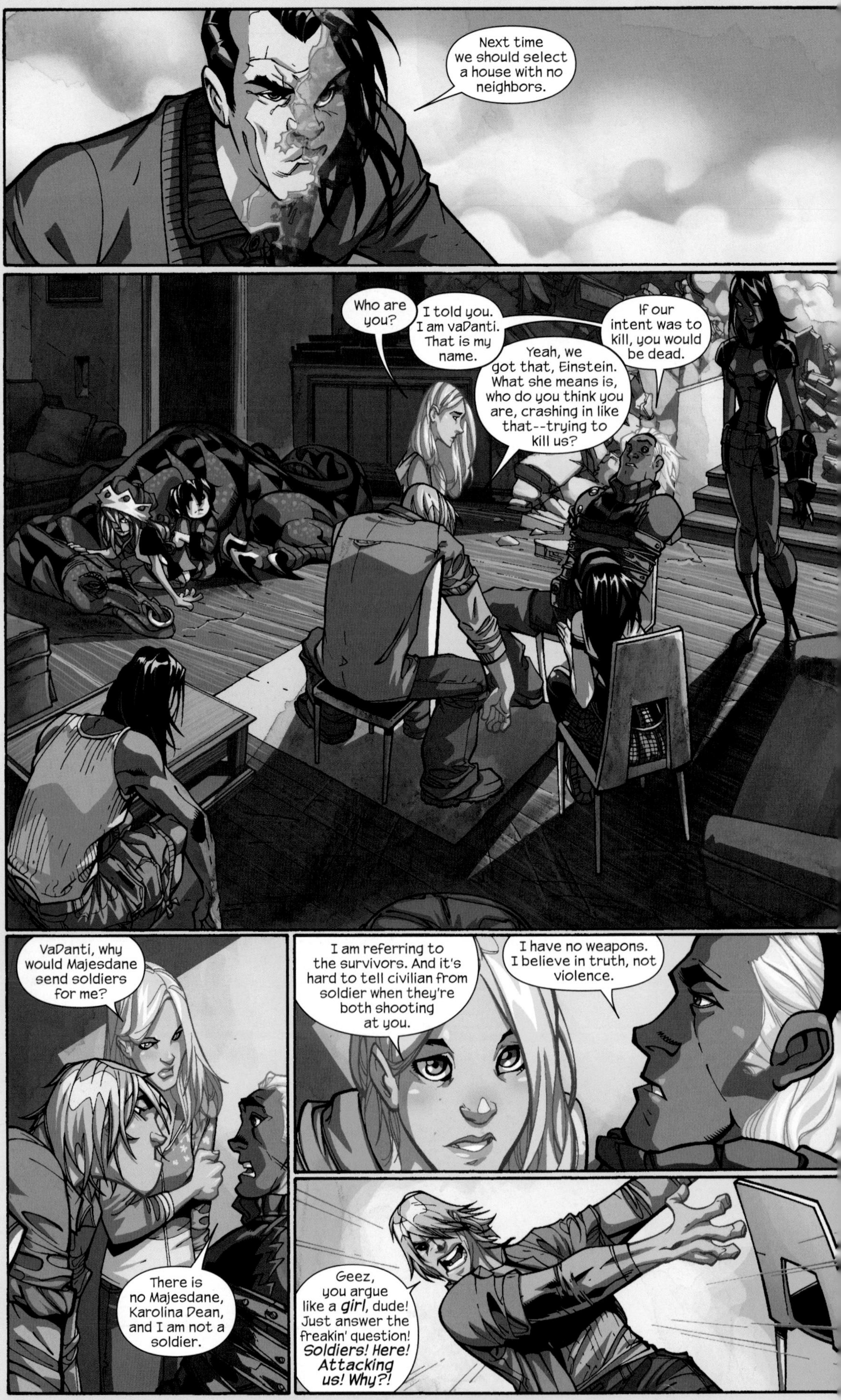

Next time we should select a house with no neighbors.
Who are you?
I told you. I am vaDanti. That is my name.
If our intent was to kill, you would be dead.
Yeah, we got that, Einstein. What she means is, who do you think you are, crashing in like that--trying to kill us?
VaDanti, why would Majesdane send soldiers for me?
There is no Majesdane, Karolina Dean, and I am not a soldier.
I am referring to the survivors. And it's hard to tell civilian from soldier when they're both shooting at you.
I have no weapons. I believe in truth, not violence.
Geez, you argue like a *girl*, dude! Just answer the freakin' question! *Soldiers! Here! Attacking us! Why?!*

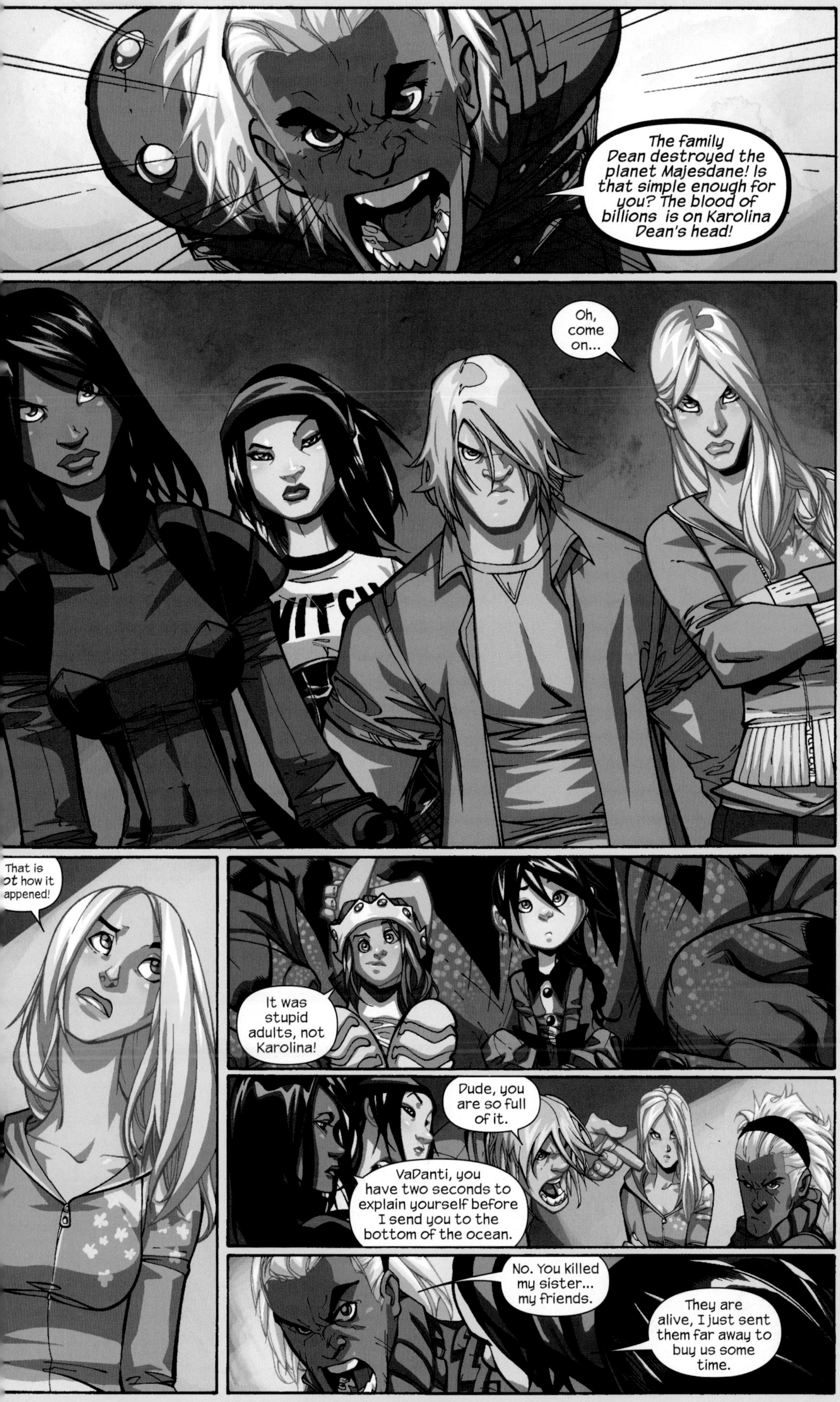
The family Dean destroyed the planet Majesdane! Is that simple enough for you? The blood of billions is on Karolina Dean's head!
Oh, come on...
That is ot how it appened!
It was stupid adults, not Karolina!
Dude, you are so full of it.
VaDanti, you have two seconds to explain yourself before I send you to the bottom of the ocean.
No. You killed my sister... my friends.
They are alive, I just sent them far away to buy us some time.

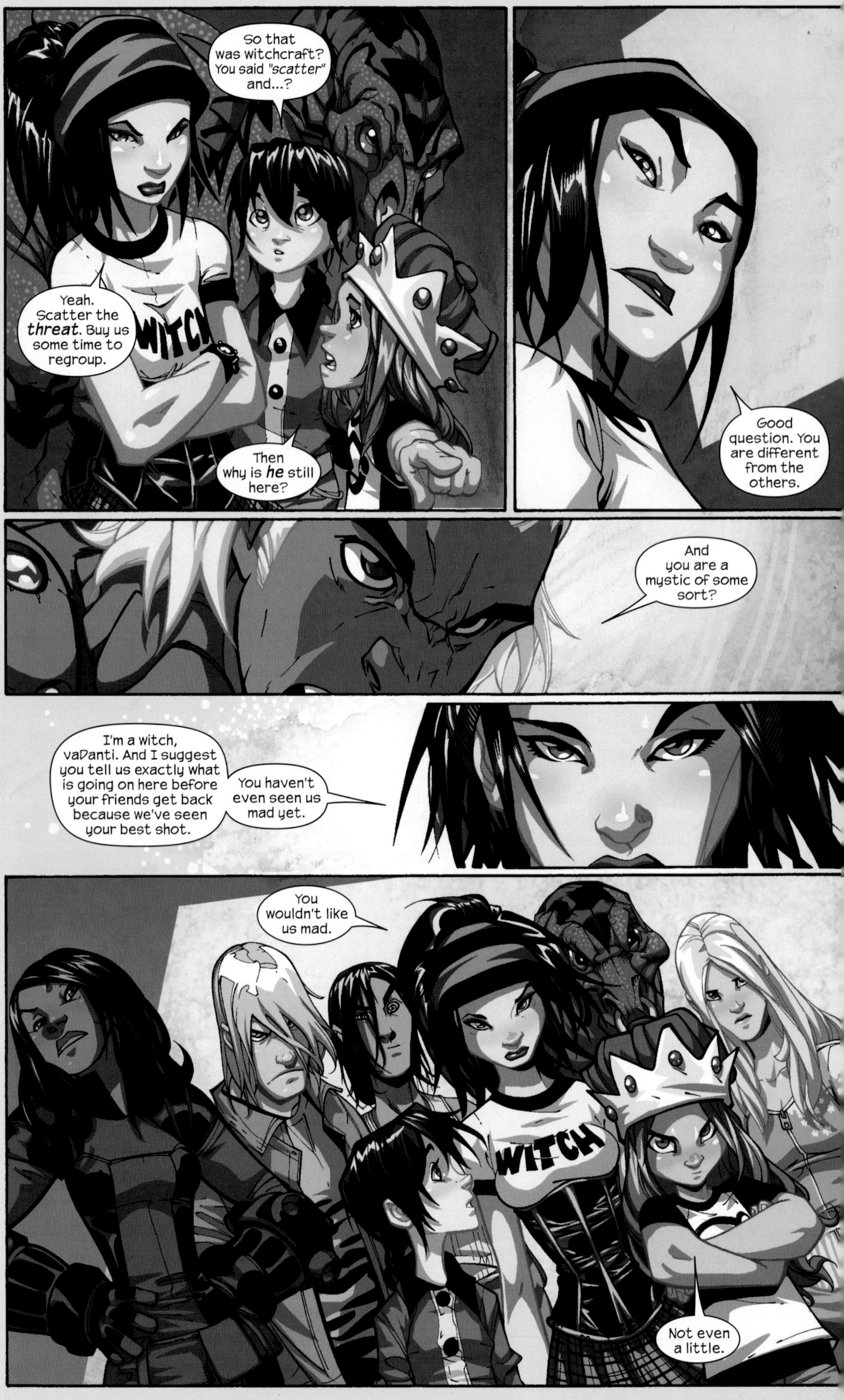
So that was witchcraft? You said "scatter" and...?
Yeah. Scatter the *threat*. Buy us some time to regroup.
Then why is *he* still here?
Good question. You are different from the others.
And you are a mystic of some sort?
I'm a witch, vaDanti. And I suggest you tell us exactly what is going on here before your friends get back because we've seen your best shot.
You haven't even seen us mad yet.
You wouldn't like us mad.
Not even a little.

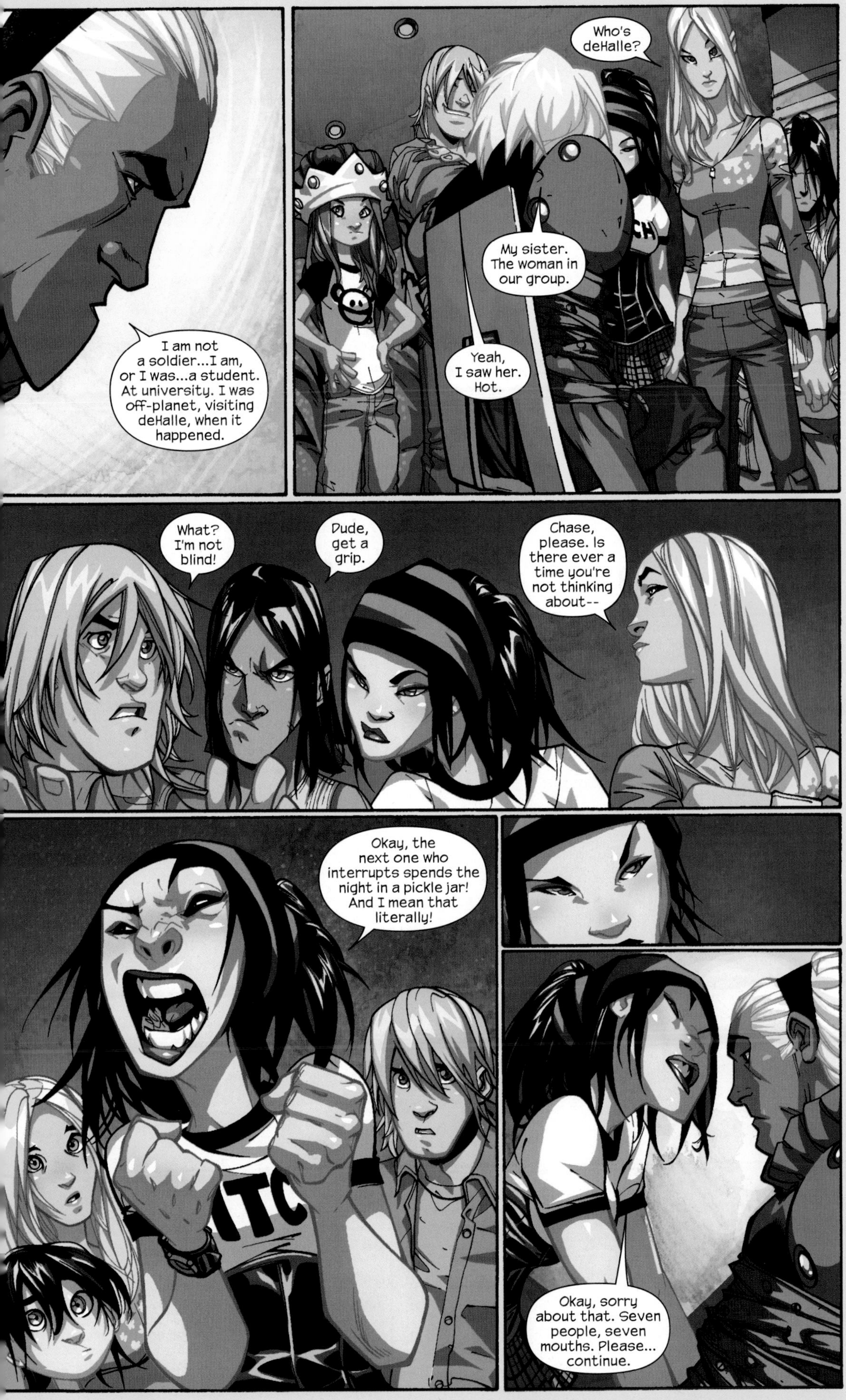
I am not a soldier...I am, or I was...a student. At university. I was off-planet, visiting deHalle, when it happened.
Who's deHalle?
My sister. The woman in our group.
Yeah, I saw her. Hot.
What? I'm not blind!
Dude, get a grip.
Chase, please. Is there ever a time you're not thinking about--
Okay, the next one who interrupts spends the night in a pickle jar! And I mean that literally!
Okay, sorry about that. Seven people, seven mouths. Please... continue.

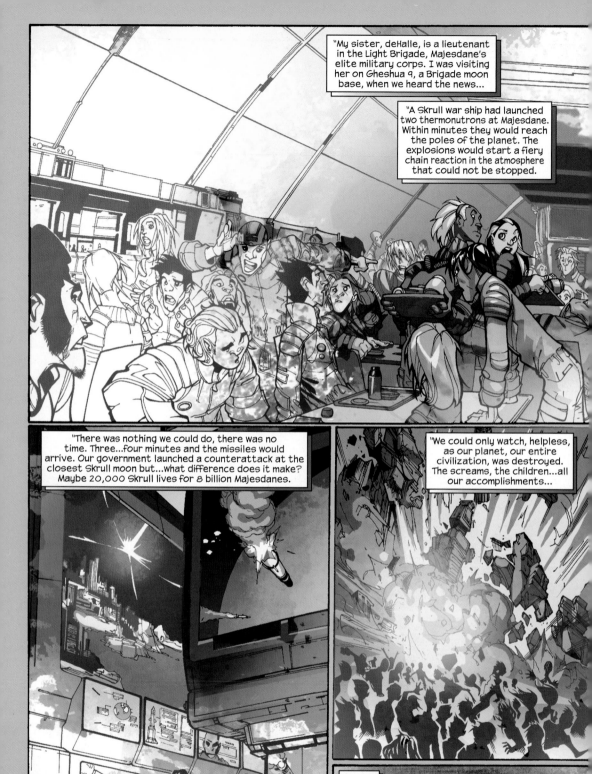

"My sister, deHalle, is a lieutenant in the Light Brigade, Majesdane's elite military corps. I was visiting her on Gheshua 9, a Brigade moon base, when we heard the news...

"A Skrull war ship had launched two thermonutrons at Majesdane. Within minutes they would reach the poles of the planet. The explosions would start a fiery chain reaction in the atmosphere that could not be stopped.

"There was nothing we could do, there was no time. Three...four minutes and the missiles would arrive. Our government launched a counterattack at the closest Skrull moon but...what difference does it make? Maybe 20,000 Skrull lives for 8 billion Majesdanes.

"We could only watch, helpless, as our planet, our entire civilization, was destroyed. The screams, the children...all our accomplishments...

"Gone.

"One minute after the missiles exploded every living thing on Majesdane was dead. Our world burned for hours before the heat disintegrated the core, splitting the planet into pieces that gradually fell into the sun."

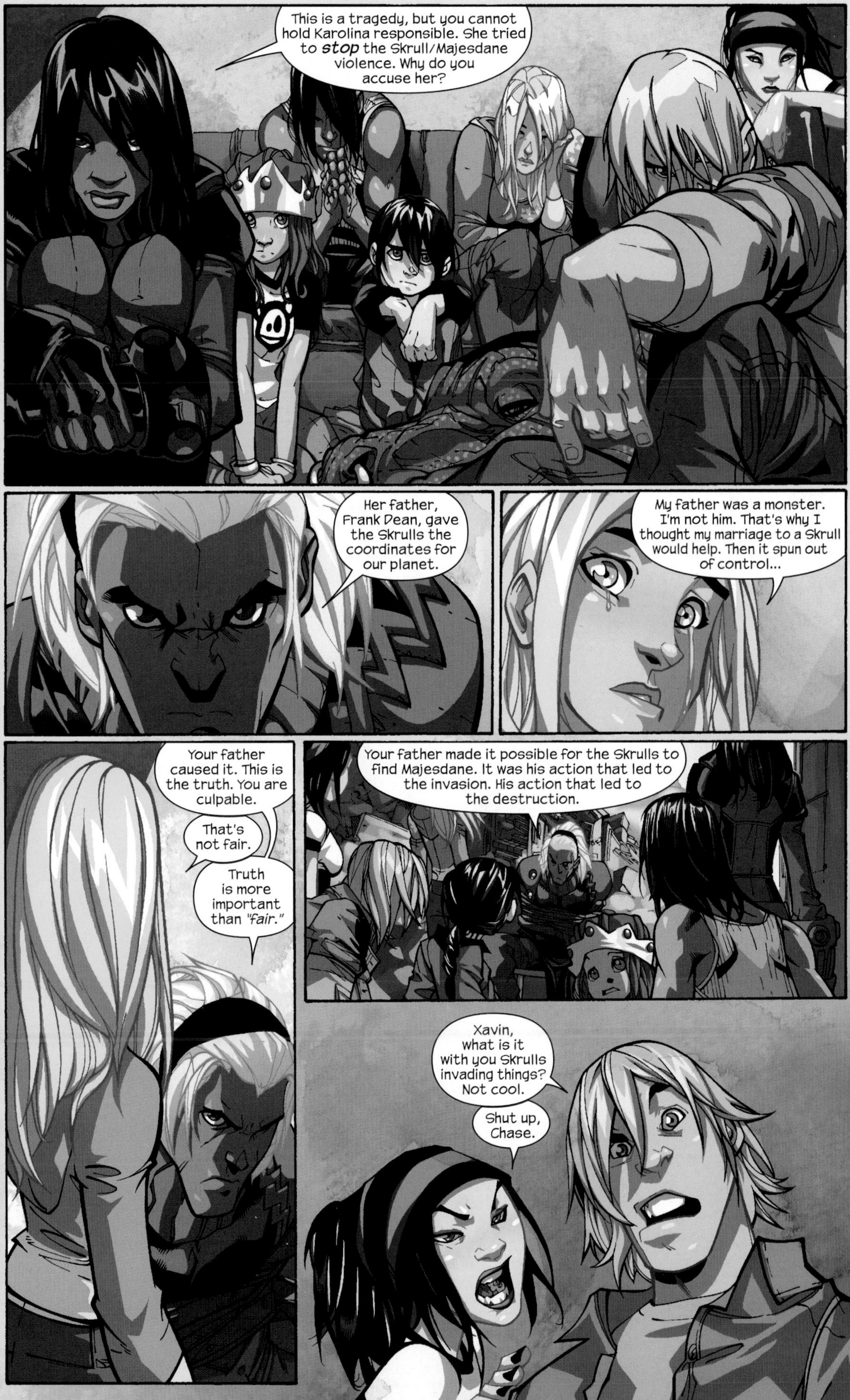
This is a tragedy, but you cannot hold Karolina responsible. She tried to **stop** the Skrull/Majesdane violence. Why do you accuse her?
Her father, Frank Dean, gave the Skrulls the coordinates for our planet.
My father was a monster. I'm not him. That's why I thought my marriage to a Skrull would help. Then it spun out of control...
Your father caused it. This is the truth. You are culpable.
That's not fair.
Truth is more important than *"fair."*
Your father made it possible for the Skrulls to find Majesdane. It was his action that led to the invasion. His action that led to the destruction.
Xavin, what is it with you Skrulls invading things? Not cool.
Shut up, Chase.

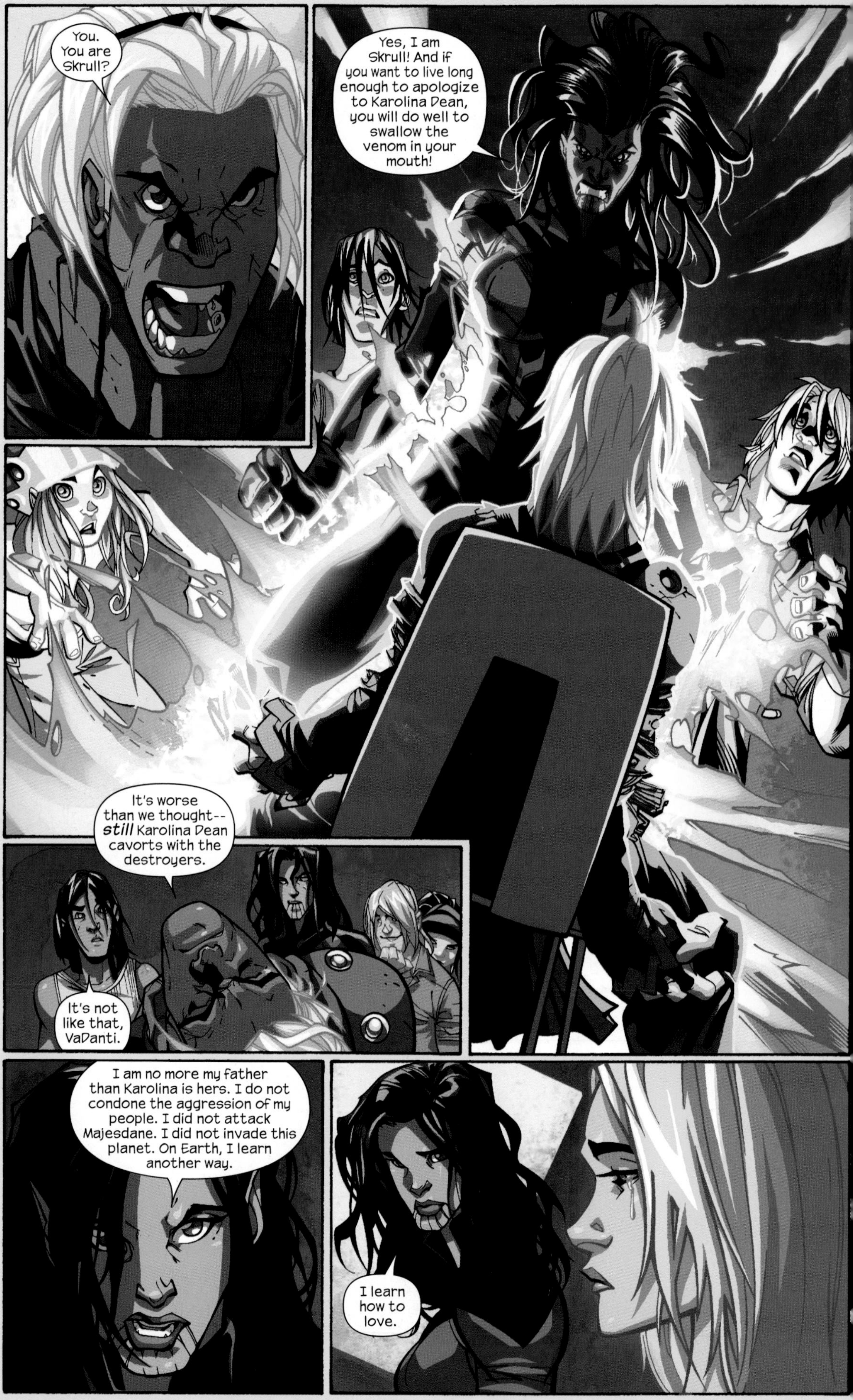
You. You are Skrull?
Yes, I am Skrull! And if you want to live long enough to apologize to Karolina Dean, you will do well to swallow the venom in your mouth!
It's worse than we thought-- *still* Karolina Dean cavorts with the destroyers.
It's not like that, VaDanti.
I am no more my father than Karolina is hers. I do not condone the aggression of my people. I did not attack Majesdane. I did not invade this planet. On Earth, I learn another way.
I learn how to love.

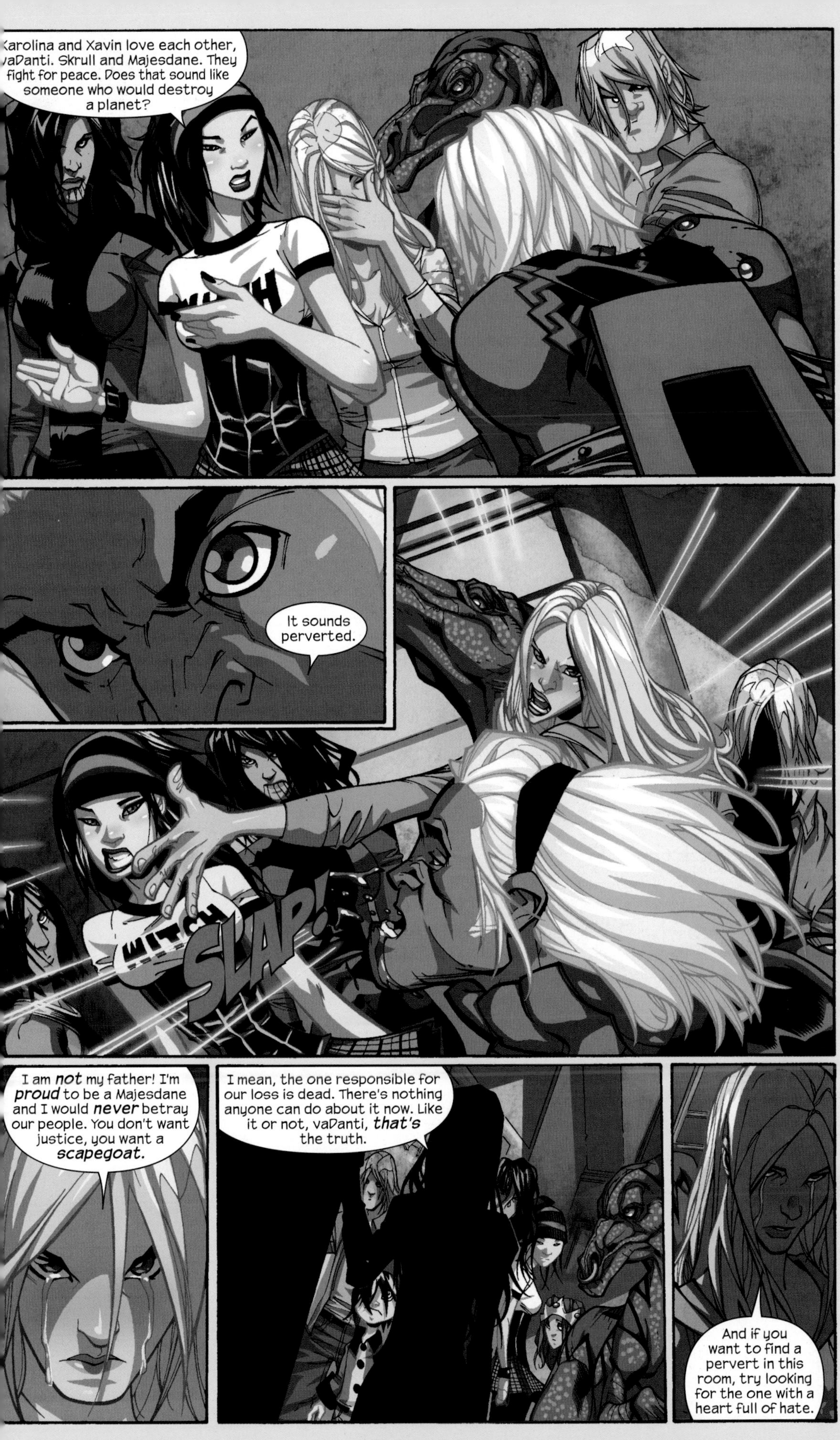

Karolina and Xavin love each other, vaDanti. Skrull and Majesdane. They fight for peace. Does that sound like someone who would destroy a planet?
It sounds perverted.
SLAP!
I am not my father! I'm proud to be a Majesdane and I would never betray our people. You don't want justice, you want a scapegoat.
I mean, the one responsible for our loss is dead. There's nothing anyone can do about it now. Like it or not, vaDanti, that's the truth.
And if you want to find a pervert in this room, try looking for the one with a heart full of hate.

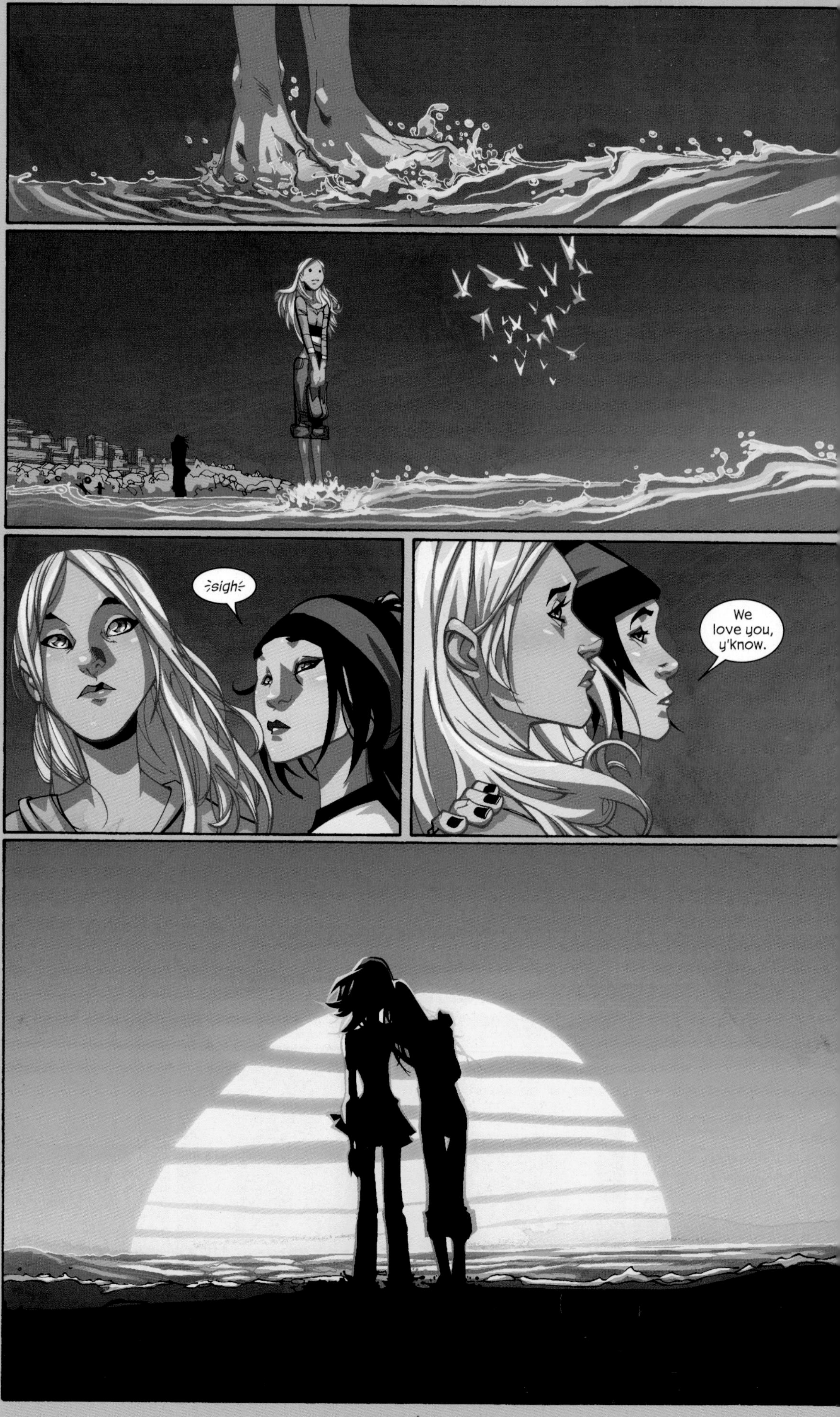

sigh
We love you, y'know.

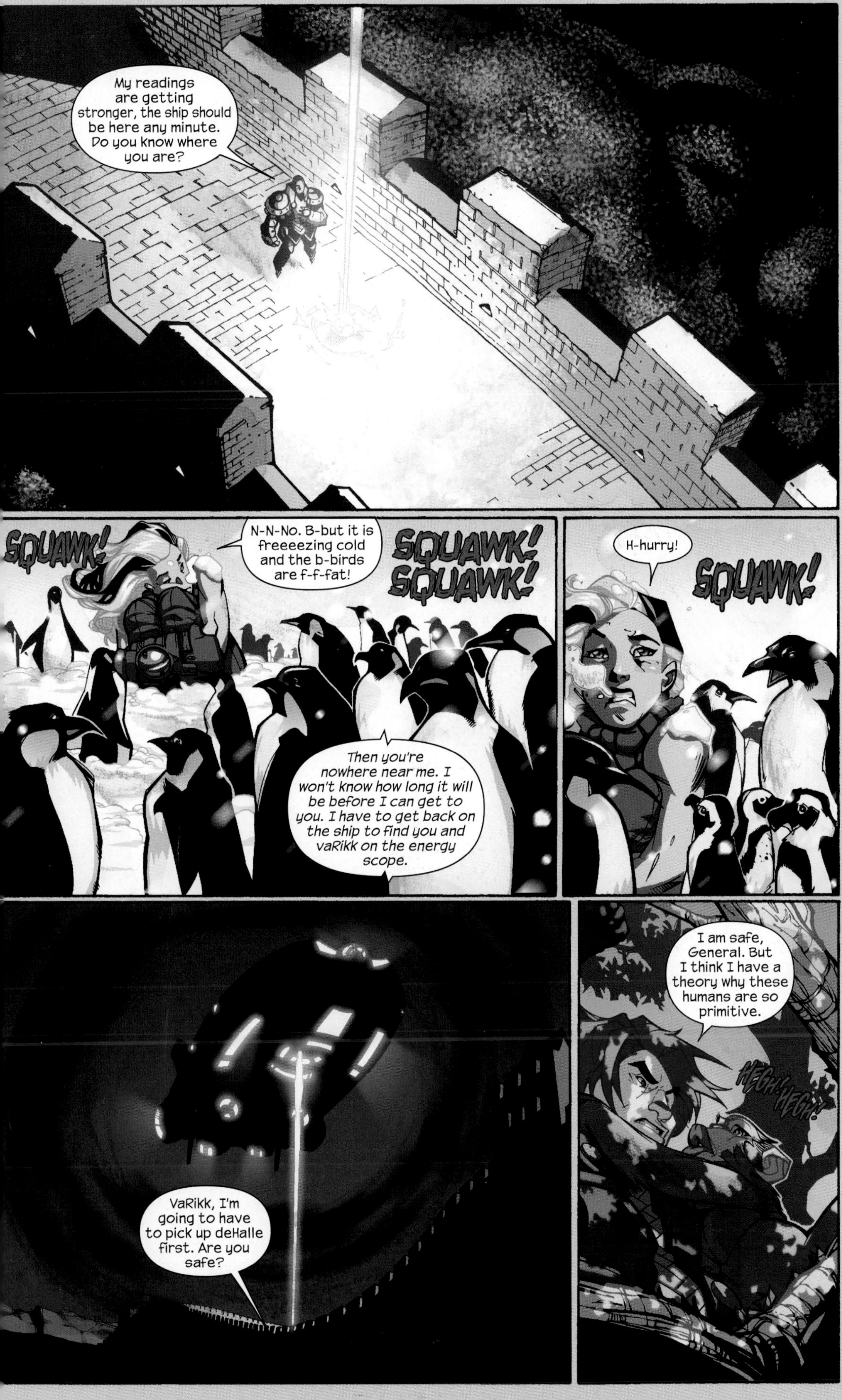
My readings are getting stronger, the ship should be here any minute. Do you know where you are?
SQUAWK!
N-N-No. B-but it is freeeezing cold and the b-birds are f-f-fat!
SQUAWK! SQUAWK!
Then you're nowhere near me. I won't know how long it will be before I can get to you. I have to get back on the ship to find you and vaRikk on the energy scope.
H-hurry!
SQUAWK!
VaRikk, I'm going to have to pick up deHalle first. Are you safe?
I am safe, General. But I think I have a theory why these humans are so primitive.
HEGH! HEGH!

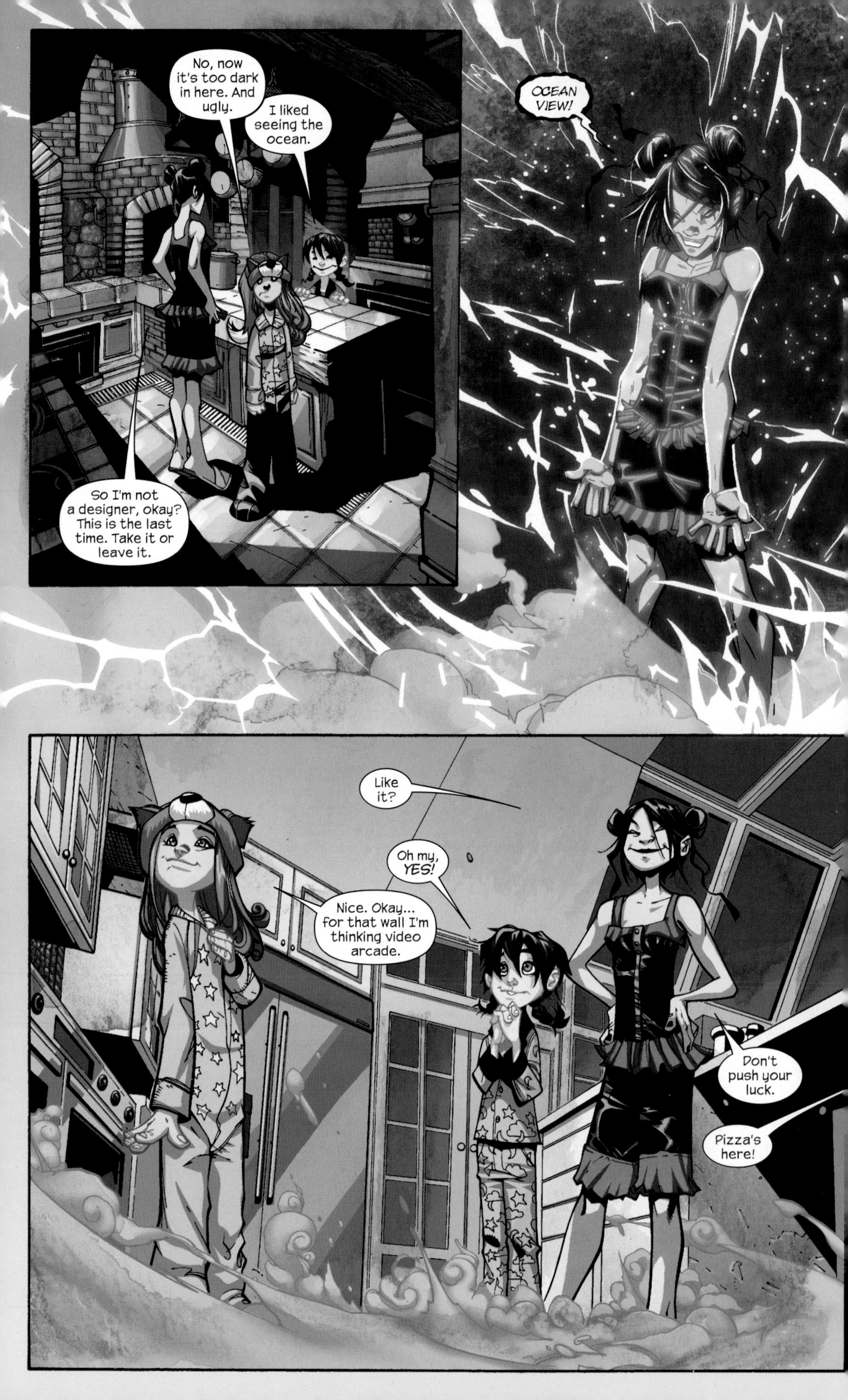
No, now it's too dark in here. And ugly.
I liked seeing the ocean.
So I'm not a designer, okay? This is the last time. Take it or leave it.
OCEAN VIEW!
Like it?
Oh my, YES!
Nice. Okay... for that wall I'm thinking video arcade.
Don't push your luck.
Pizza's here!

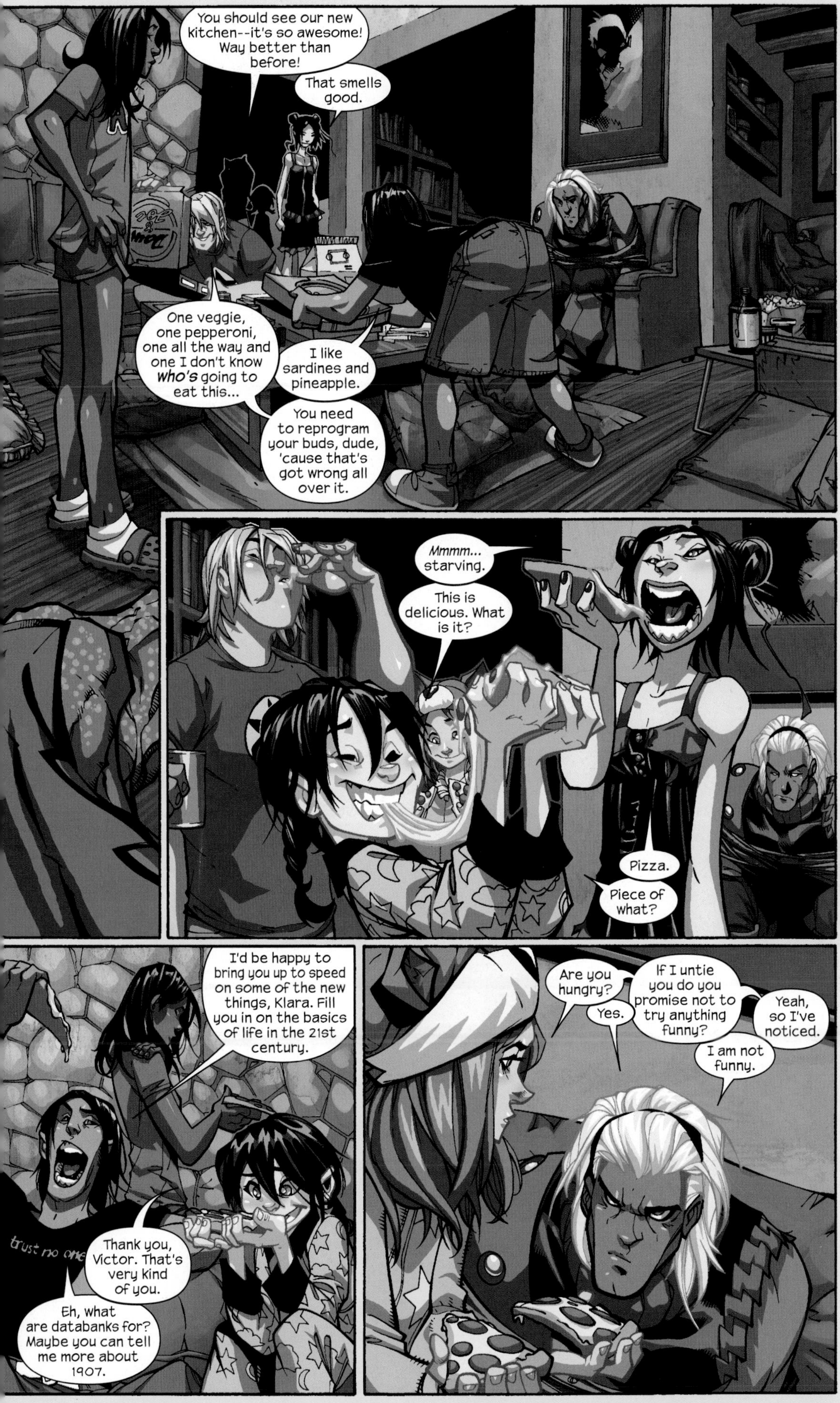
You should see our new kitchen--it's so awesome! Way better than before!
That smells good.
One veggie, one pepperoni, one all the way and one I don't know *who's* going to eat this...
I like sardines and pineapple.
You need to reprogram your buds, dude, 'cause that's got wrong all over it.
Mmmm... starving.
This is delicious. What is it?
Pizza.
Piece of what?
I'd be happy to bring you up to speed on some of the new things, Klara. Fill you in on the basics of life in the 21st century.
Thank you, Victor. That's very kind of you.
Eh, what are databanks for? Maybe you can tell me more about 1907.
trust no one
Are you hungry?
Yes.
If I untie you do you promise not to try anything funny?
I am not funny.
Yeah, so I've noticed.

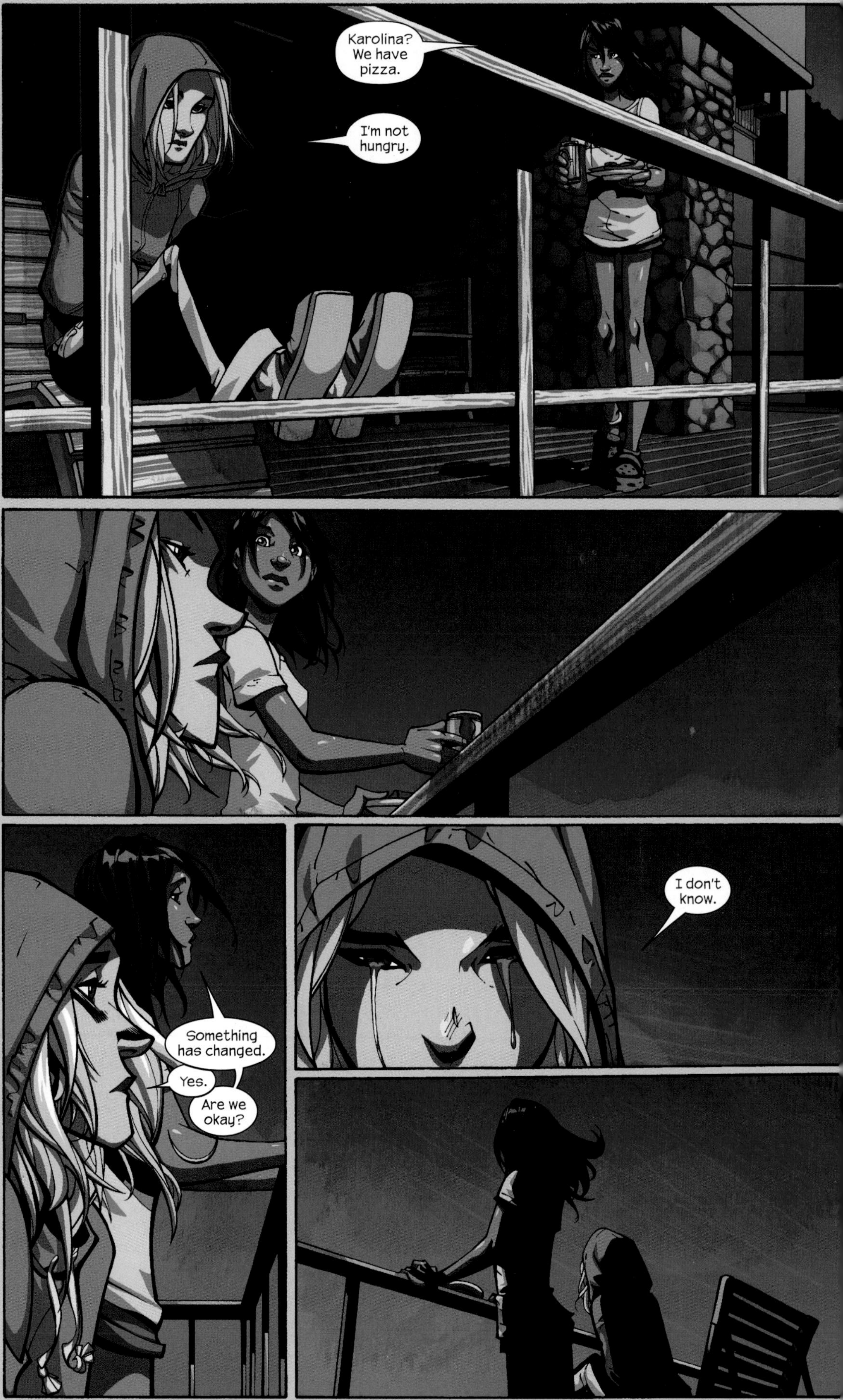
Karolina? We have pizza.
I'm not hungry.
Something has changed.
Yes.
Are we okay?
I don't know.

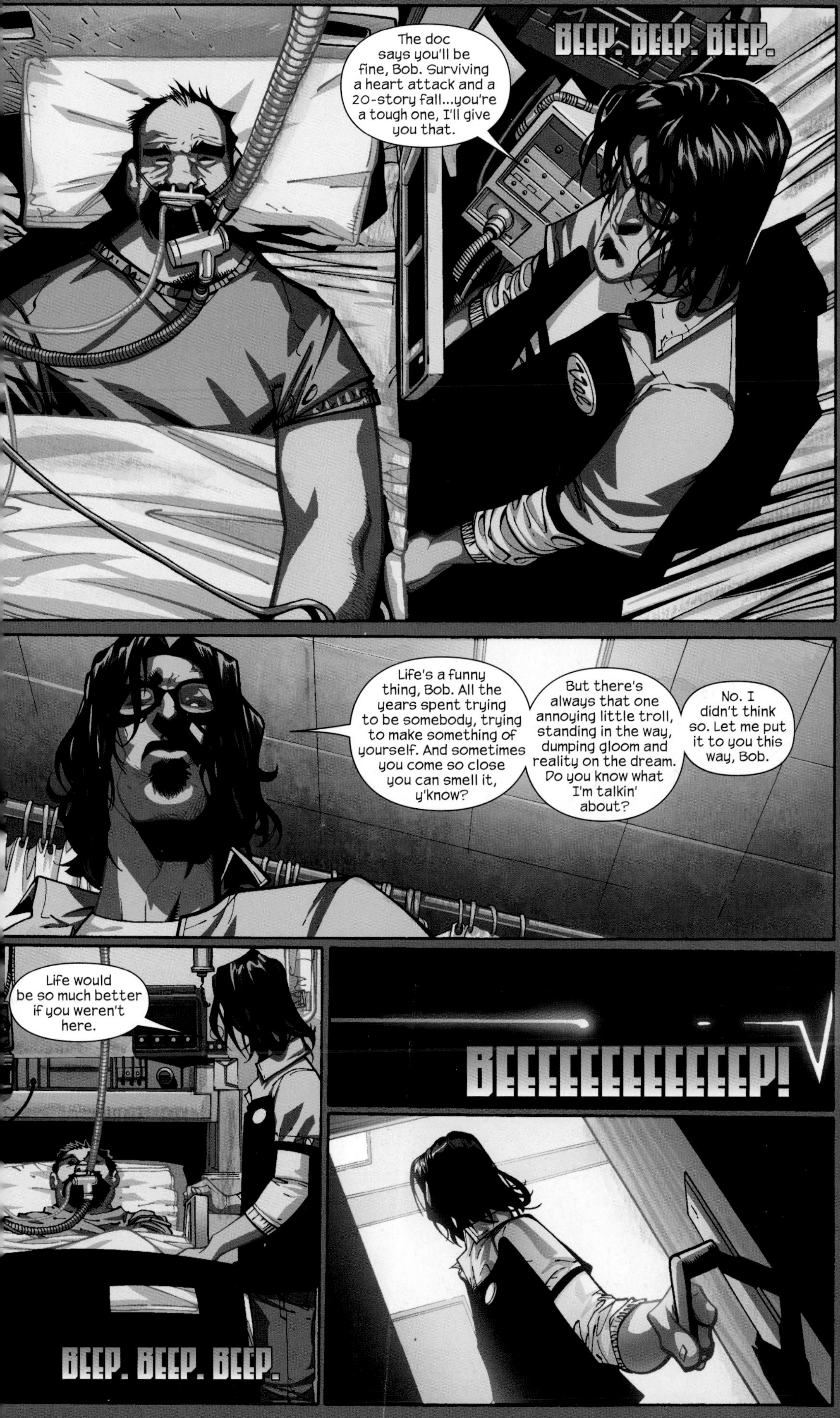
BEEP. BEEP. BEEP.
The doc says you'll be fine, Bob. Surviving a heart attack and a 20-story fall...you're a tough one, I'll give you that.
Life's a funny thing, Bob. All the years spent trying to be somebody, trying to make something of yourself. And sometimes you come so close you can smell it, y'know?
But there's always that one annoying little troll, standing in the way, dumping gloom and reality on the dream. Do you know what I'm talkin' about?
No. I didn't think so. Let me put it to you this way, Bob.
Life would be so much better if you weren't here.
BEEP. BEEP. BEEP.
BEEEEEEEEEEEEP!

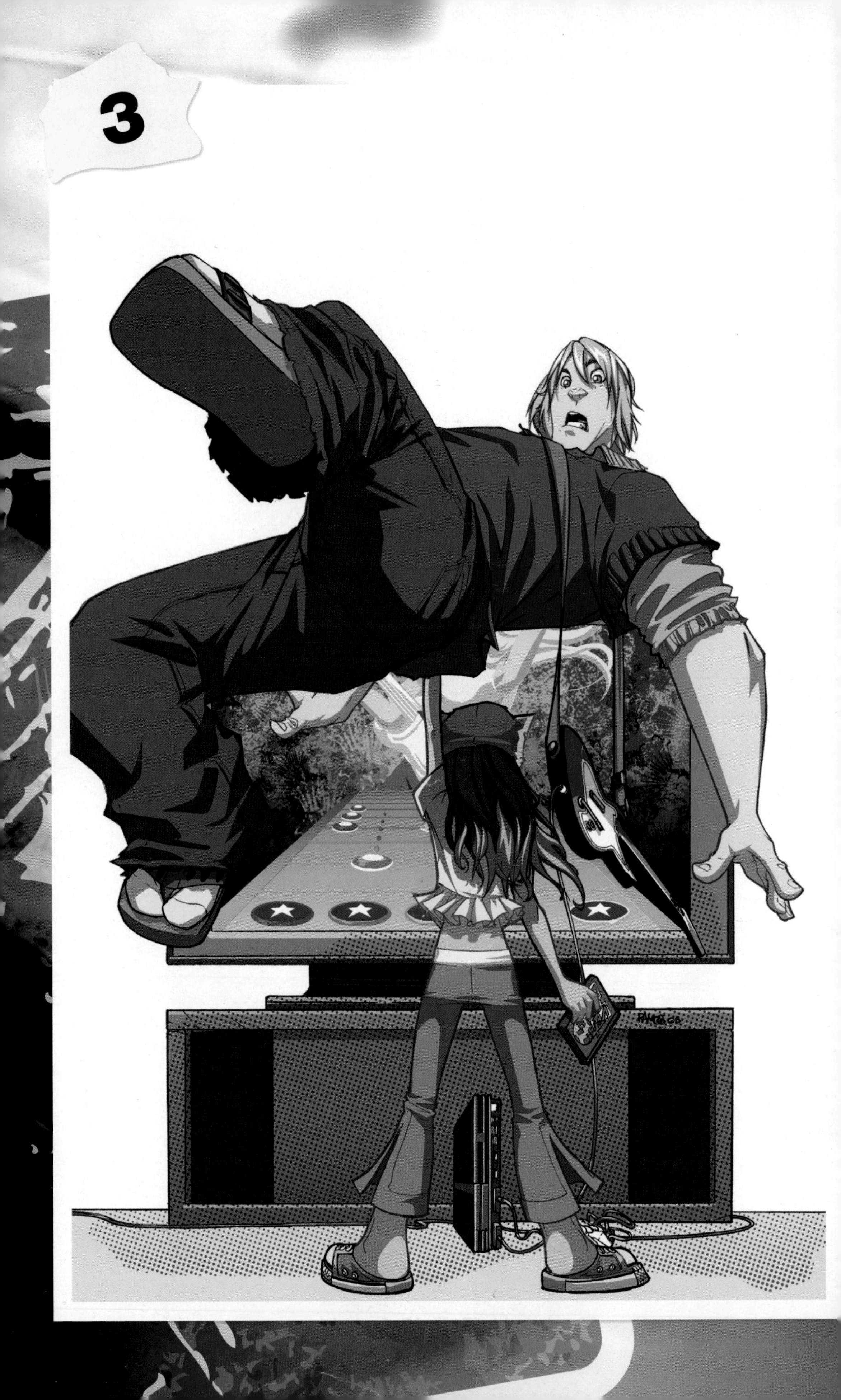
3

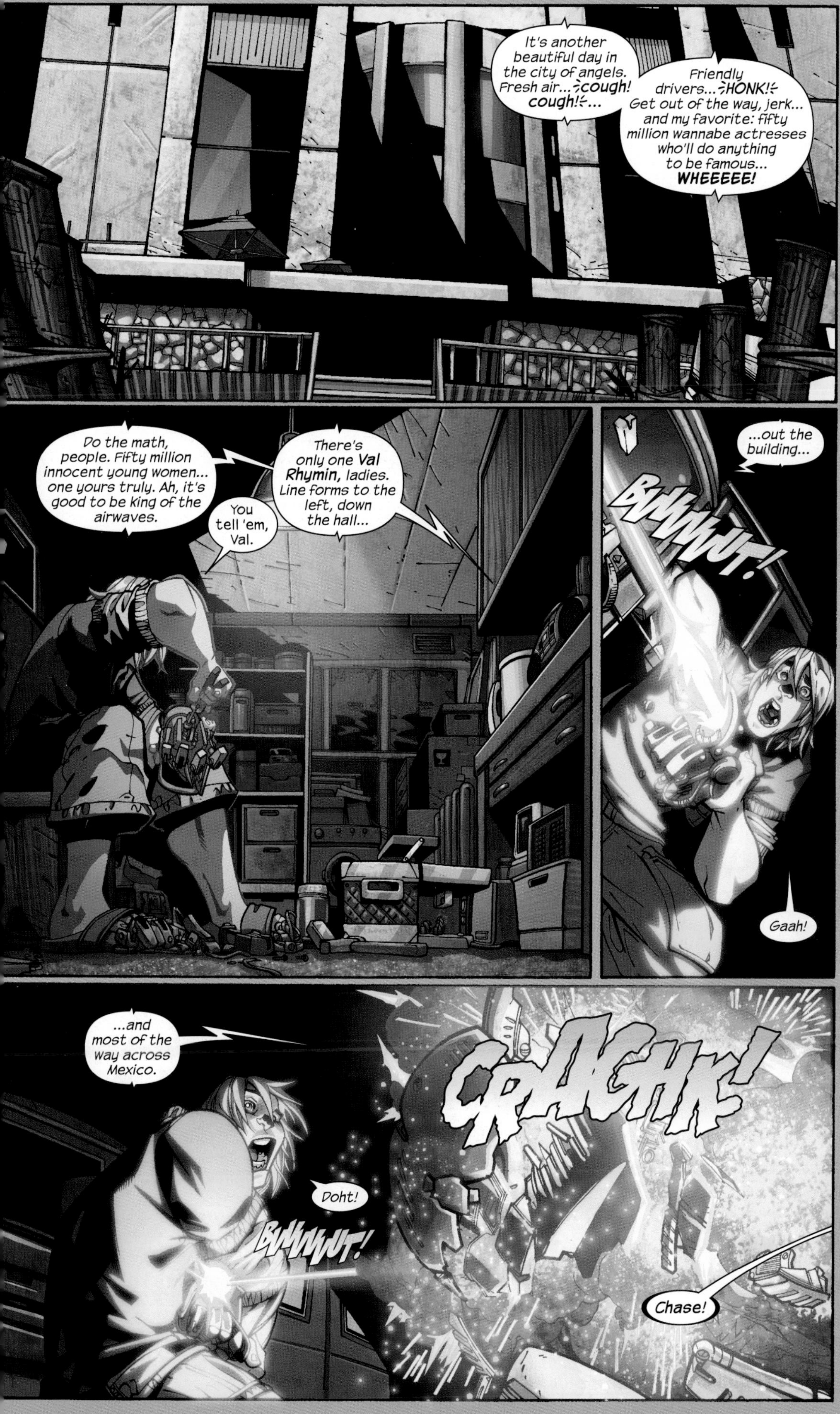
It's another beautiful day in the city of angels. Fresh air... cough! cough!...
Friendly drivers... HONK! Get out of the way, jerk... and my favorite: fifty million wannabe actresses who'll do anything to be famous... WHEEEEE!
Do the math, people. Fifty million innocent young women... one yours truly. Ah, it's good to be king of the airwaves.
There's only one Val Rhymin, ladies. Line forms to the left, down the hall...
You tell 'em, Val.
...out the building...
BWWWUT!
Gaah!
...and most of the way across Mexico.
CRAACHK!
Doht!
BWWWUT!
Chase!

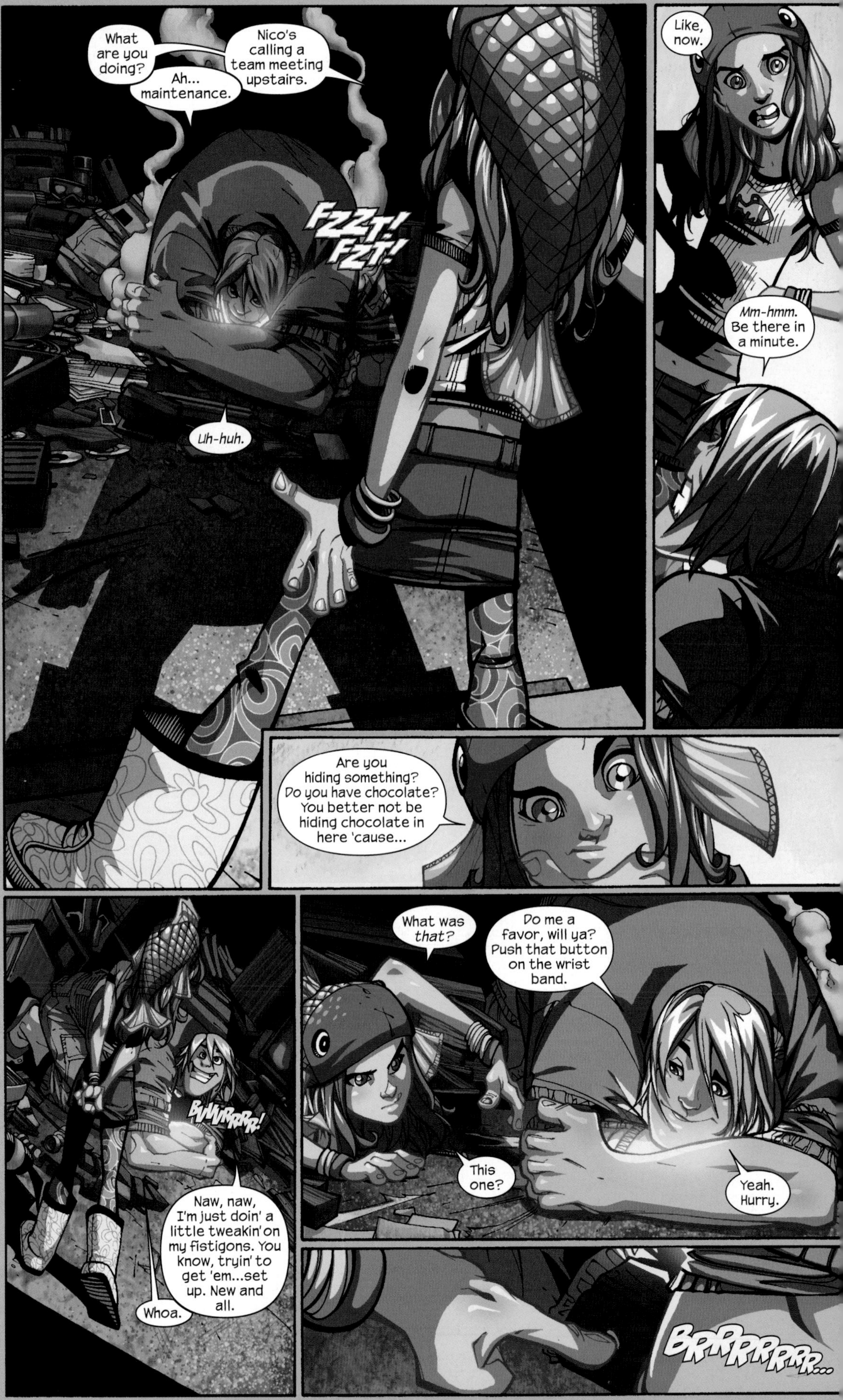

What are you doing?
Nico's calling a team meeting upstairs.
Ah... maintenance.
FZZT! FZT!
Uh-huh.
Like, now.
Mm-hmm. Be there in a minute.
Are you hiding something? Do you have chocolate? You better not be hiding chocolate in here 'cause...
BWWRRRR!
Naw, naw, I'm just doin' a little tweakin' on my fistigons. You know, tryin' to get 'em...set up. New and all.
Whoa.
What was that?
Do me a favor, will ya? Push that button on the wrist band.
This one?
Yeah. Hurry.
BRRRRRRR...

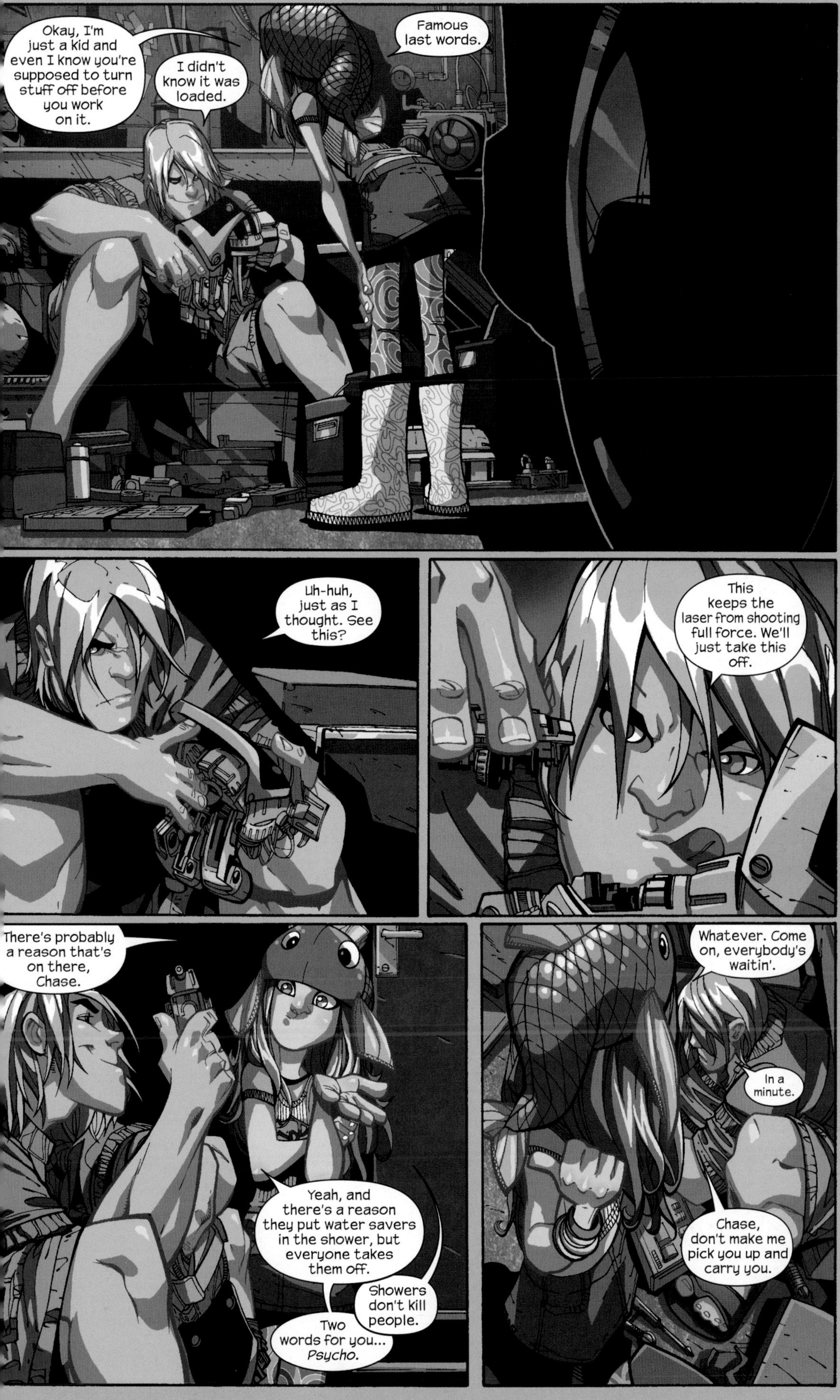
Okay, I'm just a kid and even I know you're supposed to turn stuff off before you work on it.
I didn't know it was loaded.
Famous last words.
Uh-huh, just as I thought. See this?
This keeps the laser from shooting full force. We'll just take this off.
There's probably a reason that's on there, Chase.
Yeah, and there's a reason they put water savers in the shower, but everyone takes them off.
Showers don't kill people.
Two words for you... *Psycho*.
Whatever. Come on, everybody's waitin'.
In a minute.
Chase, don't make me pick you up and carry you.

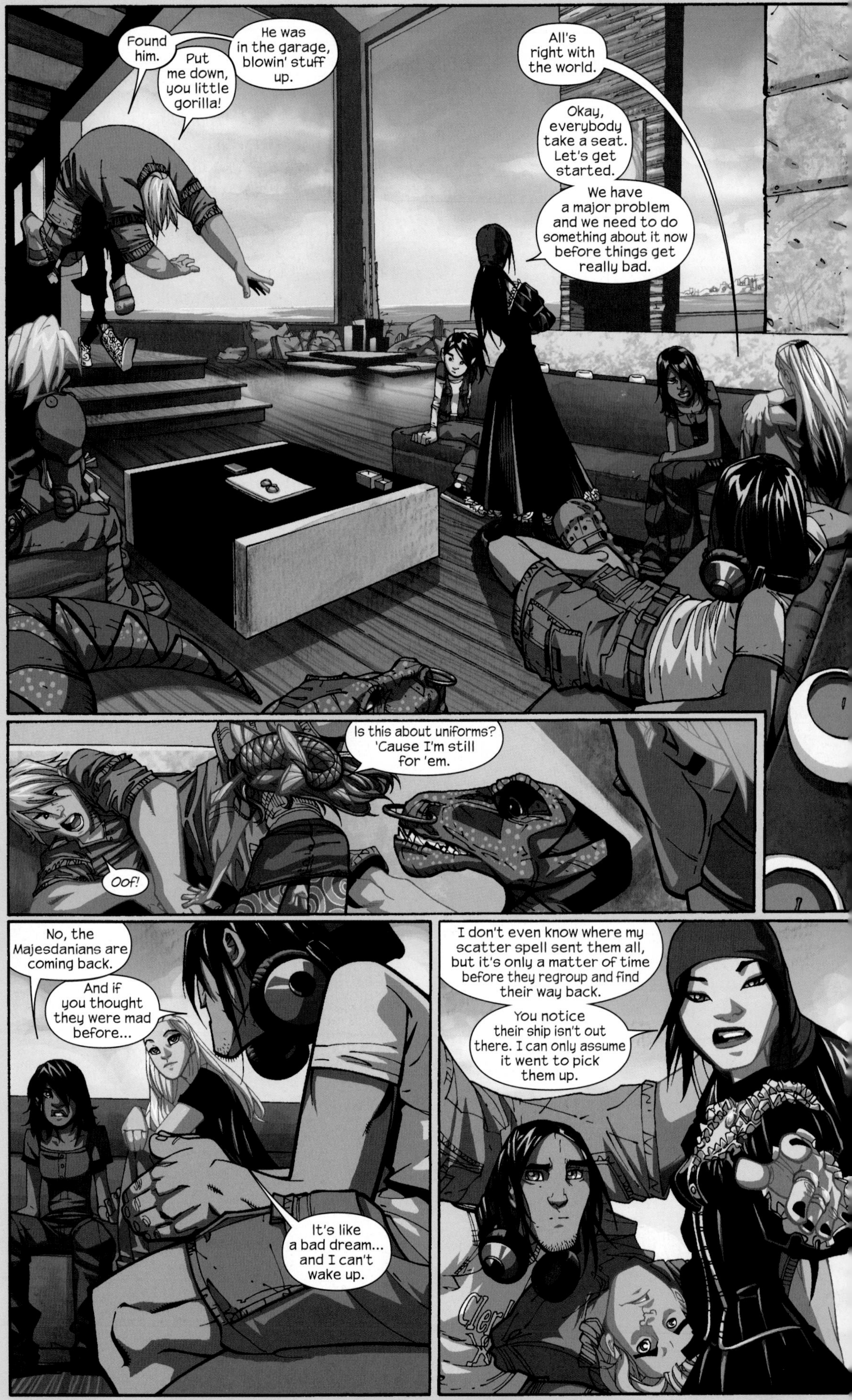
Found him.
He was in the garage, blowin' stuff up.
Put me down, you little gorilla!
All's right with the world.
Okay, everybody take a seat. Let's get started.
We have a major problem and we need to do something about it now before things get really bad.
Is this about uniforms? 'Cause I'm still for 'em.
Oof!
No, the Majesdanians are coming back.
And if you thought they were mad before...
It's like a bad dream... and I can't wake up.
I don't even know where my scatter spell sent them all, but it's only a matter of time before they regroup and find their way back.
You notice their ship isn't out there. I can only assume it went to pick them up.

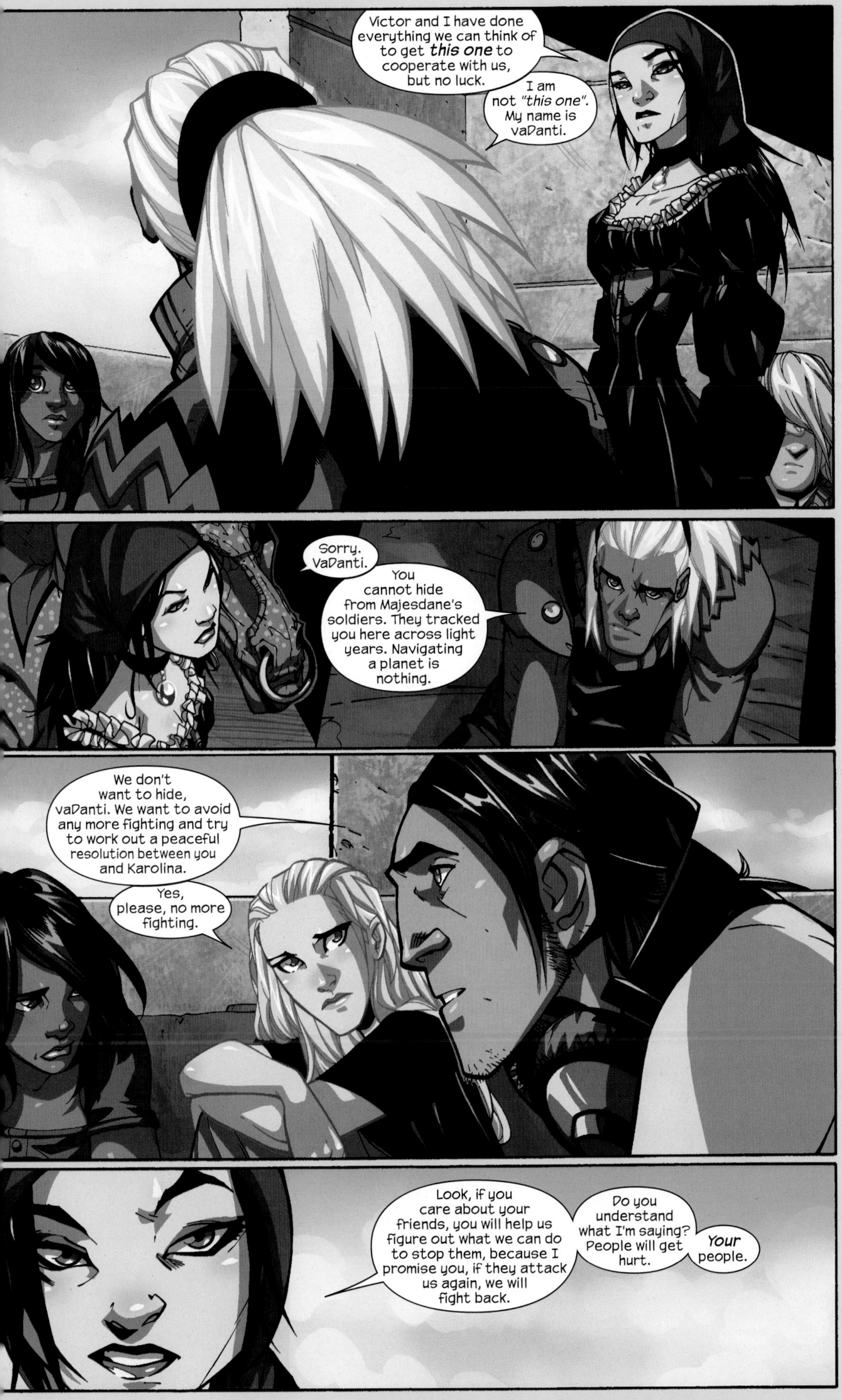
Victor and I have done everything we can think of to get *this one* to cooperate with us, but no luck.
I am not *"this one"*. My name is vaDanti.
Sorry. VaDanti.
You cannot hide from Majesdane's soldiers. They tracked you here across light years. Navigating a planet is nothing.
We don't want to hide, vaDanti. We want to avoid any more fighting and try to work out a peaceful resolution between you and Karolina.
Yes, please, no more fighting.
Look, if you care about your friends, you will help us figure out what we can do to stop them, because I promise you, if they attack us again, we will fight back.
Do you understand what I'm saying? People will get hurt.
Your people.

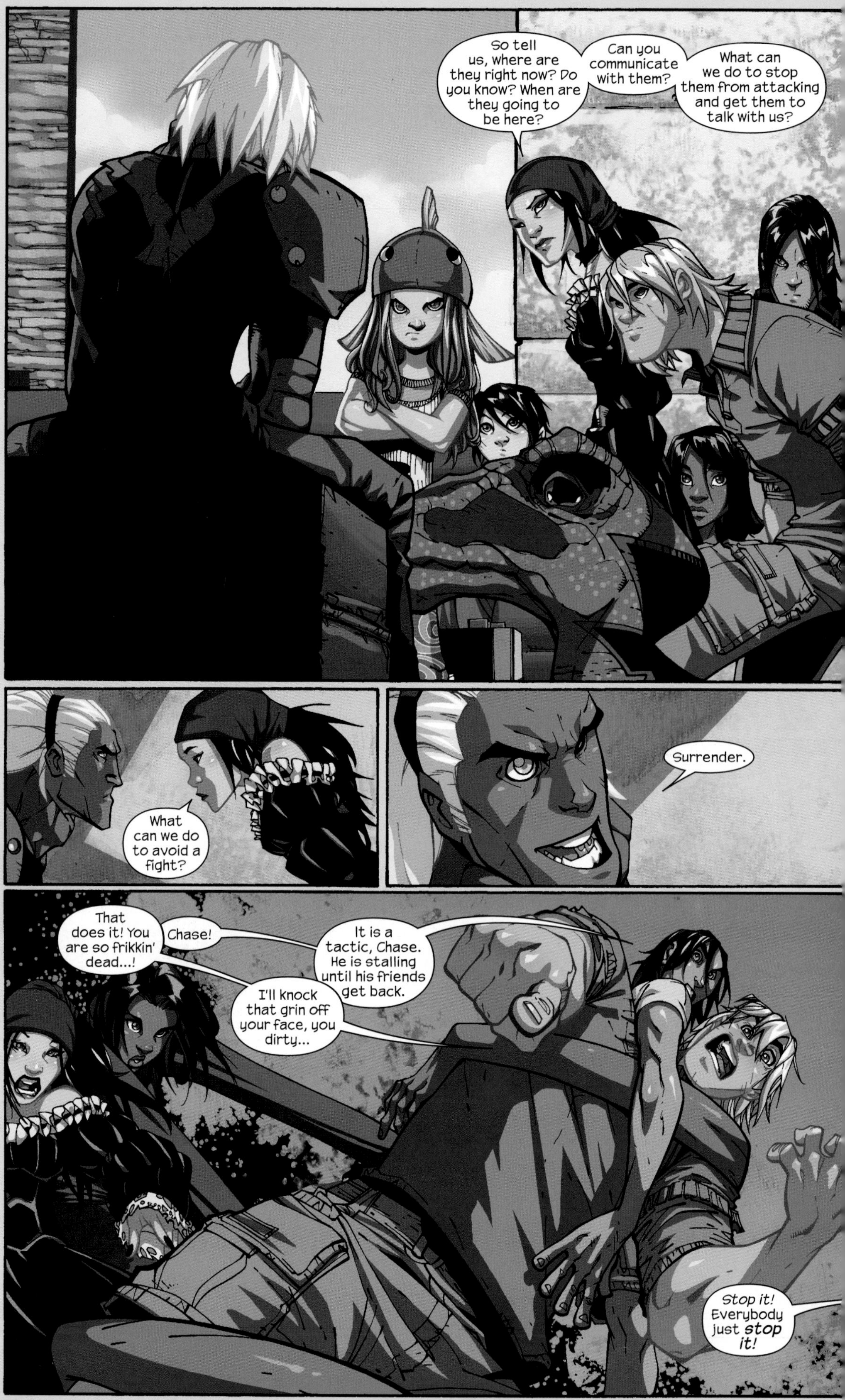
So tell us, where are they right now? Do you know? When are they going to be here?
Can you communicate with them?
What can we do to stop them from attacking and get them to talk with us?
What can we do to avoid a fight?
Surrender.
That does it! You are so frikkin' dead...!
Chase!
It is a tactic, Chase. He is stalling until his friends get back.
I'll knock that grin off your face, you dirty...
Stop it! Everybody just *stop it!*

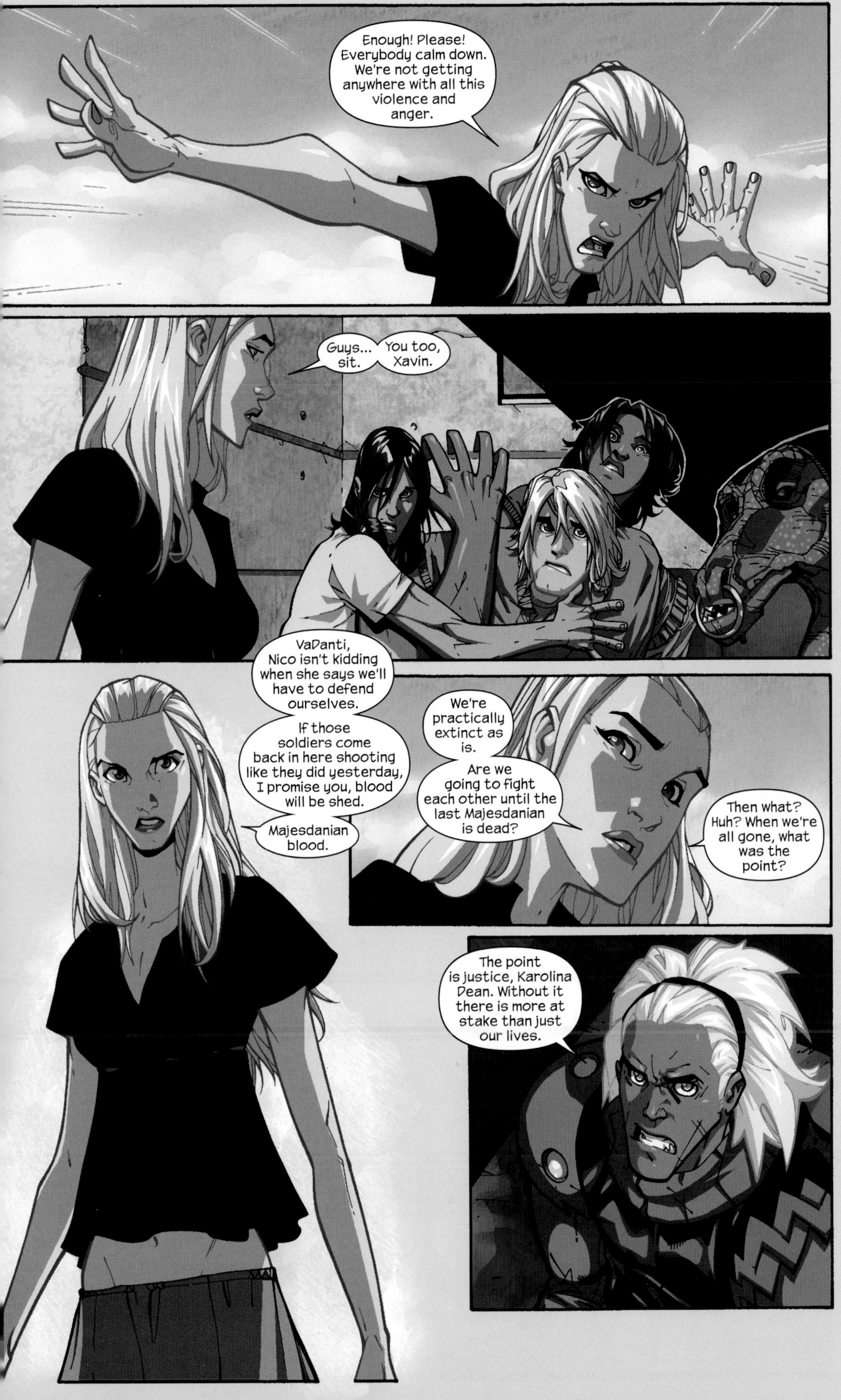
Enough! Please! Everybody calm down. We're not getting anywhere with all this violence and anger.
Guys... sit.
You too, Xavin.
VaDanti, Nico isn't kidding when she says we'll have to defend ourselves.
If those soldiers come back in here shooting like they did yesterday, I promise you, blood will be shed.
Majesdanian blood.
We're practically extinct as is.
Are we going to fight each other until the last Majesdanian is dead?
Then what? Huh? When we're all gone, what was the point?
The point is justice, Karolina Dean. Without it there is more at stake than just our lives.

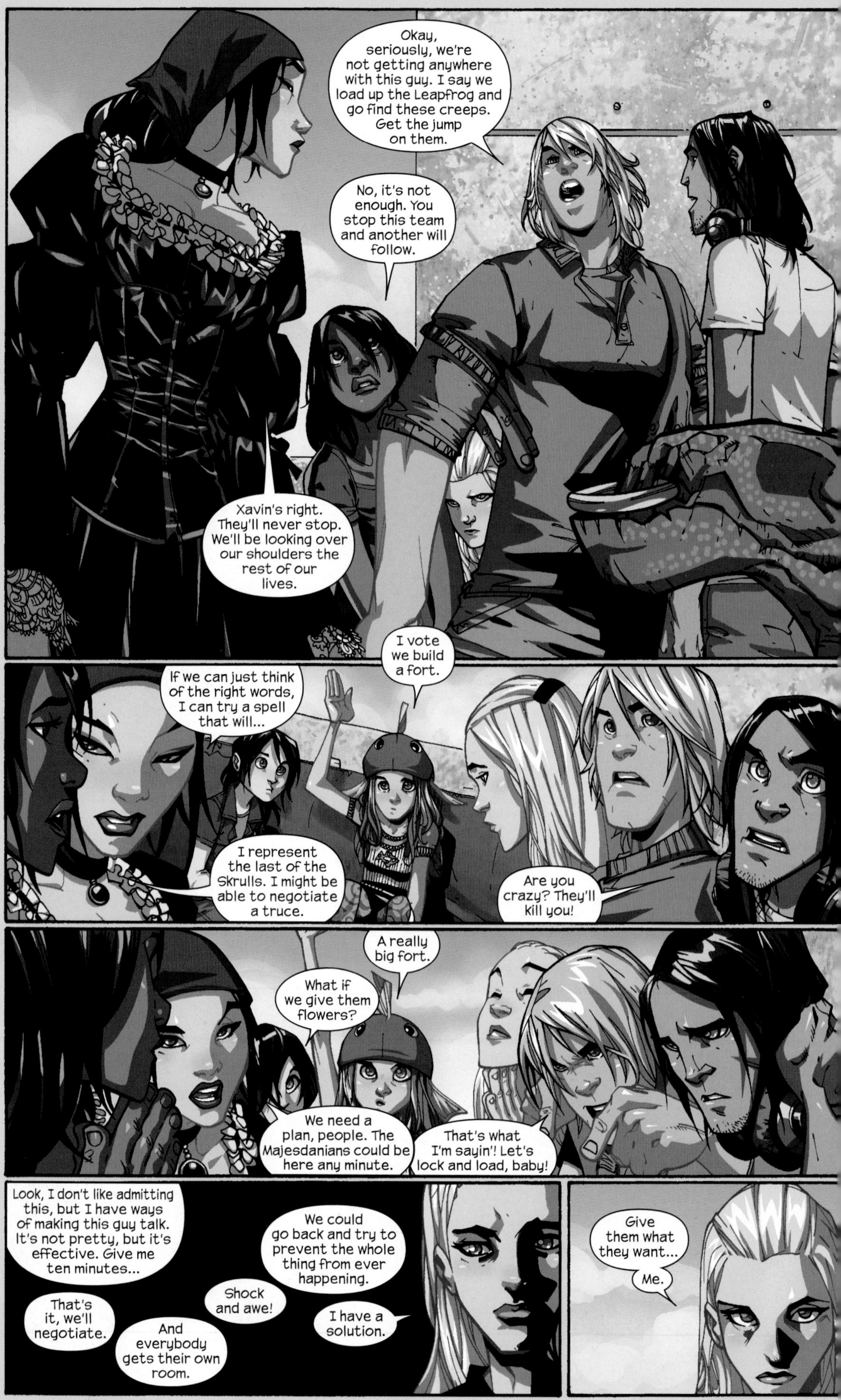
Okay, seriously, we're not getting anywhere with this guy. I say we load up the Leapfrog and go find these creeps. Get the jump on them.
No, it's not enough. You stop this team and another will follow.
Xavin's right. They'll never stop. We'll be looking over our shoulders the rest of our lives.
If we can just think of the right words, I can try a spell that will...
I vote we build a fort.
I represent the last of the Skrulls. I might be able to negotiate a truce.
Are you crazy? They'll kill you!
A really big fort.
What if we give them flowers?
We need a plan, people. The Majesdanians could be here any minute.
That's what I'm sayin'! Let's lock and load, baby!
Look, I don't like admitting this, but I have ways of making this guy talk. It's not pretty, but it's effective. Give me ten minutes...
We could go back and try to prevent the whole thing from ever happening.
That's it, we'll negotiate.
Shock and awe!
And everybody gets their own room.
I have a solution.
Give them what they want...
Me.

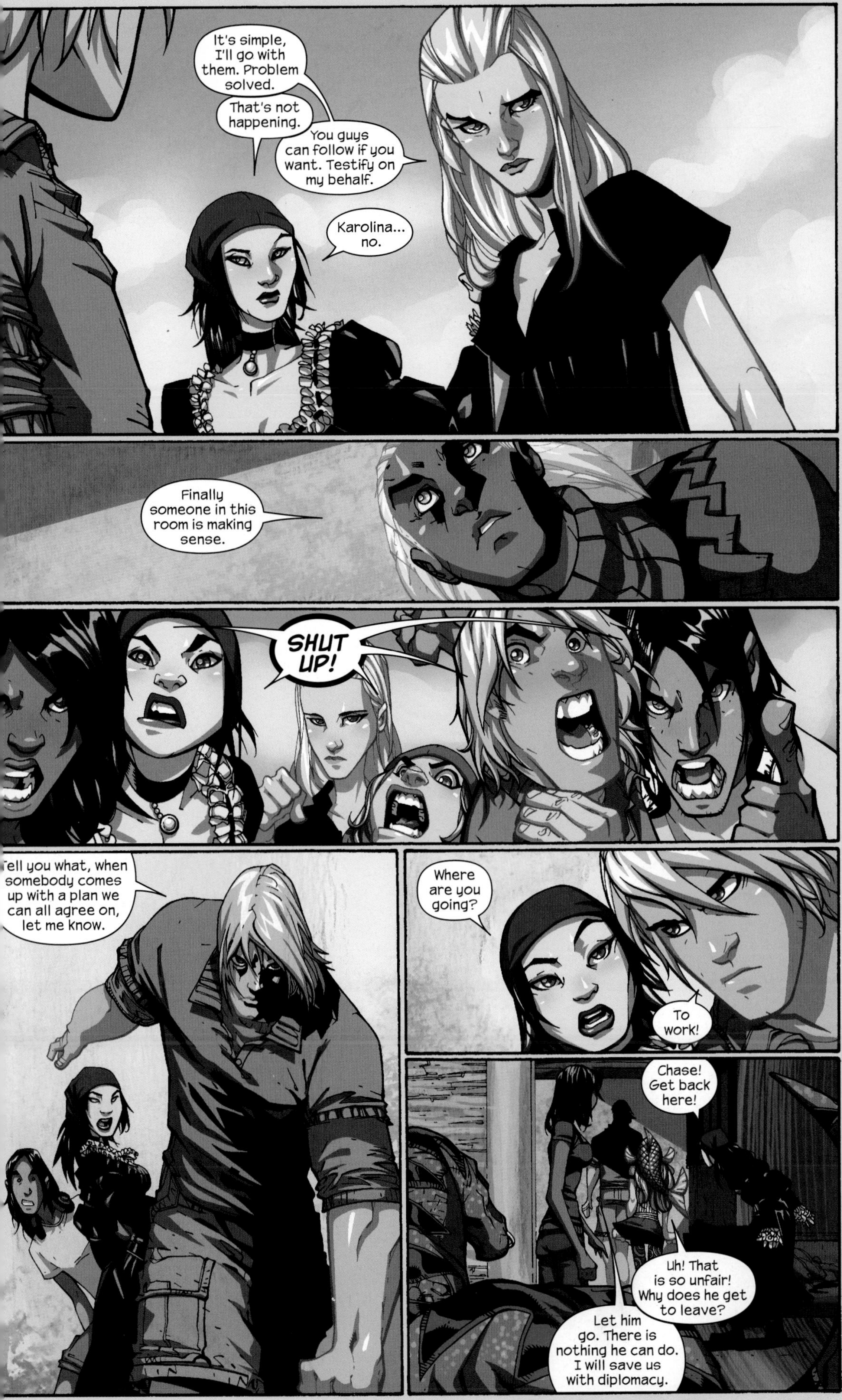
It's simple, I'll go with them. Problem solved.
That's not happening.
You guys can follow if you want. Testify on my behalf.
Karolina... no.
Finally someone in this room is making sense.
SHUT UP!
Tell you what, when somebody comes up with a plan we can all agree on, let me know.
Where are you going?
To work!
Chase! Get back here!
Uh! That is so unfair! Why does he get to leave?
Let him go. There is nothing he can do. I will save us with diplomacy.

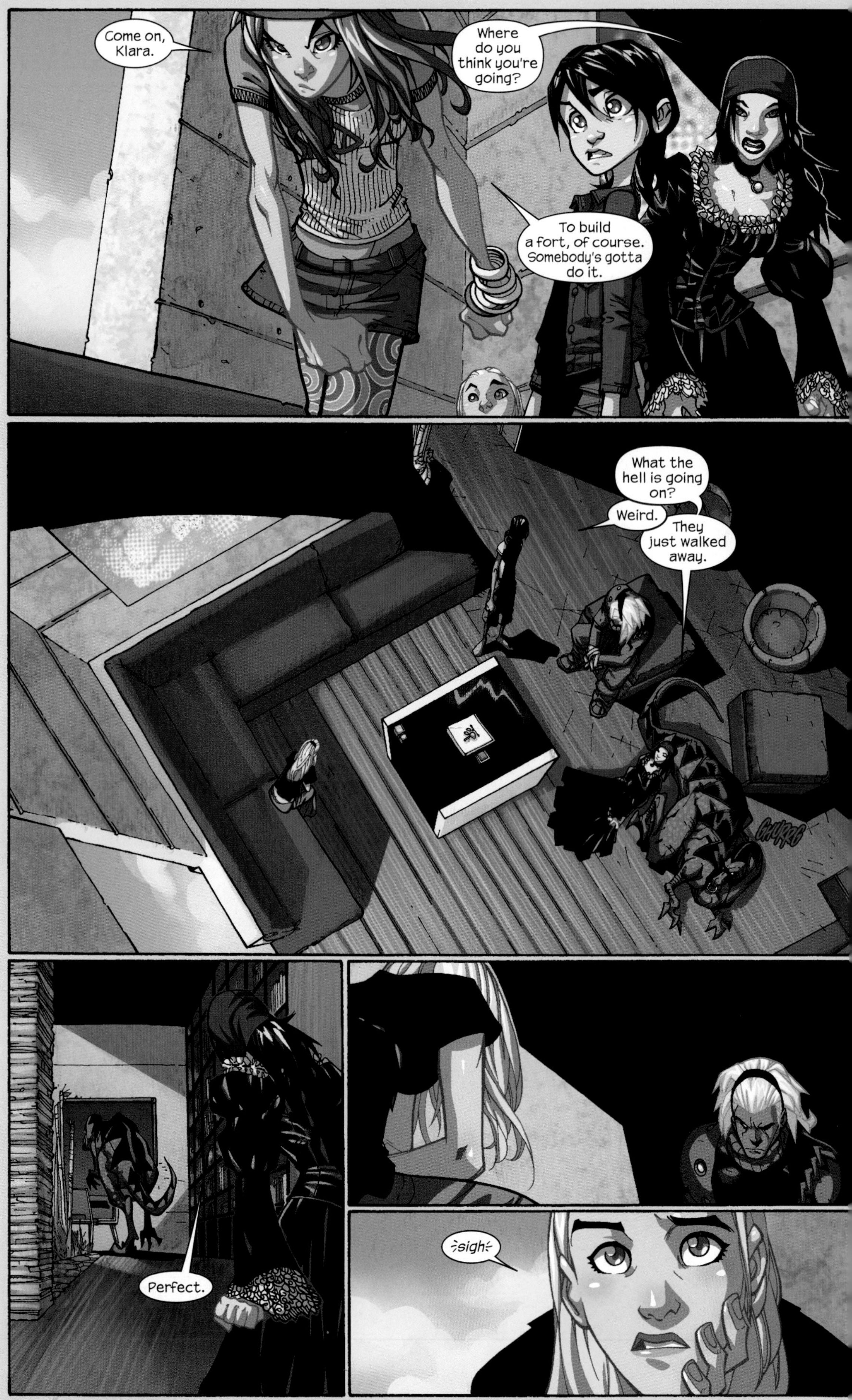
Come on, Klara.
Where do you think you're going?
To build a fort, of course. Somebody's gotta do it.
What the hell is going on?
Weird.
They just walked away.
GHURRG
Perfect.
sigh

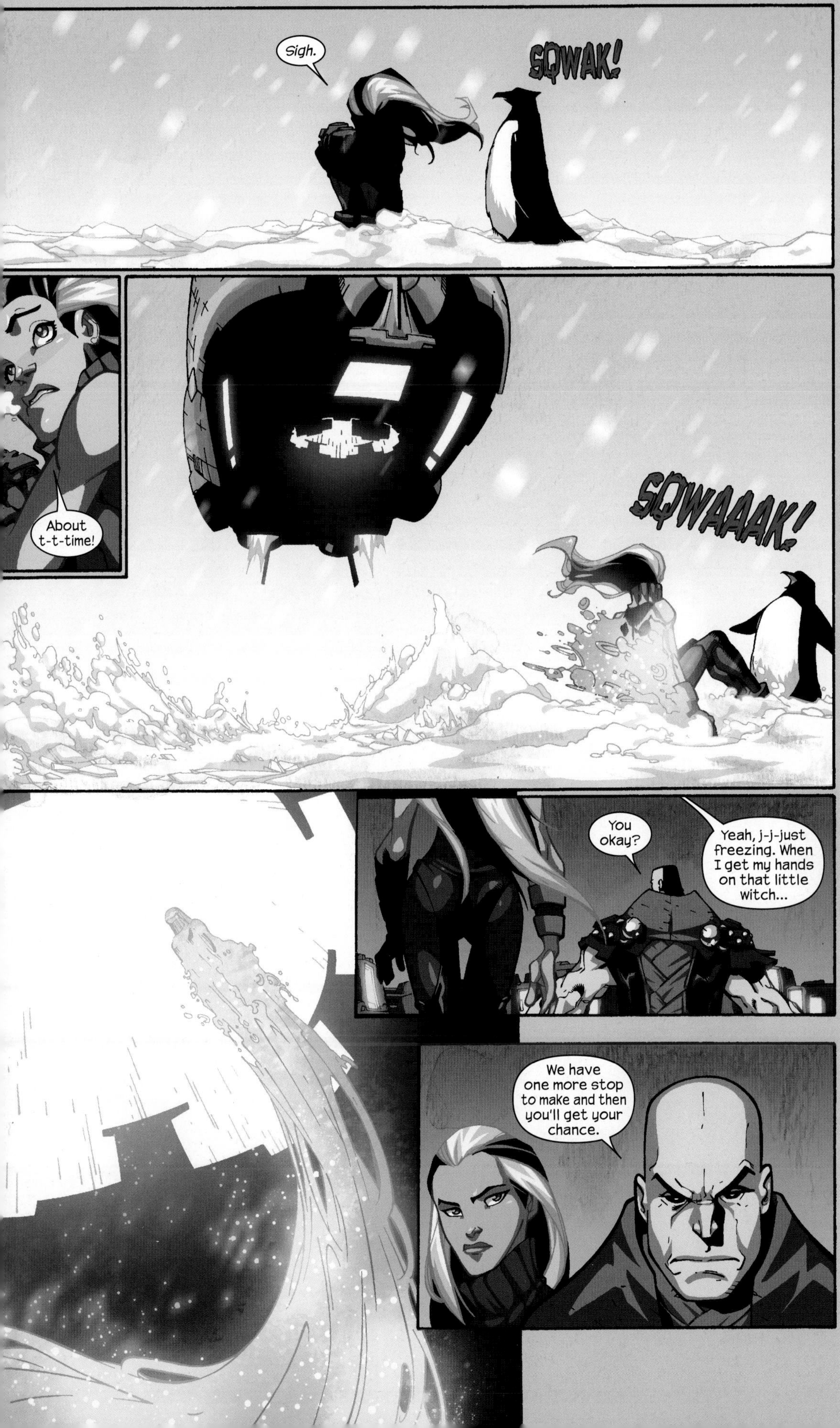
Sigh.
SQWAK!
About t-t-time!
SQWAAAK!
You okay?
Yeah, j-j-just freezing. When I get my hands on that little witch...
We have one more stop to make and then you'll get your chance.

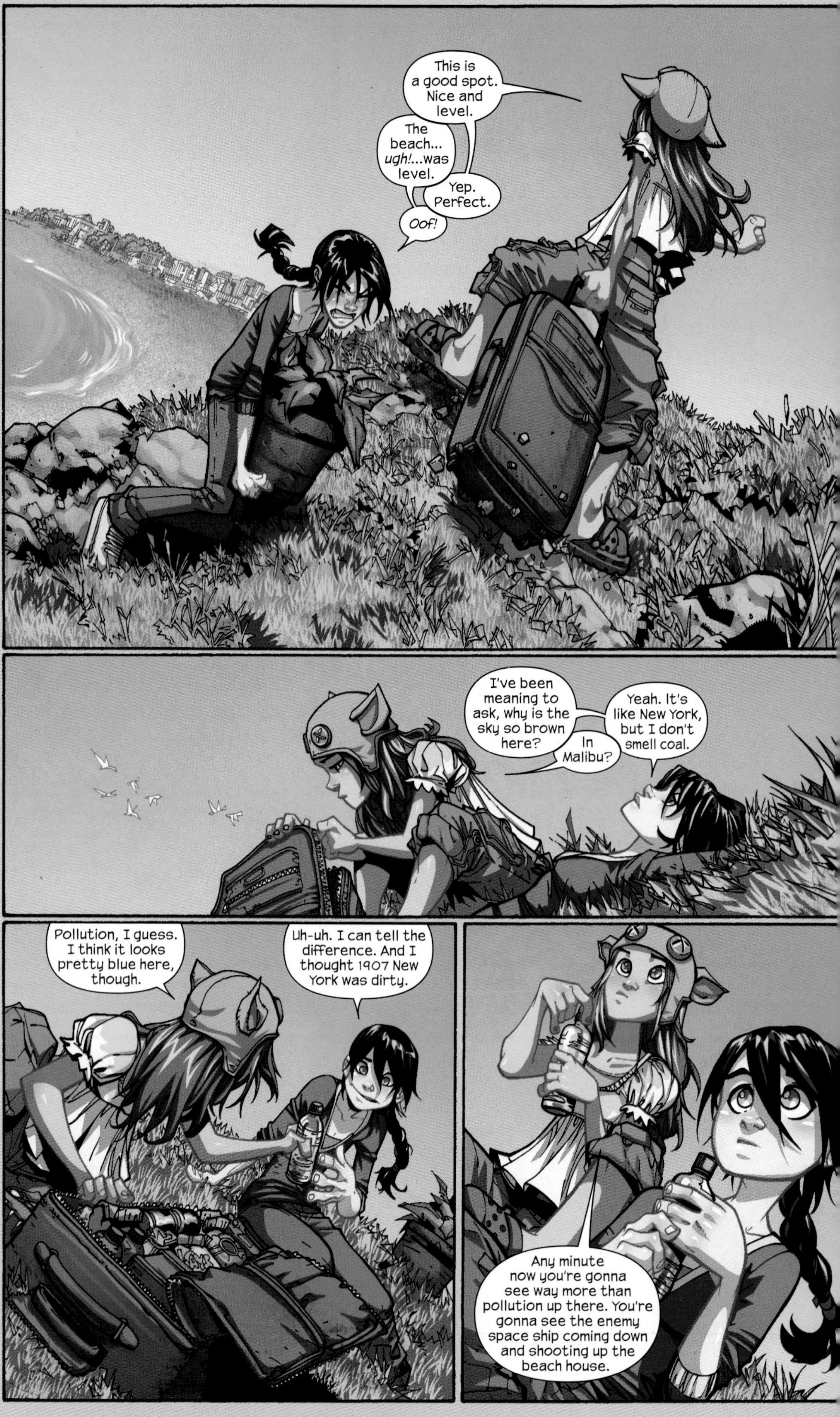
This is a good spot. Nice and level.
The beach... *ugh!*...was level.
Yep. Perfect.
Oof!
I've been meaning to ask, why is the sky so brown here?
In Malibu?
Yeah. It's like New York, but I don't smell coal.
Pollution, I guess. I think it looks pretty blue here, though.
Uh-uh. I can tell the difference. And I thought 1907 New York was dirty.
Any minute now you're gonna see way more than pollution up there. You're gonna see the enemy space ship coming down and shooting up the beach house.

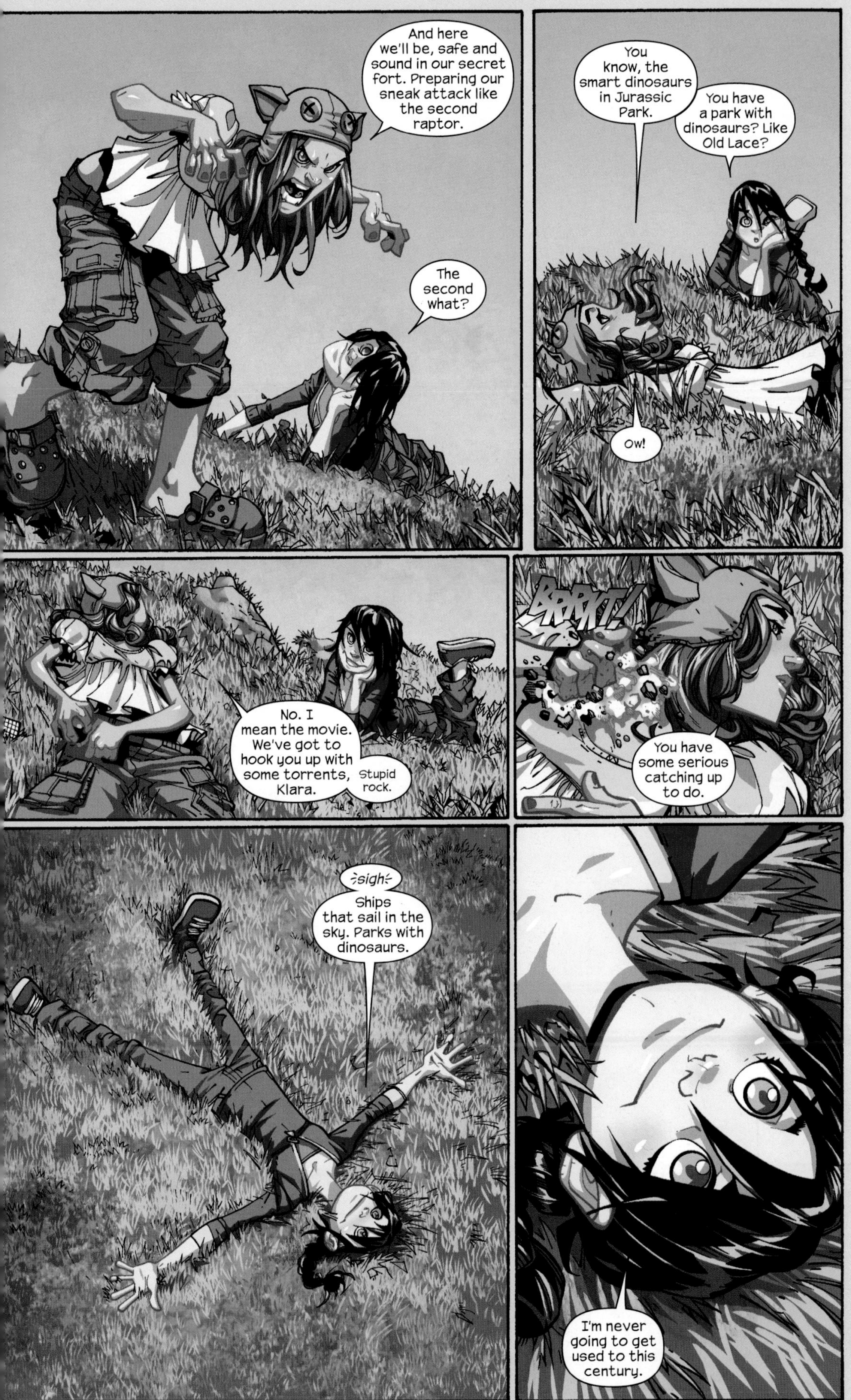
And here we'll be, safe and sound in our secret fort. Preparing our sneak attack like the second raptor.
The second what?
You know, the smart dinosaurs in Jurassic Park.
You have a park with dinosaurs? Like Old Lace?
Ow!
No. I mean the movie. We've got to hook you up with some torrents, Klara.
Stupid rock.
BRRKT!
You have some serious catching up to do.
sigh
Ships that sail in the sky. Parks with dinosaurs.
I'm never going to get used to this century.

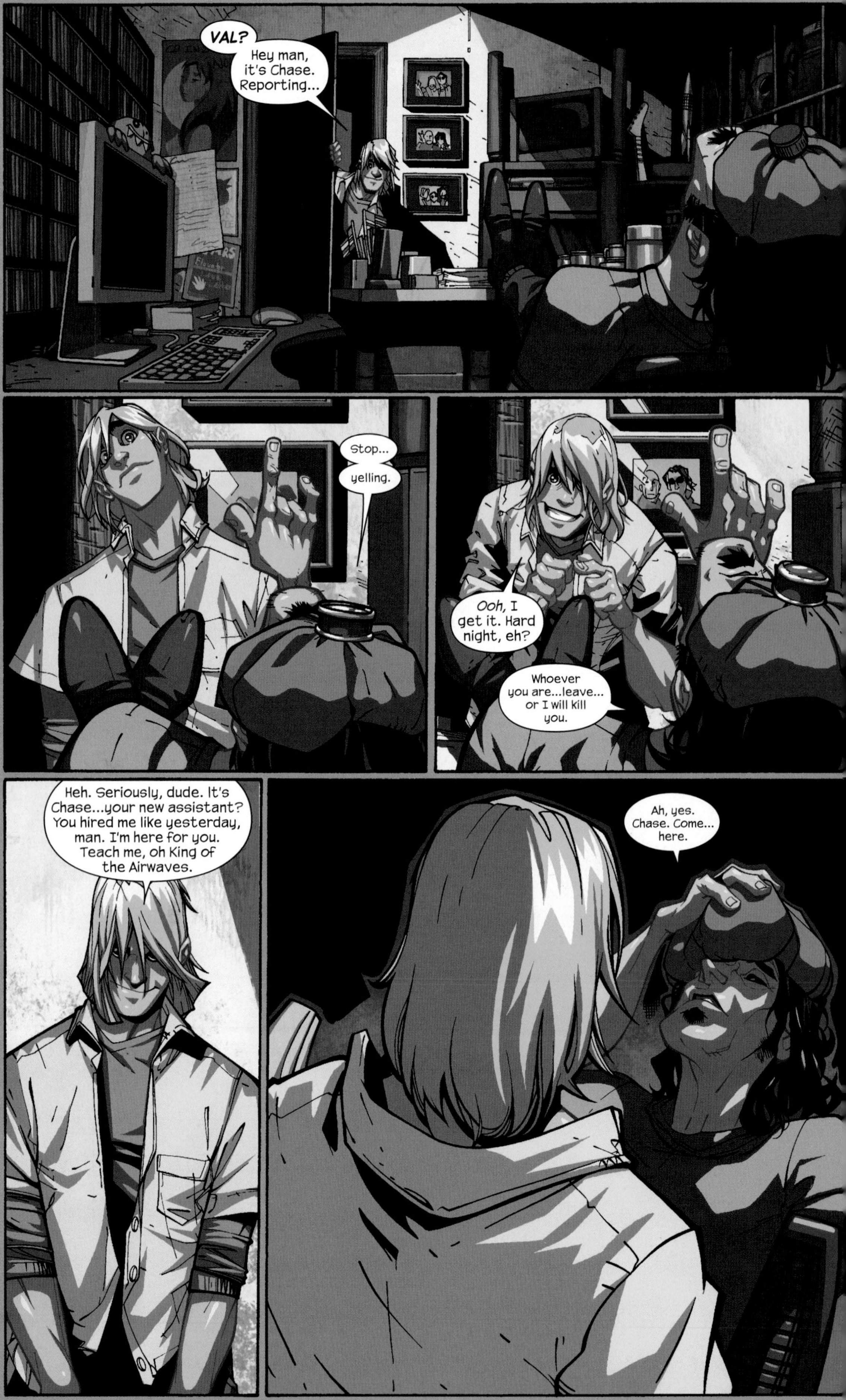
VAL?
Hey man, it's Chase. Reporting...
Stop...
yelling.
Ooh, I get it. Hard night, eh?
Whoever you are...leave... or I will kill you.
Heh. Seriously, dude. It's Chase...your new assistant? You hired me like yesterday, man. I'm here for you. Teach me, oh King of the Airwaves.
Ah, yes. Chase. Come... here.

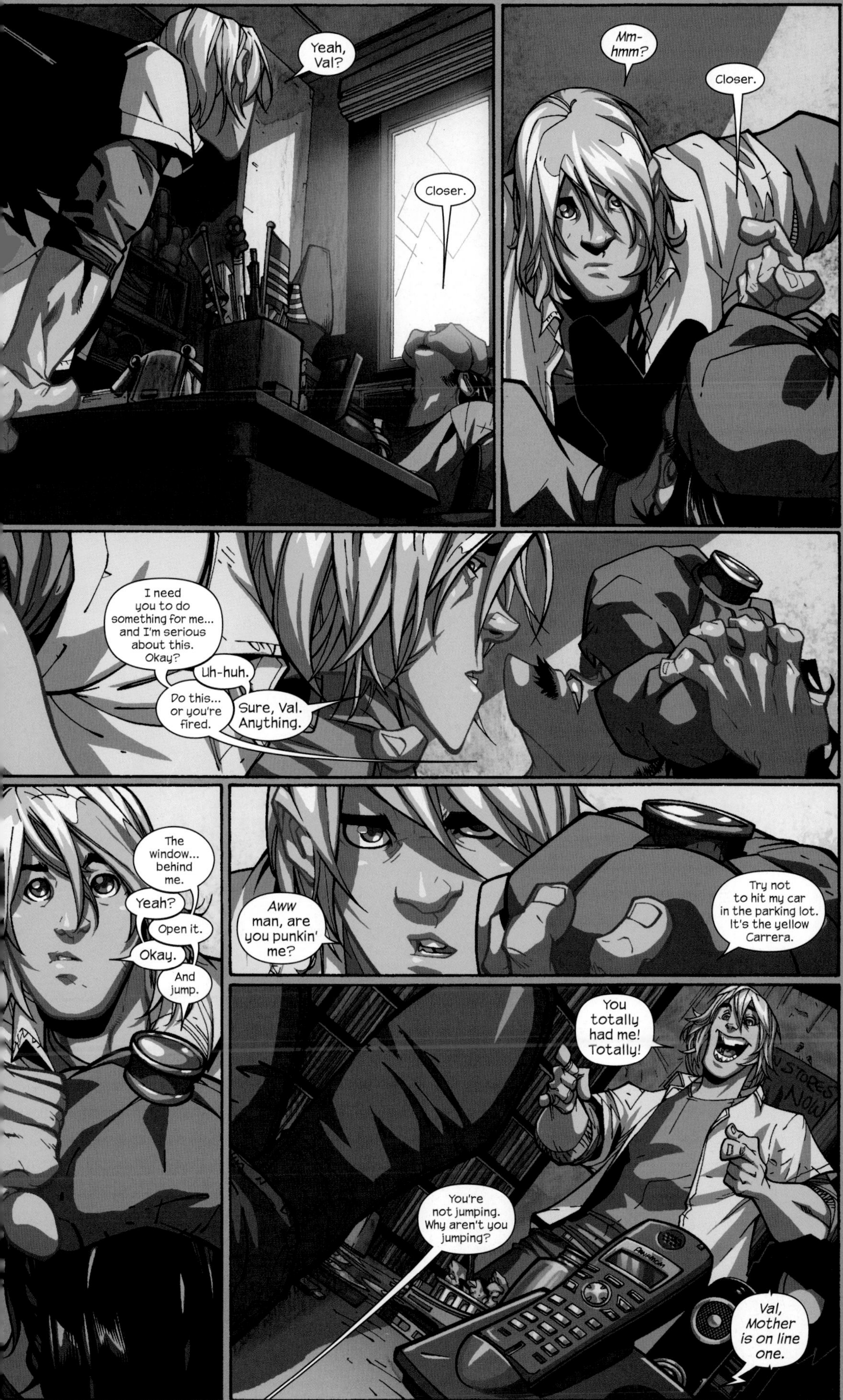
Yeah, Val?
Closer.
Mm-hmm?
Closer.
I need you to do something for me... and I'm serious about this. Okay?
Uh-huh.
Do this... or you're fired.
Sure, Val. Anything.
The window... behind me.
Yeah?
Open it.
Okay.
And jump.
Aww man, are you punkin' me?
Try not to hit my car in the parking lot. It's the yellow Carrera.
You totally had me! Totally!
You're not jumping. Why aren't you jumping?
Val, Mother is on line one.

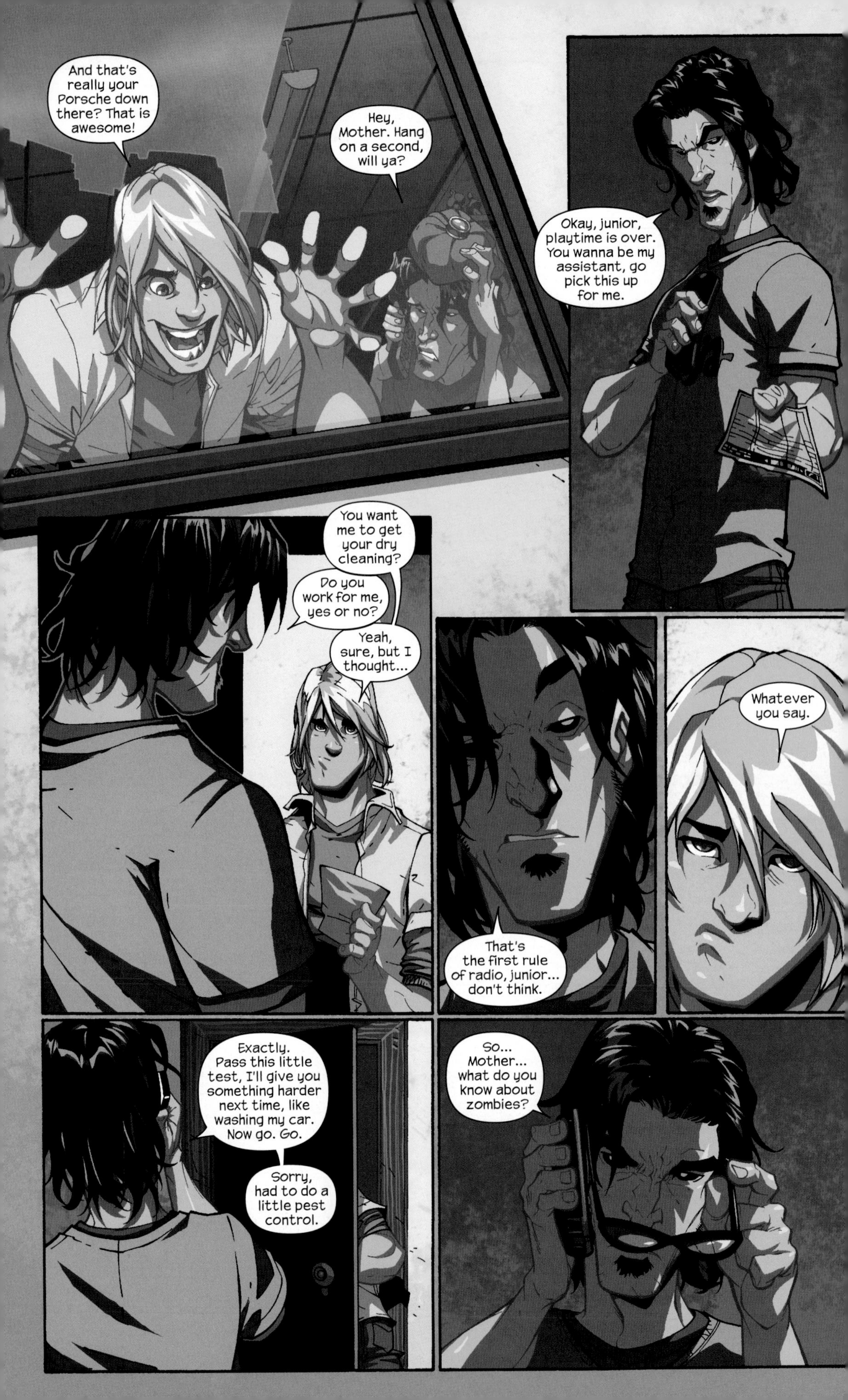
And that's really your Porsche down there? That is awesome!
Hey, Mother. Hang on a second, will ya?
Okay, junior, playtime is over. You wanna be my assistant, go pick this up for me.
You want me to get your dry cleaning?
Do you work for me, yes or no?
Yeah, sure, but I thought...
That's the first rule of radio, junior... don't think.
Whatever you say.
Exactly. Pass this little test, I'll give you something harder next time, like washing my car. Now go. Go.
Sorry, had to do a little pest control.
So... Mother... what do you know about zombies?

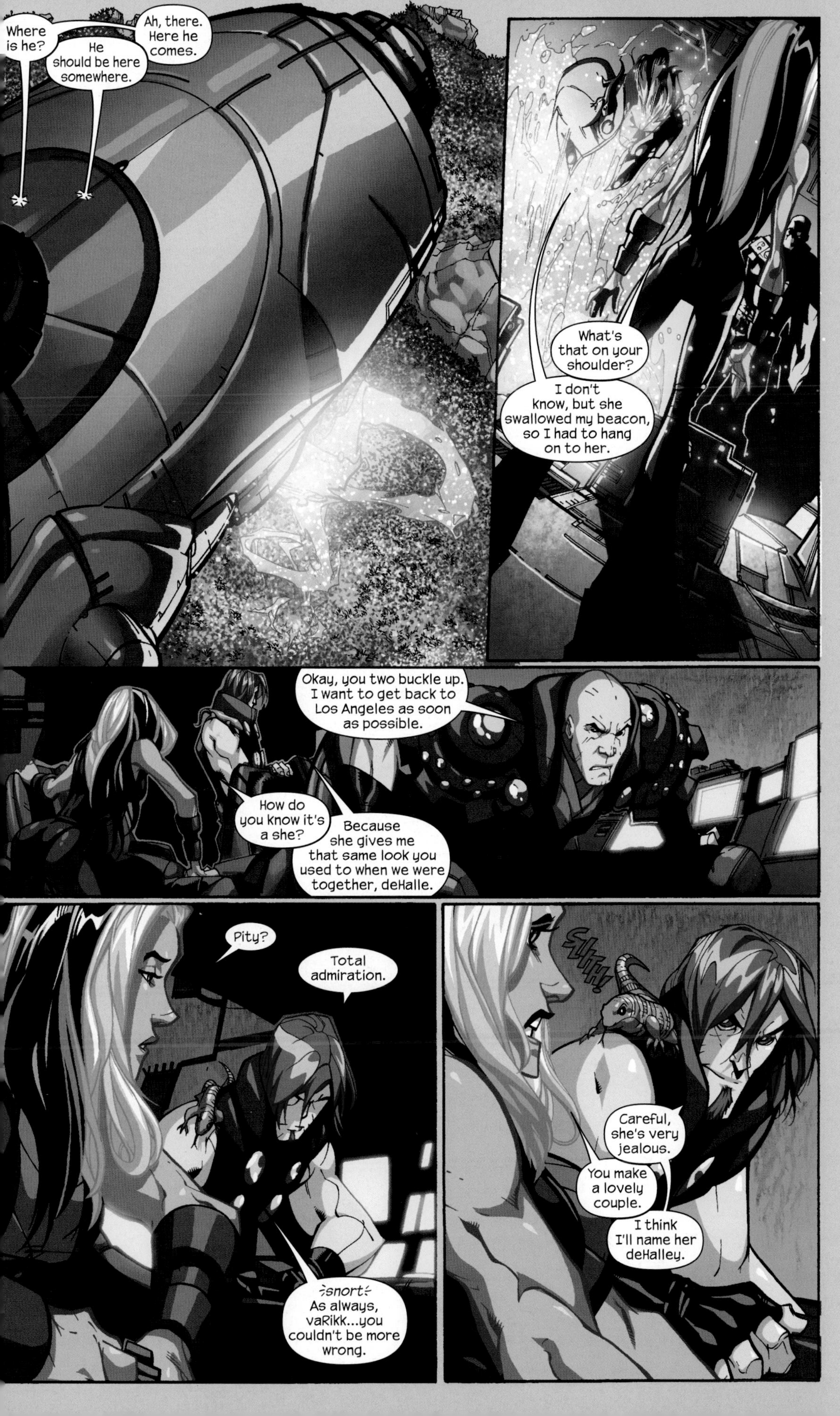

Where is he?
He should be here somewhere.
Ah, there. Here he comes.
What's that on your shoulder?
I don't know, but she swallowed my beacon, so I had to hang on to her.
Okay, you two buckle up. I want to get back to Los Angeles as soon as possible.
How do you know it's a she?
Because she gives me that same look you used to when we were together, deHalle.
Pity?
Total admiration.
snort As always, vaRikk...you couldn't be more wrong.
SLITH!
Careful, she's very jealous.
You make a lovely couple.
I think I'll name her deHalley.

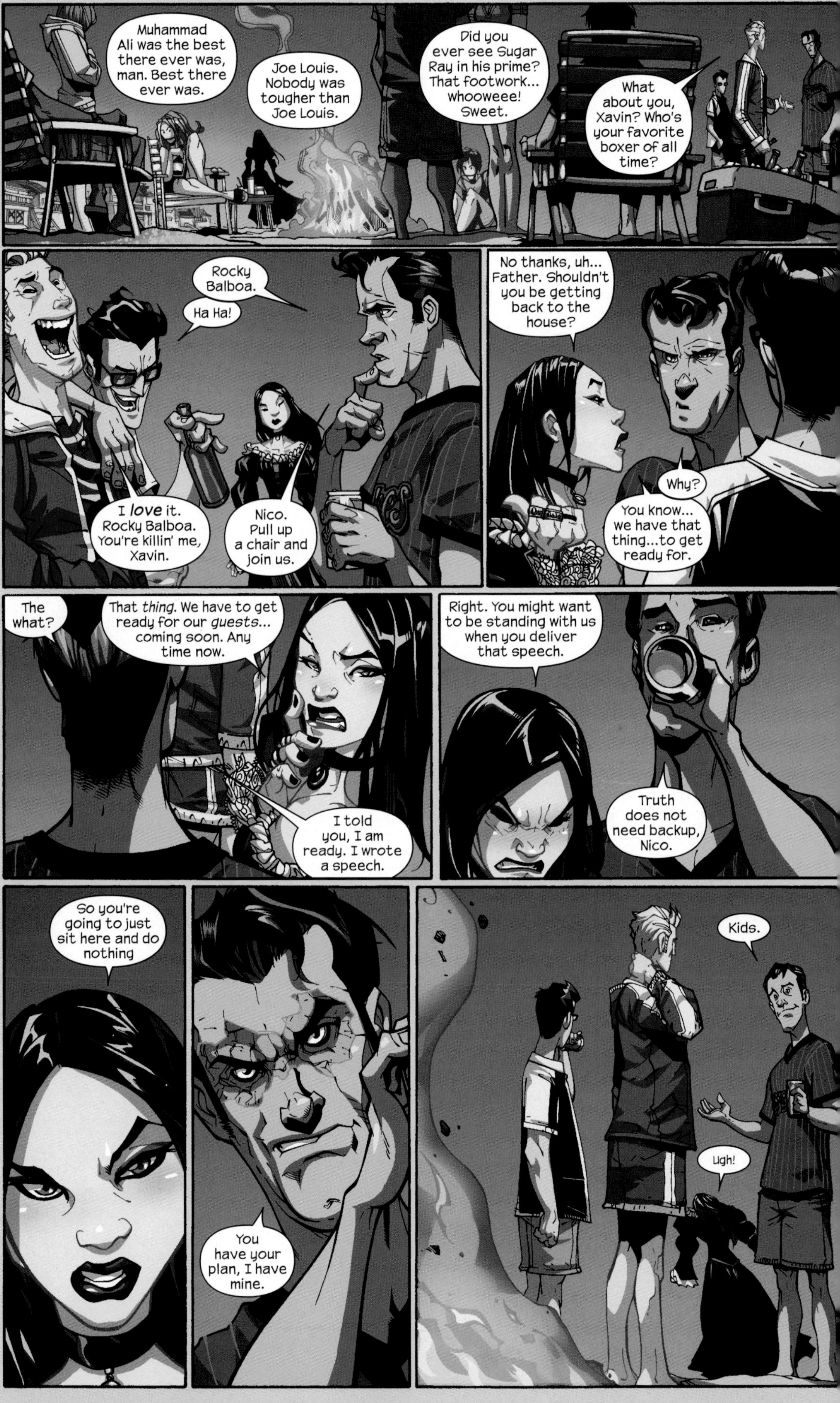
Muhammad Ali was the best there ever was, man. Best there ever was.
Joe Louis. Nobody was tougher than Joe Louis.
Did you ever see Sugar Ray in his prime? That footwork... whooweee! Sweet.
What about you, Xavin? Who's your favorite boxer of all time?
Rocky Balboa.
Ha Ha!
I *love* it. Rocky Balboa. You're killin' me, Xavin.
Nico. Pull up a chair and join us.
No thanks, uh... Father. Shouldn't you be getting back to the house?
Why?
You know... we have that thing...to get ready for.
The what?
That *thing*. We have to get ready for our *guests*... coming soon. Any time now.
I told you, I am ready. I wrote a speech.
Right. You might want to be standing with us when you deliver that speech.
Truth does not need backup, Nico.
So you're going to just sit here and do nothing
You have your plan, I have mine.
Kids.
Ugh!

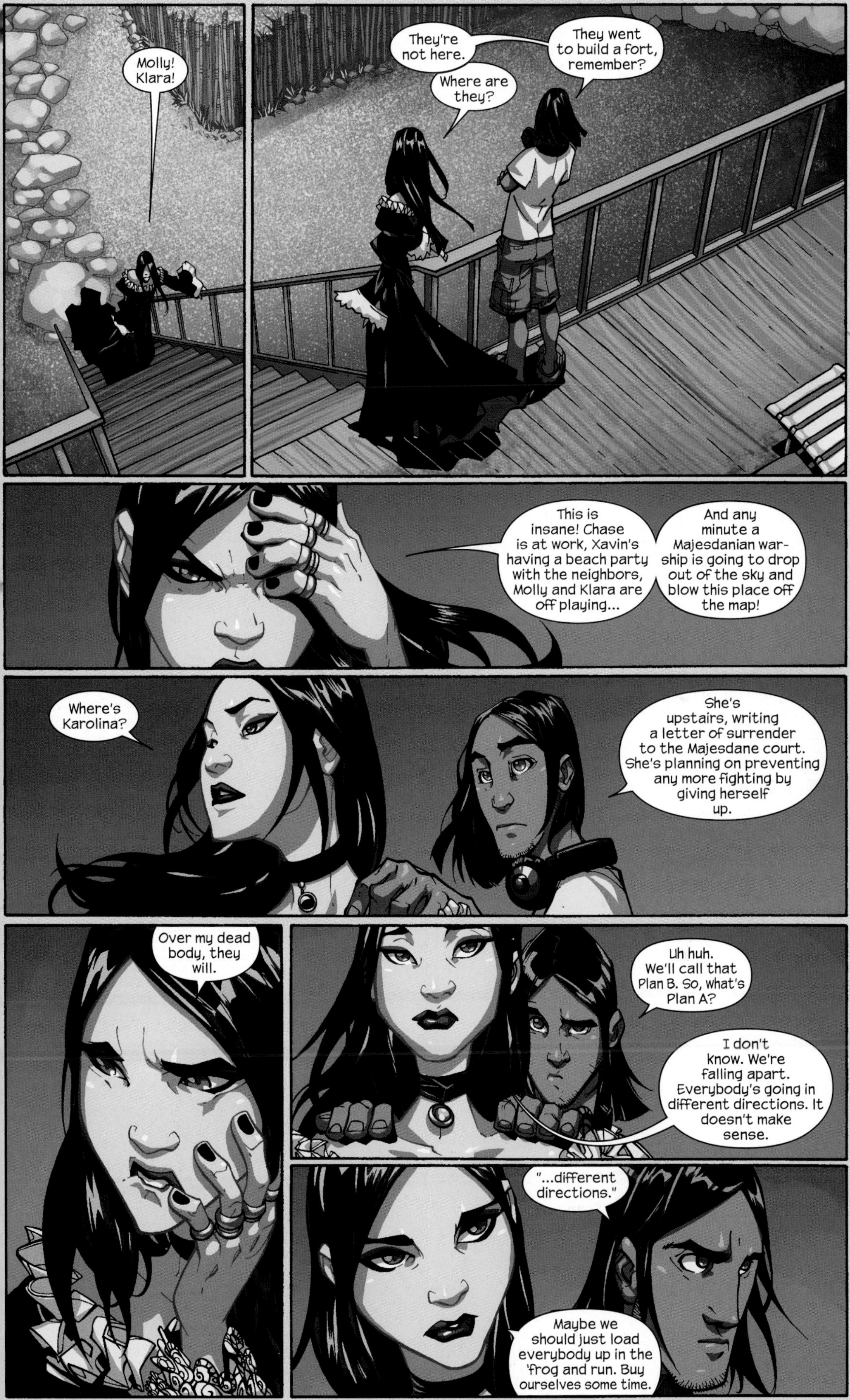
Molly! Klara!
They're not here.
Where are they?
They went to build a fort, remember?
This is insane! Chase is at work, Xavin's having a beach party with the neighbors, Molly and Klara are off playing...
And any minute a Majesdanian war-ship is going to drop out of the sky and blow this place off the map!
Where's Karolina?
She's upstairs, writing a letter of surrender to the Majesdane court. She's planning on preventing any more fighting by giving herself up.
Over my dead body, they will.
Uh huh. We'll call that Plan B. So, what's Plan A?
I don't know. We're falling apart. Everybody's going in different directions. It doesn't make sense.
"...different directions."
Maybe we should just load everybody up in the 'frog and run. Buy ourselves some time.

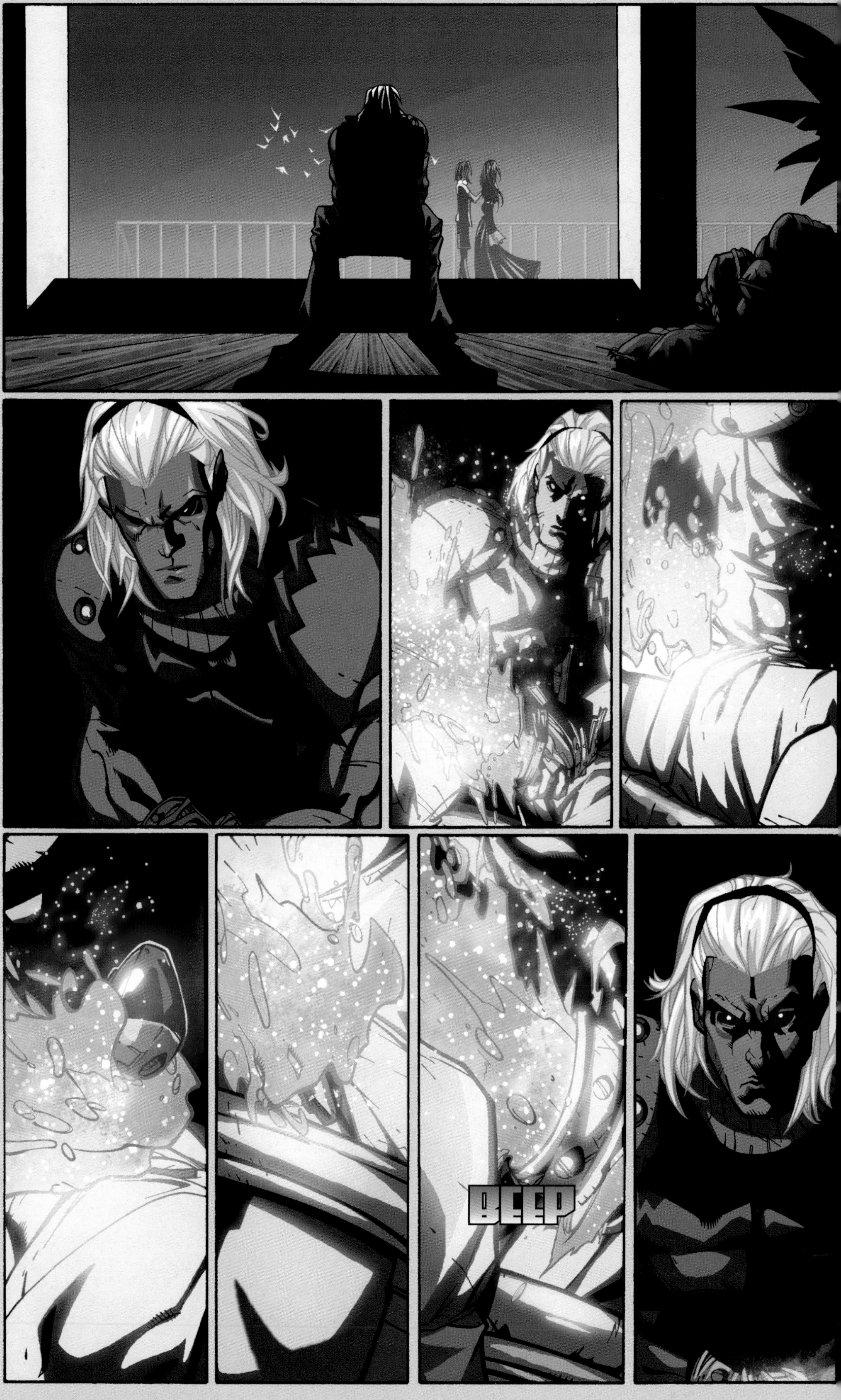
BEEP

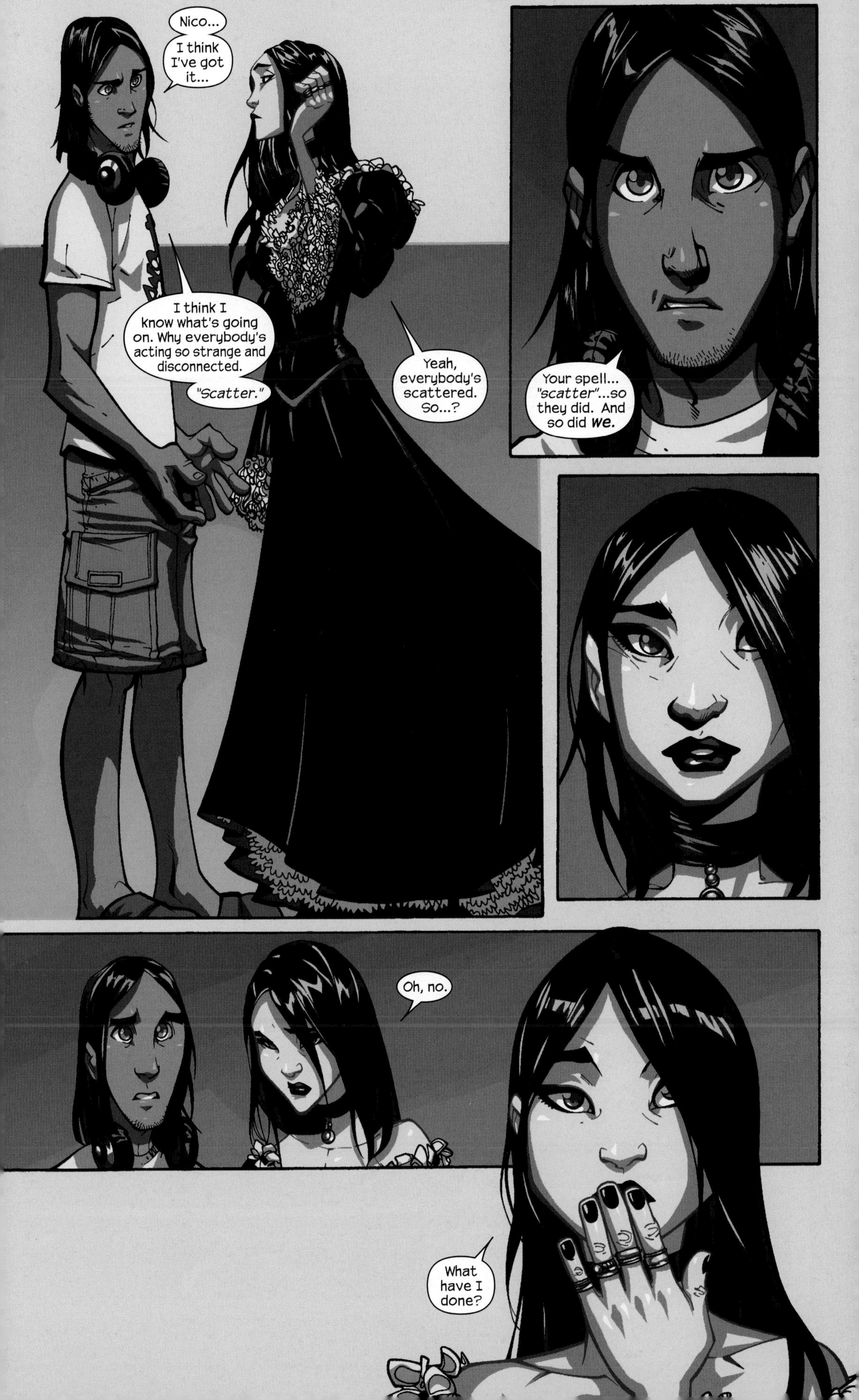
Nico...
I think I've got it...
I think I know what's going on. Why everybody's acting so strange and disconnected.
"Scatter."
Yeah, everybody's scattered. So...?
Your spell... "scatter"...so they did. And so did we.
Oh, no.
What have I done?

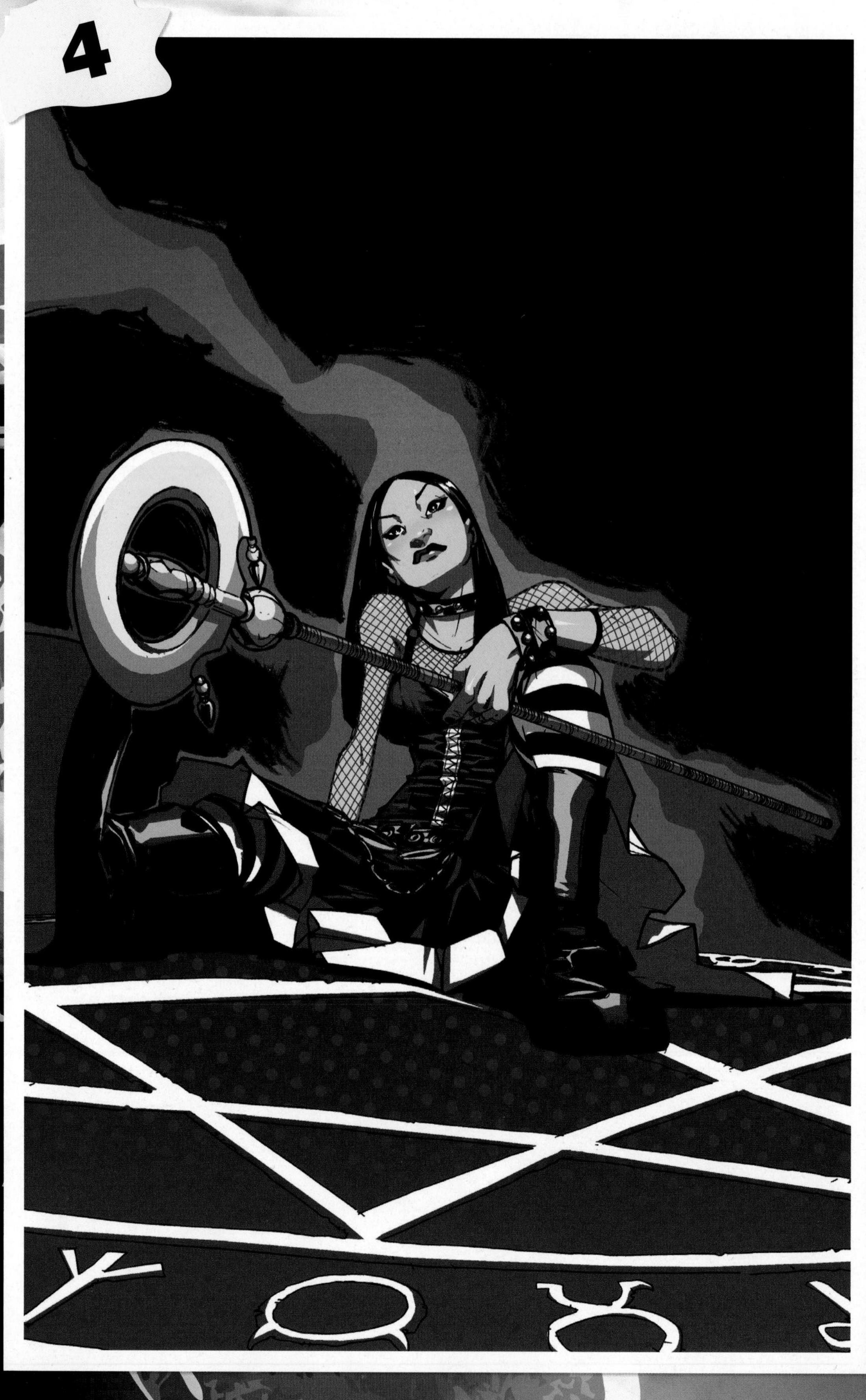
4

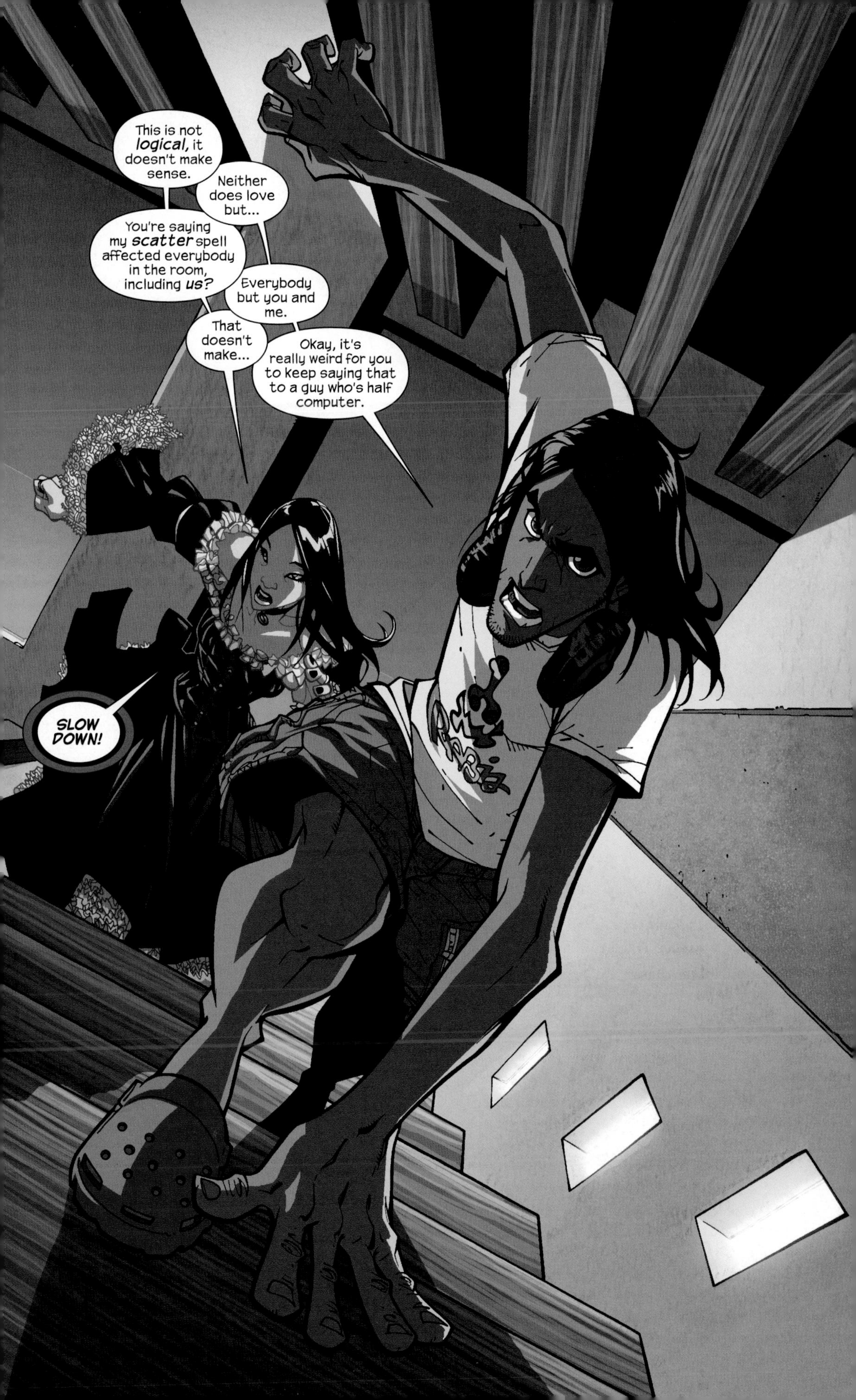
This is not logical, it doesn't make sense.
Neither does love but...
You're saying my scatter spell affected everybody in the room, including us?
Everybody but you and me.
That doesn't make...
Okay, it's really weird for you to keep saying that to a guy who's half computer.
SLOW DOWN!

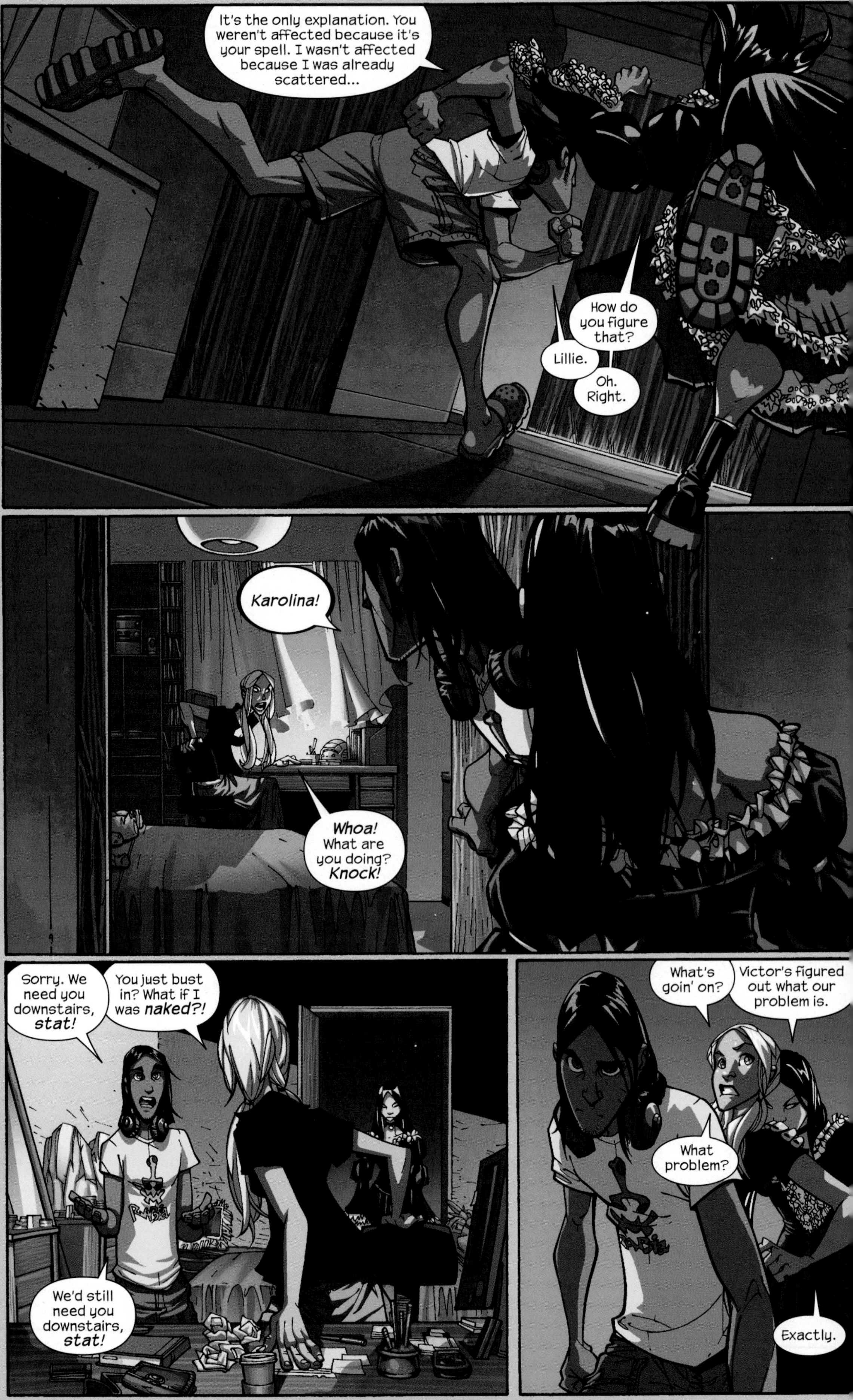
It's the only explanation. You weren't affected because it's your spell. I wasn't affected because I was already scattered...
How do you figure that?
Lillie.
Oh. Right.
Karolina!
Whoa! What are you doing? Knock!
Sorry. We need you downstairs, stat!
You just bust in? What if I was naked?!
We'd still need you downstairs, stat!
What's goin' on?
Victor's figured out what our problem is.
What problem?
Exactly.

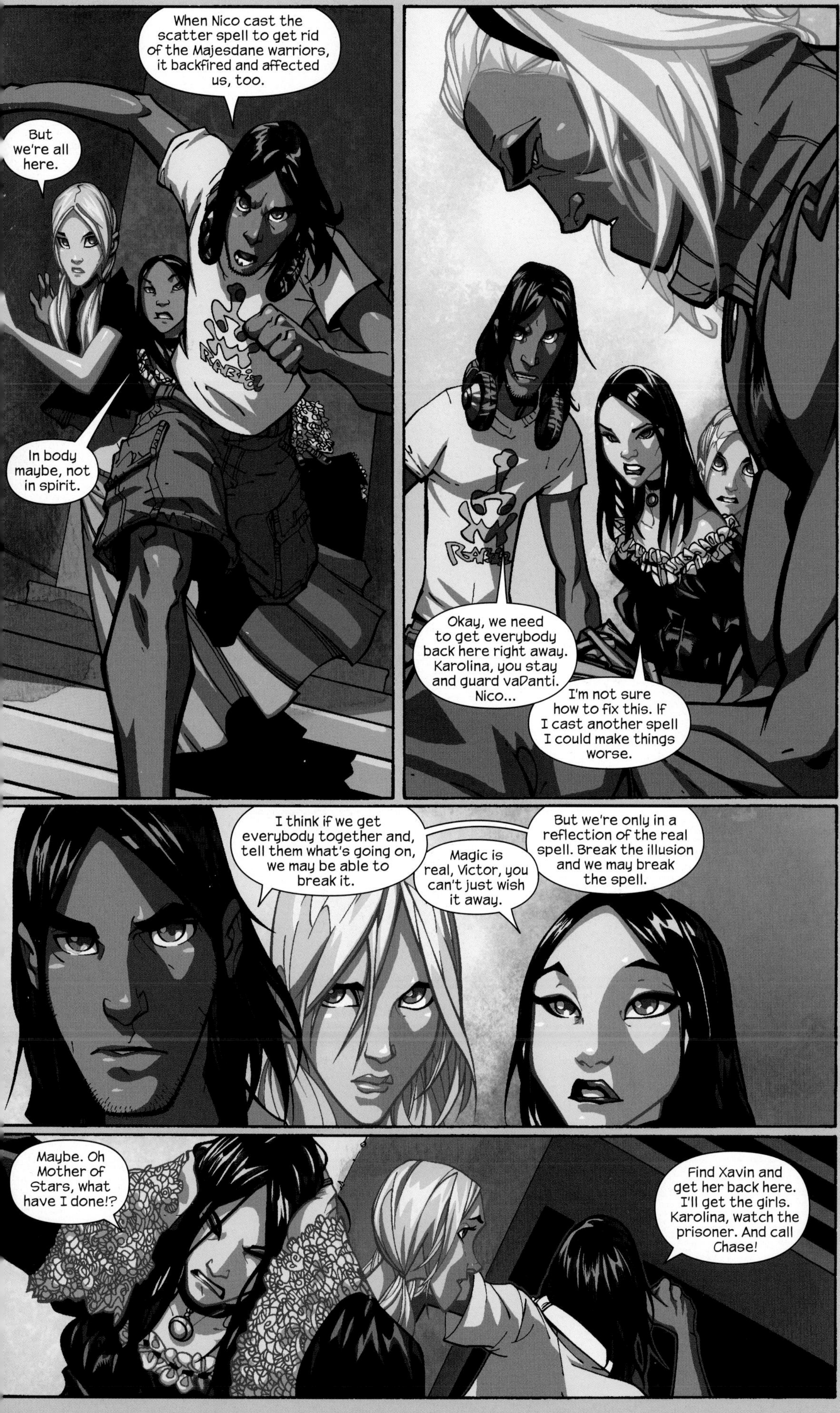
When Nico cast the scatter spell to get rid of the Majesdane warriors, it backfired and affected us, too.
But we're all here.
In body maybe, not in spirit.
Okay, we need to get everybody back here right away. Karolina, you stay and guard vaDanti. Nico...
I'm not sure how to fix this. If I cast another spell I could make things worse.
I think if we get everybody together and, tell them what's going on, we may be able to break it.
Magic is real, Victor, you can't just wish it away.
But we're only in a reflection of the real spell. Break the illusion and we may break the spell.
Maybe. Oh Mother of Stars, what have I done!?
Find Xavin and get her back here. I'll get the girls. Karolina, watch the prisoner. And call Chase!

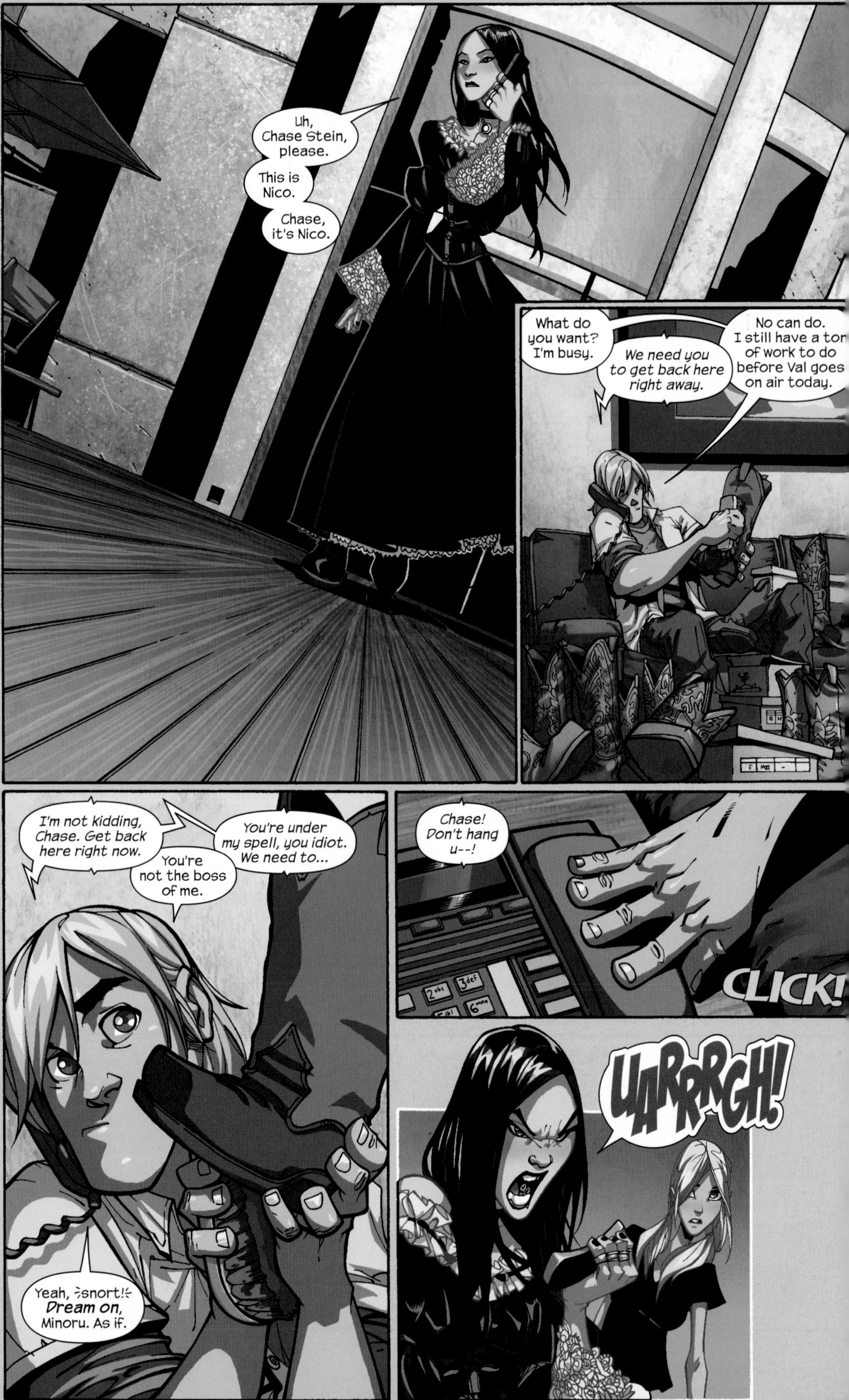
Uh, Chase Stein, please.
This is Nico.
Chase, it's Nico.
What do you want? I'm busy.
We need you to get back here right away.
No can do. I still have a ton of work to do before Val goes on air today.
I'm not kidding, Chase. Get back here right now.
You're not the boss of me.
You're under my spell, you idiot. We need to...
Yeah, *snort!* Dream on, Minoru. As if.
Chase! Don't hang u--!
CLICK!
UARRRGH!

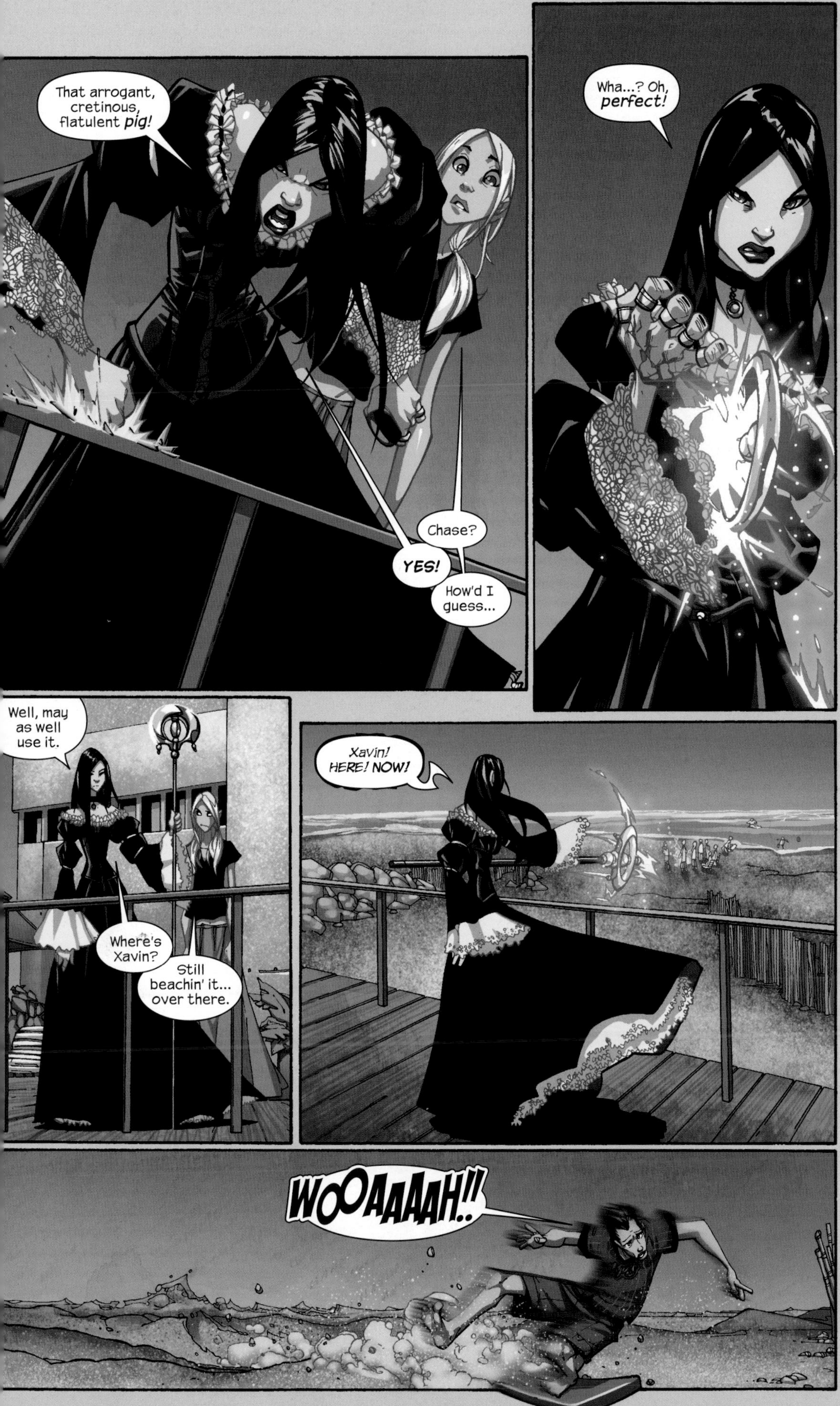
That arrogant, cretinous, flatulent *pig!*
Chase?
YES!
How'd I guess...
Wha...? Oh, *perfect!*
Well, may as well use it.
Where's Xavin?
Still beachin' it... over there.
Xavin! HERE! NOW!
WOOAAAAH!!

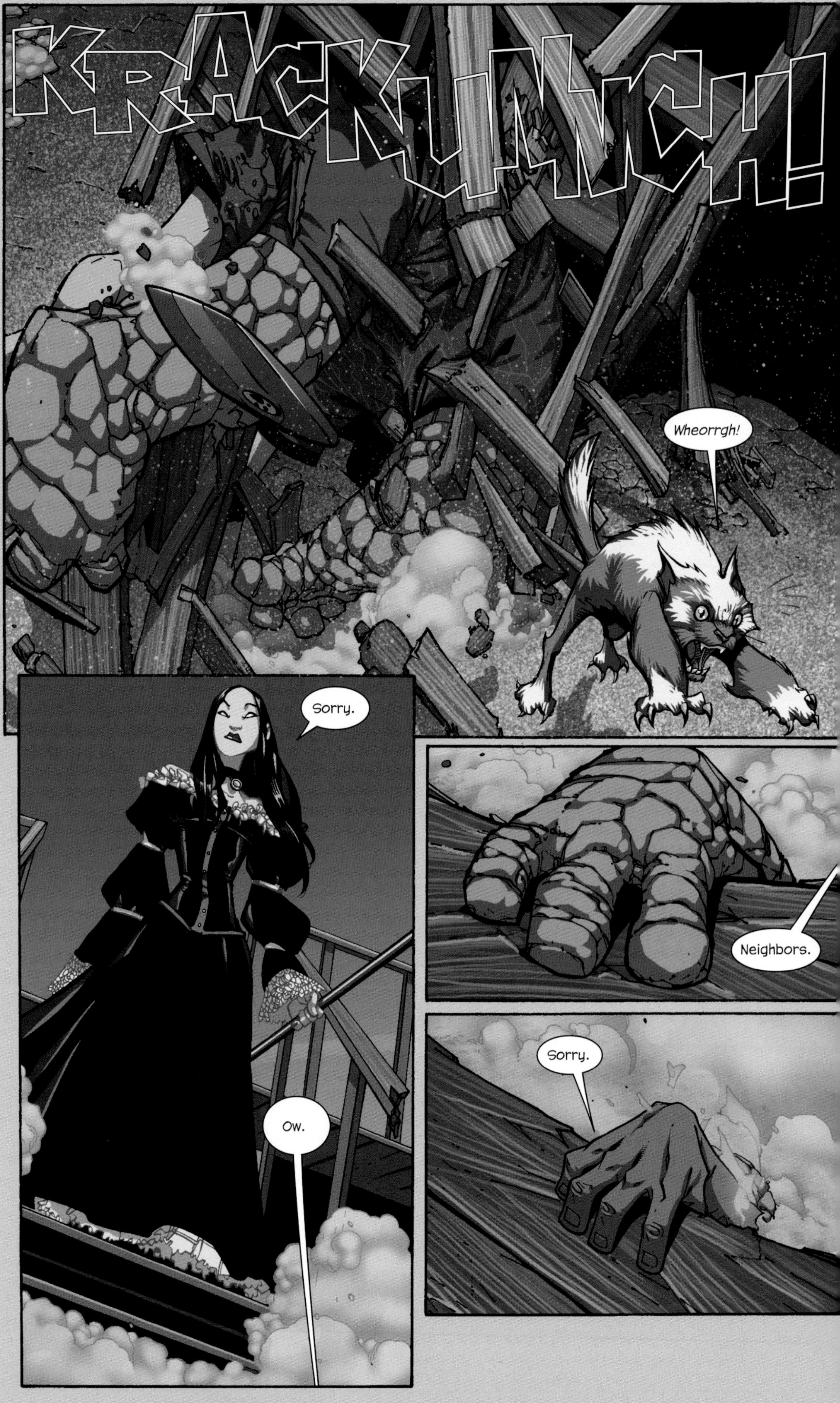
KRACKUNNCH!
Wheorrgh!
Sorry.
Ow.
Neighbors.
Sorry.

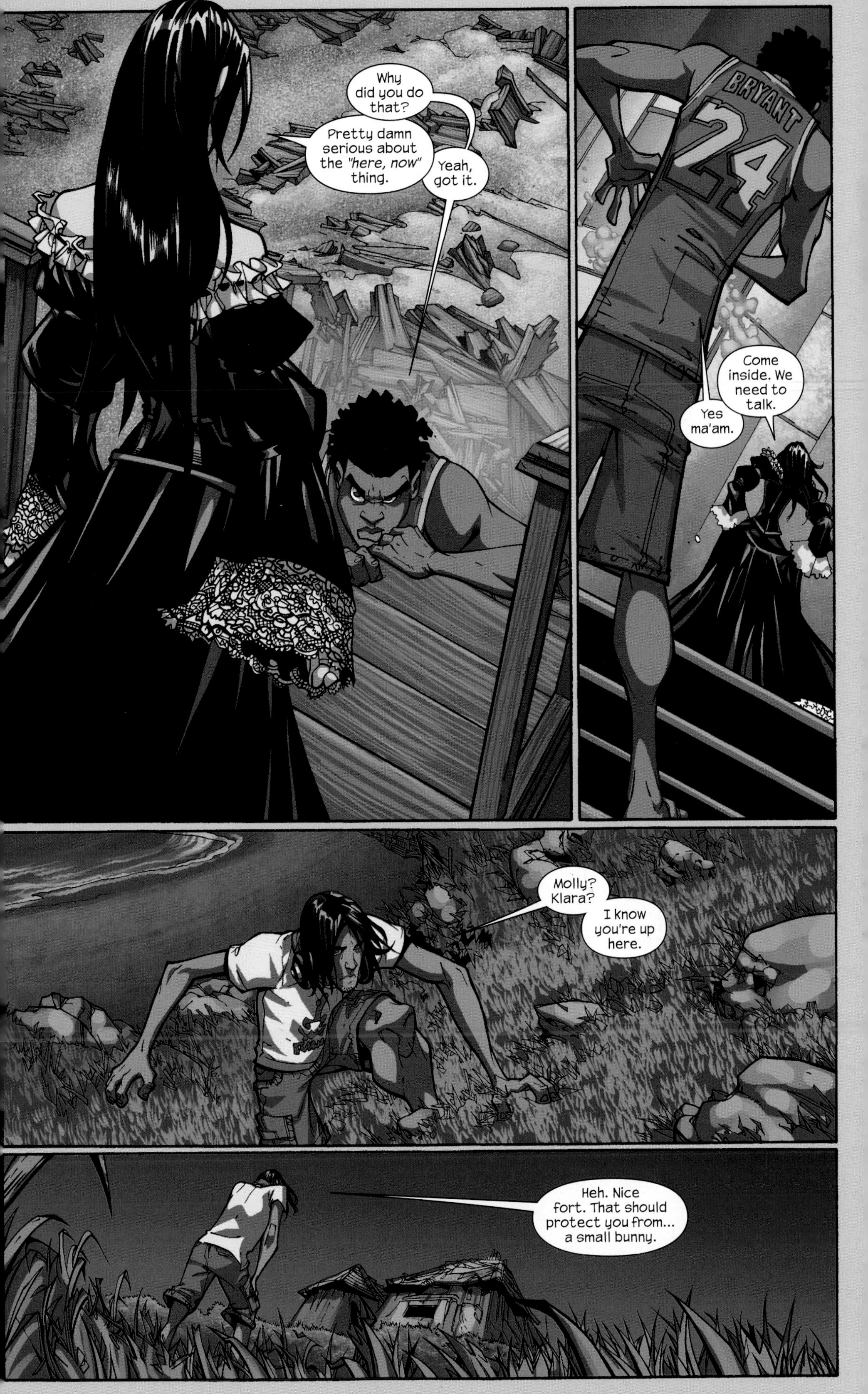
Why did you do that?
Pretty damn serious about the "here, now" thing.
Yeah, got it.
BRYANT 24
Come inside. We need to talk.
Yes ma'am.
Molly? Klara?
I know you're up here.
Heh. Nice fort. That should protect you from... a small bunny.

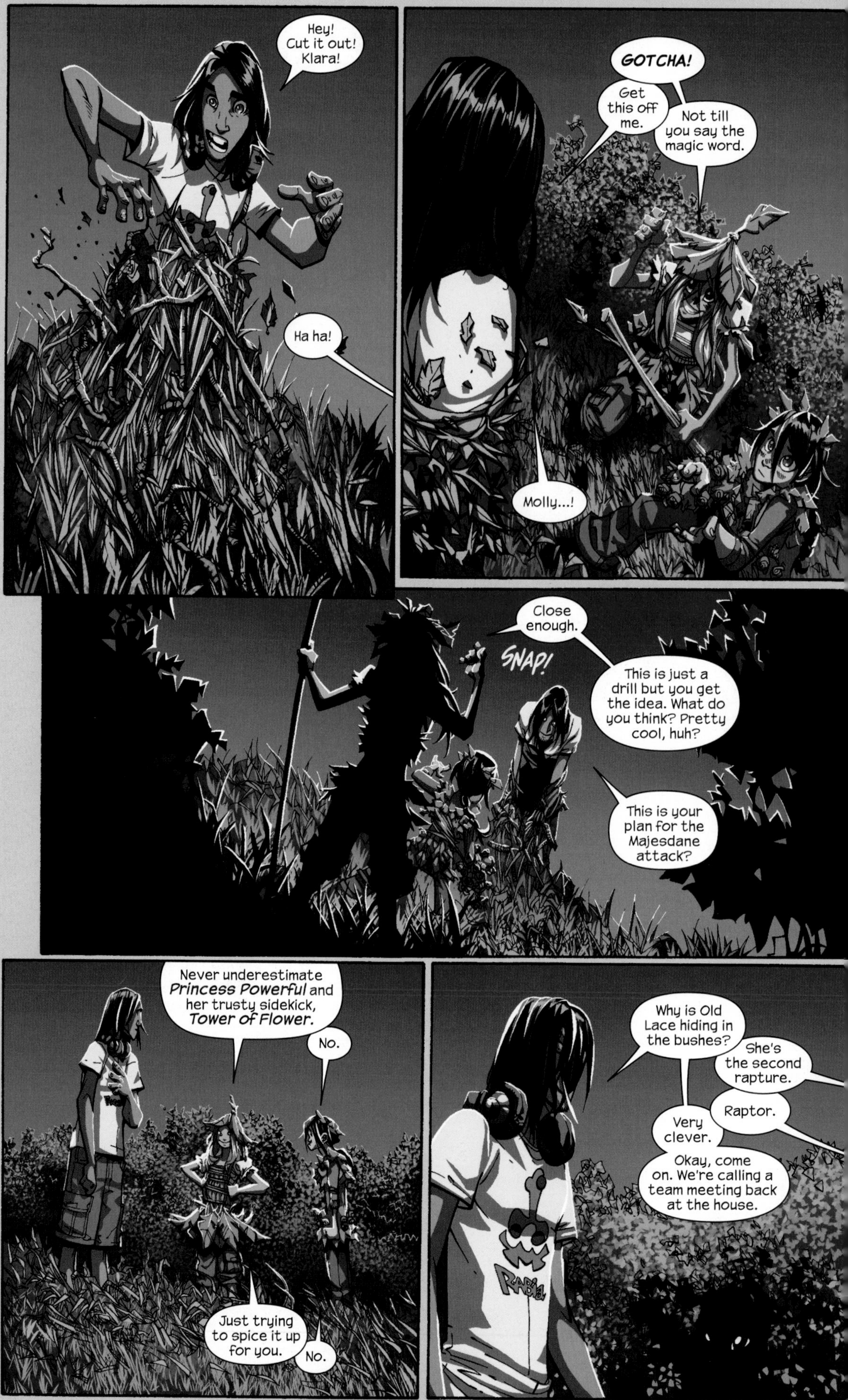
Hey! Cut it out! Klara!
Ha ha!
GOTCHA!
Get this off me.
Not till you say the magic word.
Molly...!
Close enough.
SNAP!
This is just a drill but you get the idea. What do you think? Pretty cool, huh?
This is your plan for the Majesdane attack?
Never underestimate Princess Powerful and her trusty sidekick, Tower of Flower.
No.
Just trying to spice it up for you.
No.
Why is Old Lace hiding in the bushes?
She's the second rapture.
Raptor.
Very clever.
Okay, come on. We're calling a team meeting back at the house.

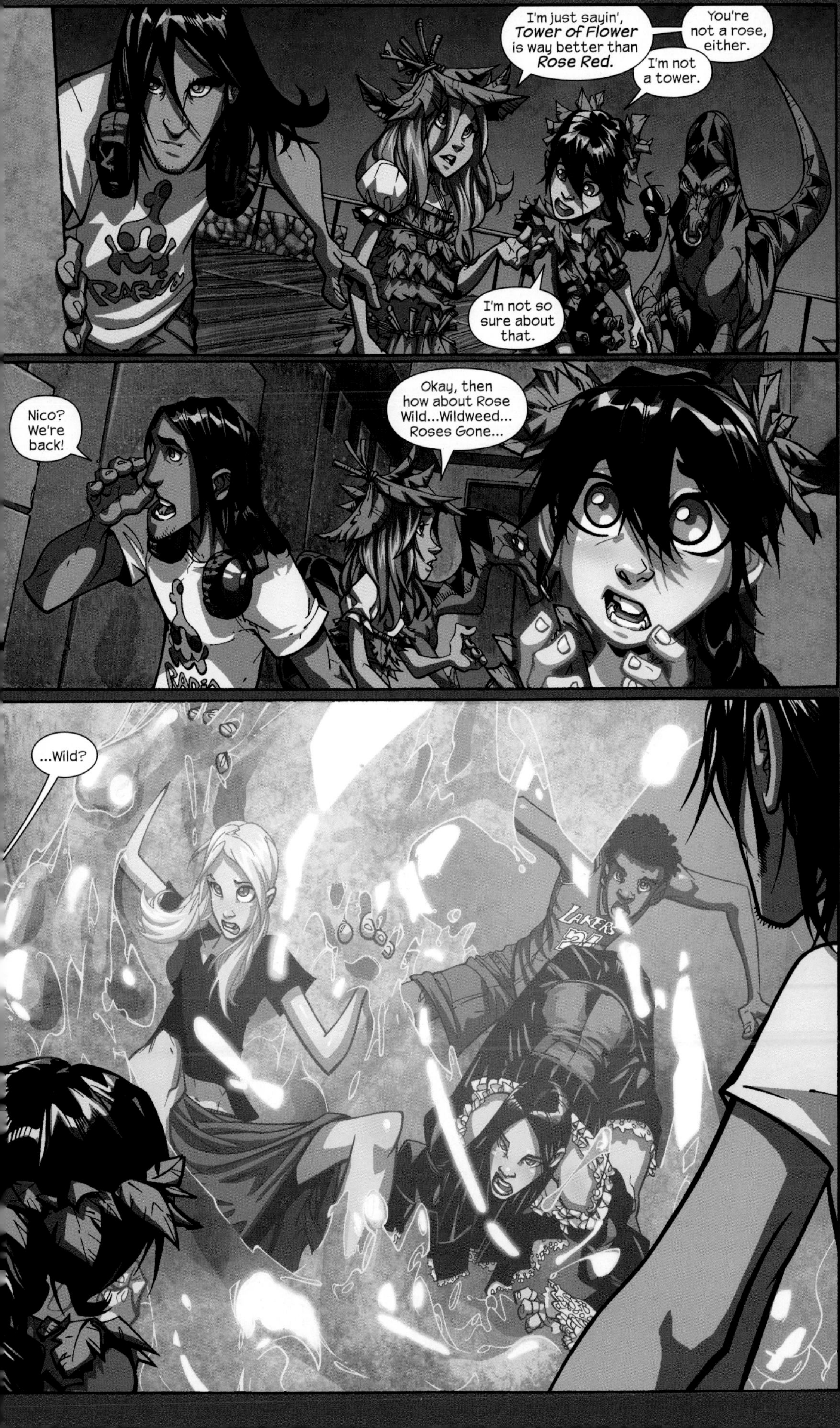

I'm just sayin', Tower of Flower is way better than Rose Red.
You're not a rose, either.
I'm not a tower.
I'm not so sure about that.
Nico? We're back!
Okay, then how about Rose Wild...Wildweed... Roses Gone...
...Wild?
LAKERS

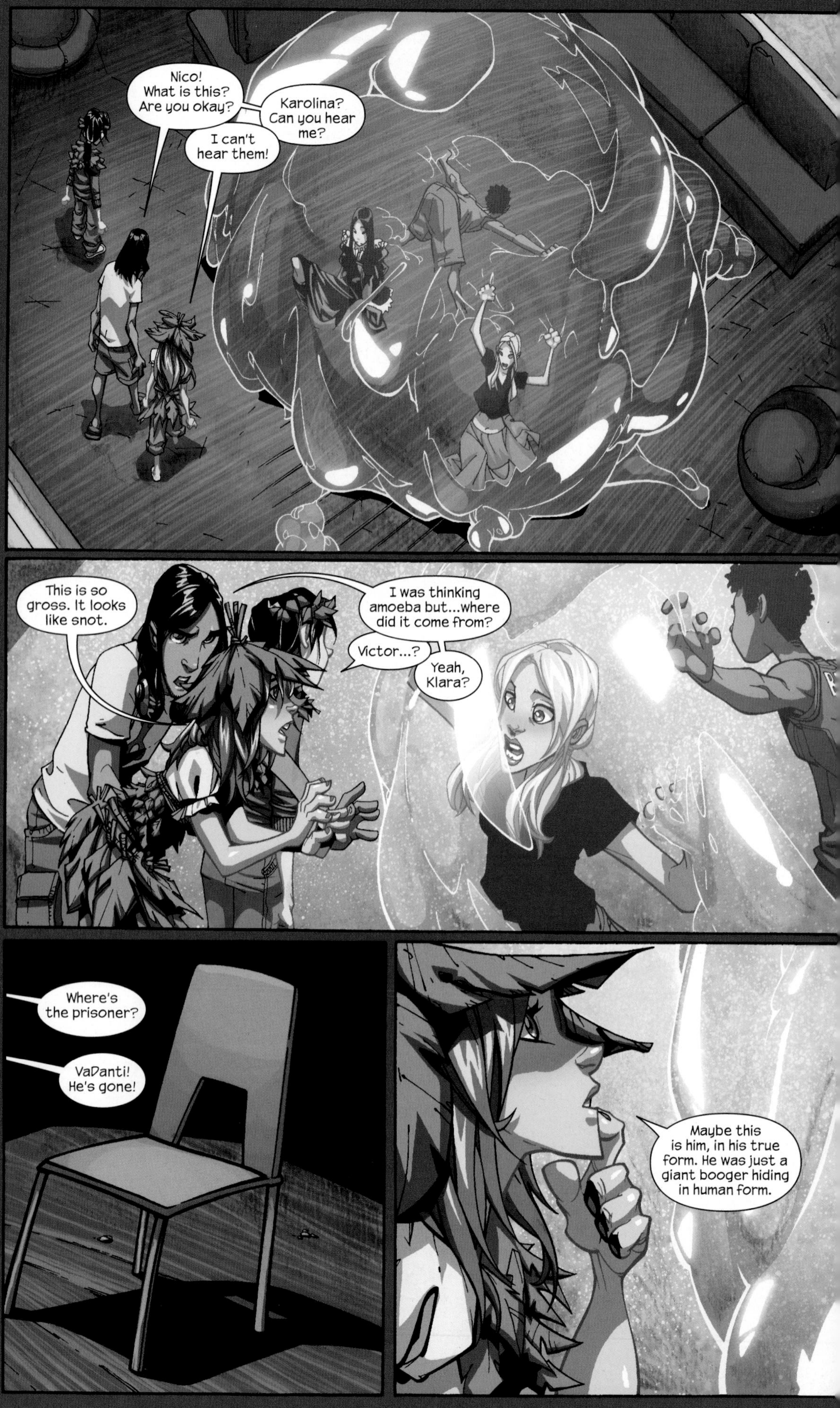
Nico!
What is this?
Are you okay?
Karolina?
Can you hear
me?
I can't
hear them!
This is so
gross. It looks
like snot.
I was thinking
amoeba but...where
did it come from?
Victor...?
Yeah,
Klara?
Where's
the prisoner?
VaDanti!
He's gone!
Maybe this
is him, in his true
form. He was just a
giant booger hiding
in human form.

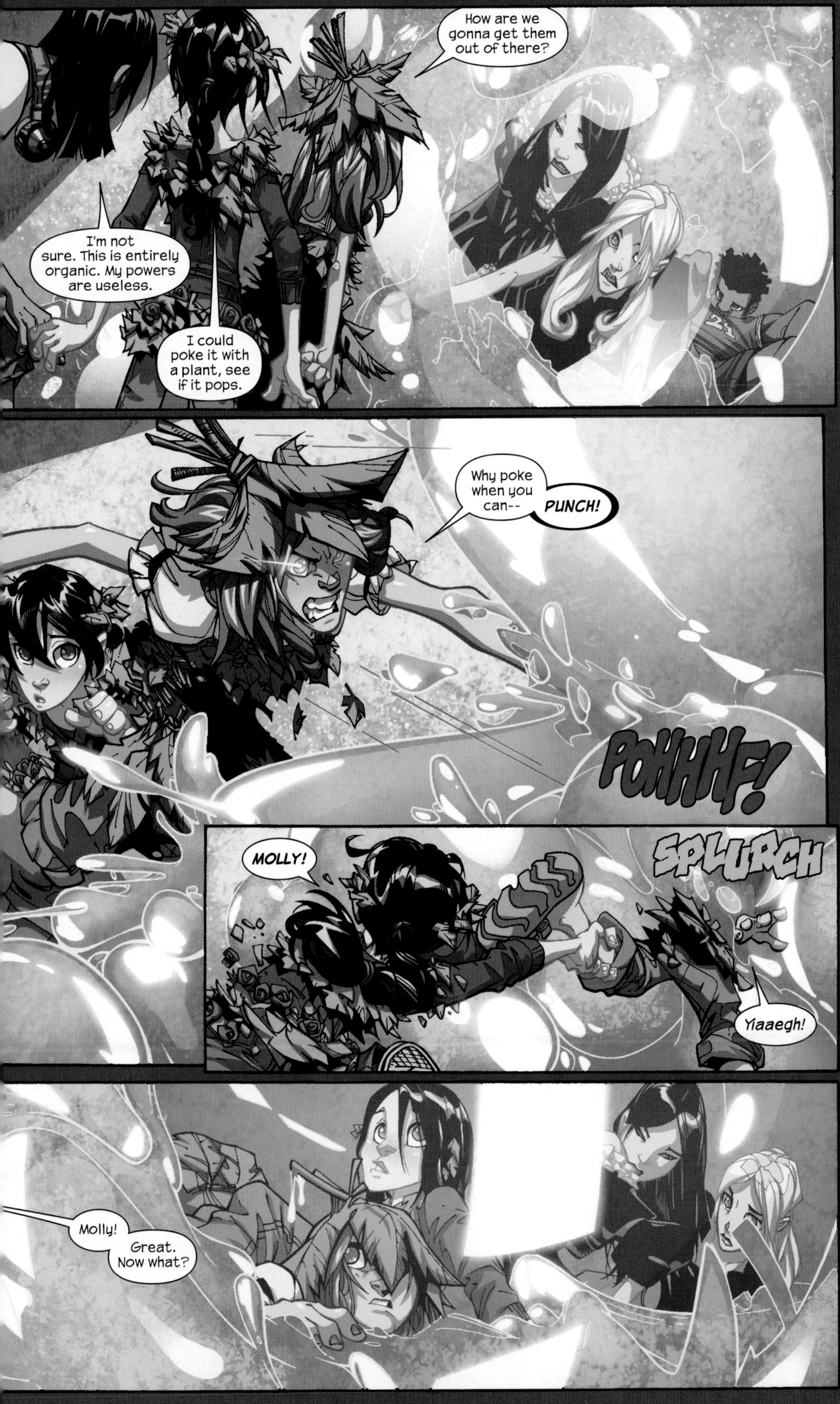
How are we gonna get them out of there?
I'm not sure. This is entirely organic. My powers are useless.
I could poke it with a plant, see if it pops.
Why poke when you can--
PUNCH!
POHHHF!
MOLLY!
SPLURCH
Yiaaegh!
Molly!
Great. Now what?

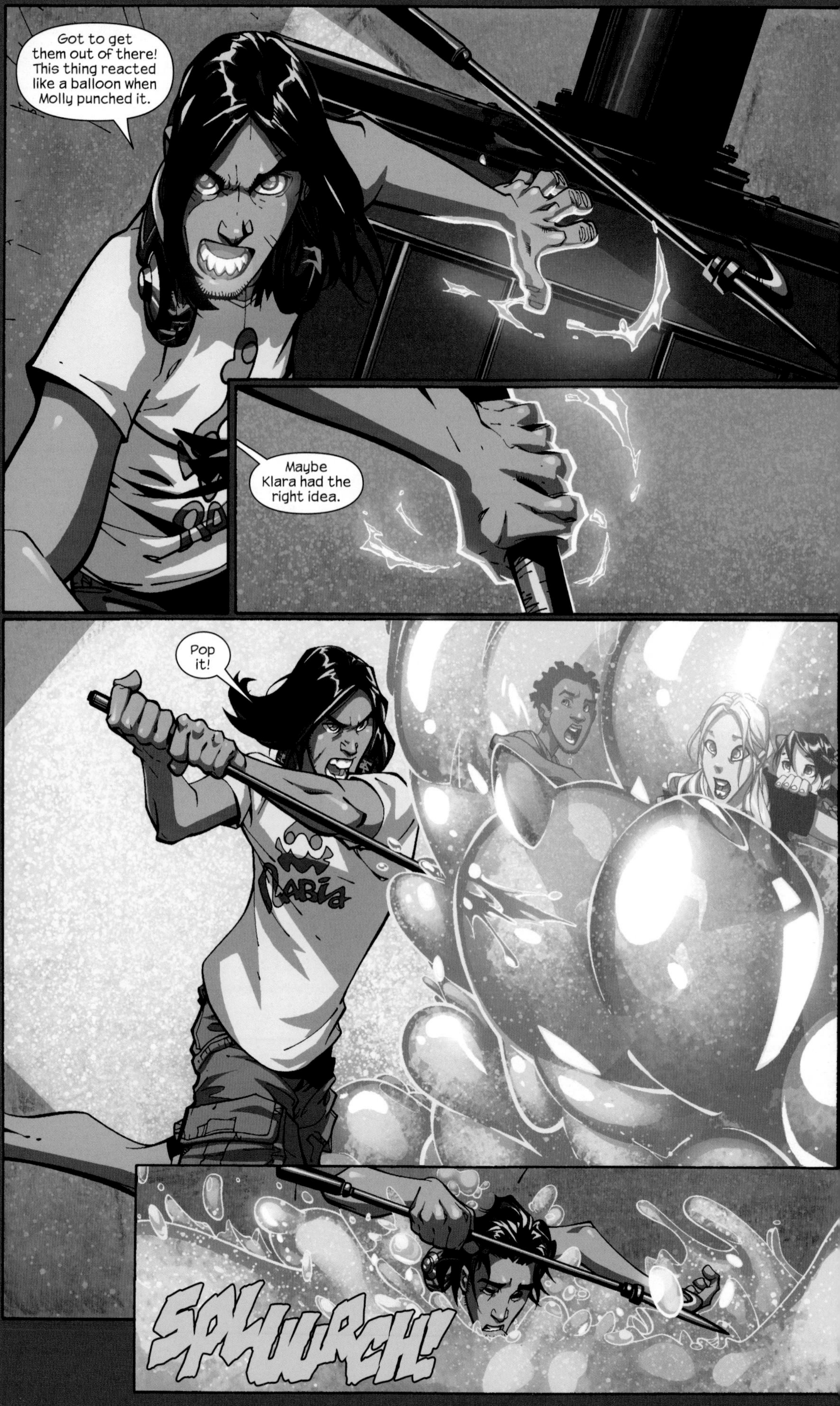
Got to get them out of there! This thing reacted like a balloon when Molly punched it.
Maybe Klara had the right idea.
Pop it!
SPLUURCH!

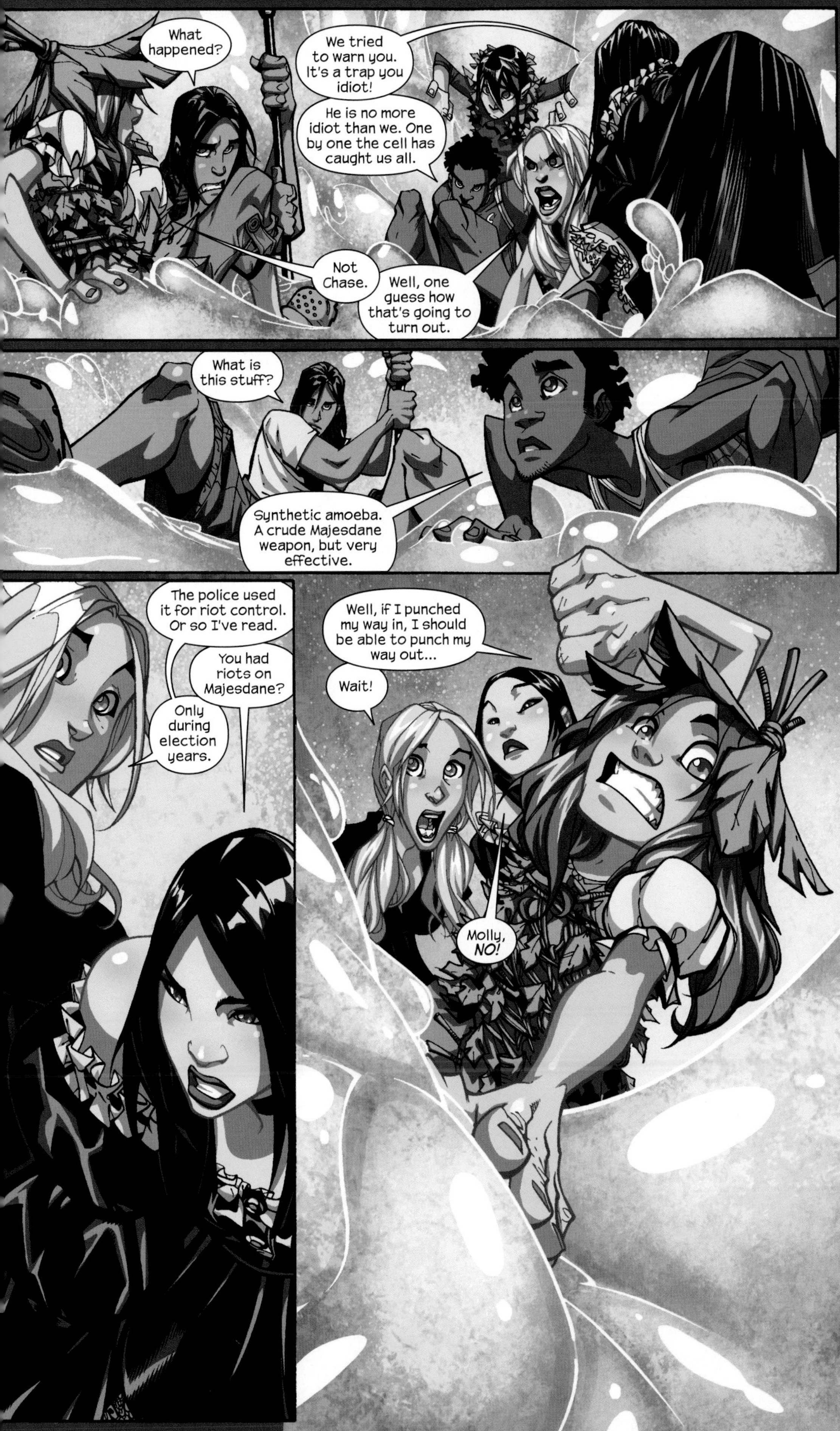

What happened?
We tried to warn you. It's a trap you idiot!
He is no more idiot than we. One by one the cell has caught us all.
Not Chase.
Well, one guess how that's going to turn out.
What is this stuff?
Synthetic amoeba. A crude Majesdane weapon, but very effective.
The police used it for riot control. Or so I've read.
You had riots on Majesdane?
Only during election years.
Well, if I punched my way in, I should be able to punch my way out...
Wait!
Molly, NO!

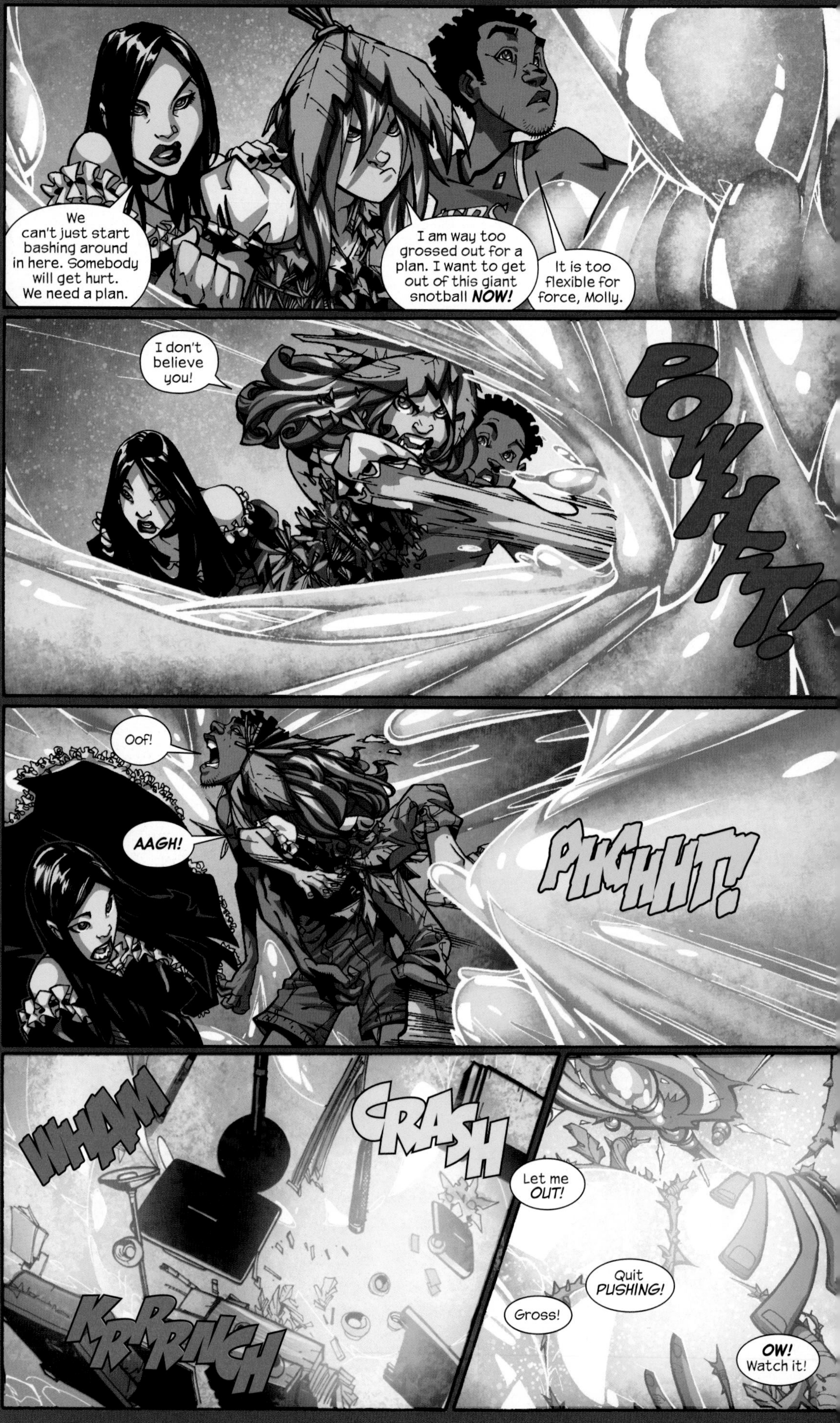
We can't just start bashing around in here. Somebody will get hurt. We need a plan.
I am way too grossed out for a plan. I want to get out of this giant snotball NOW!
It is too flexible for force, Molly.
I don't believe you!
POWHT!!
Oof!
AAGH!
PHGHHT!
WHAM
CRASH
KRRRNCH
Let me OUT!
Quit PUSHING!
Gross!
OW! Watch it!

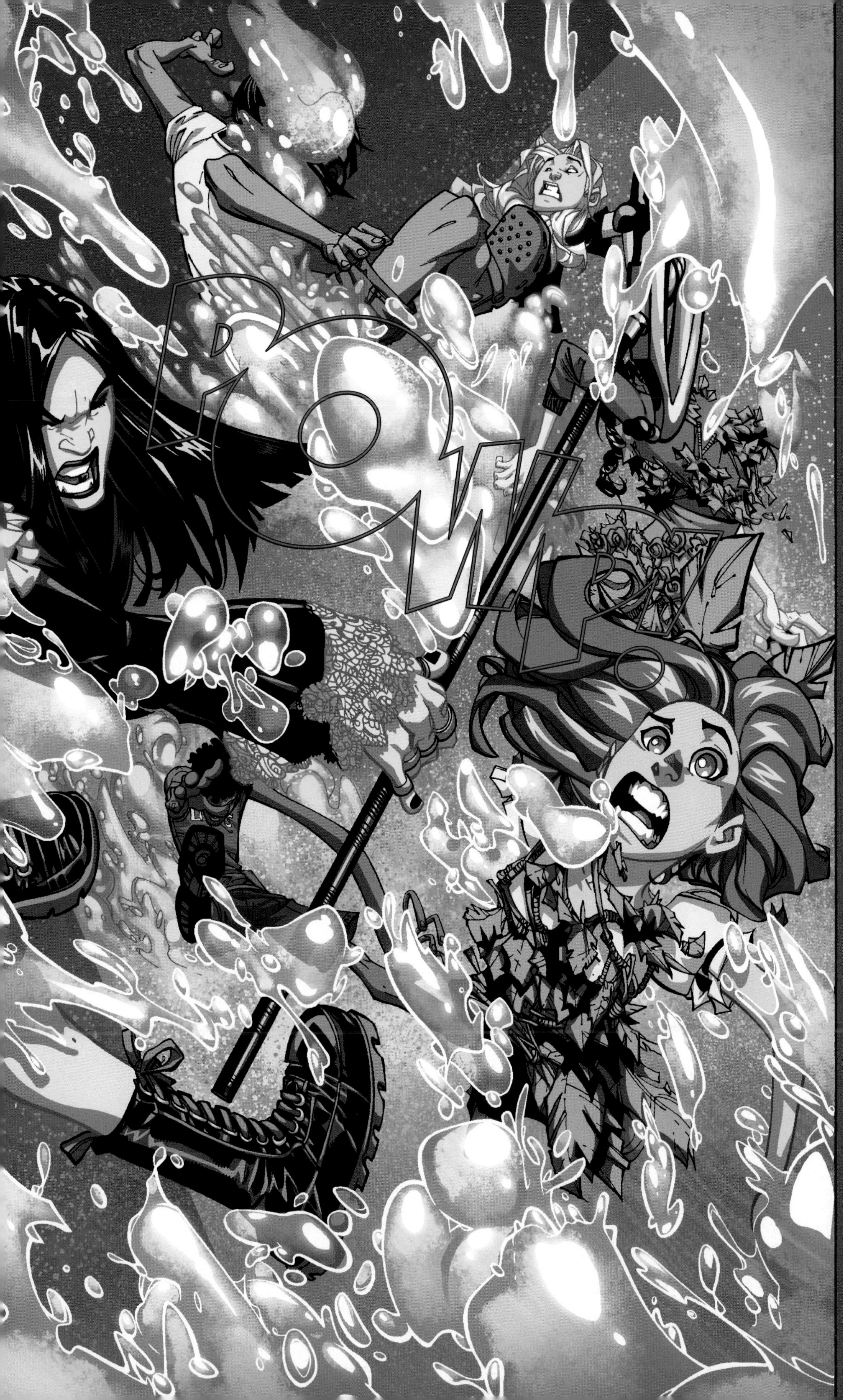

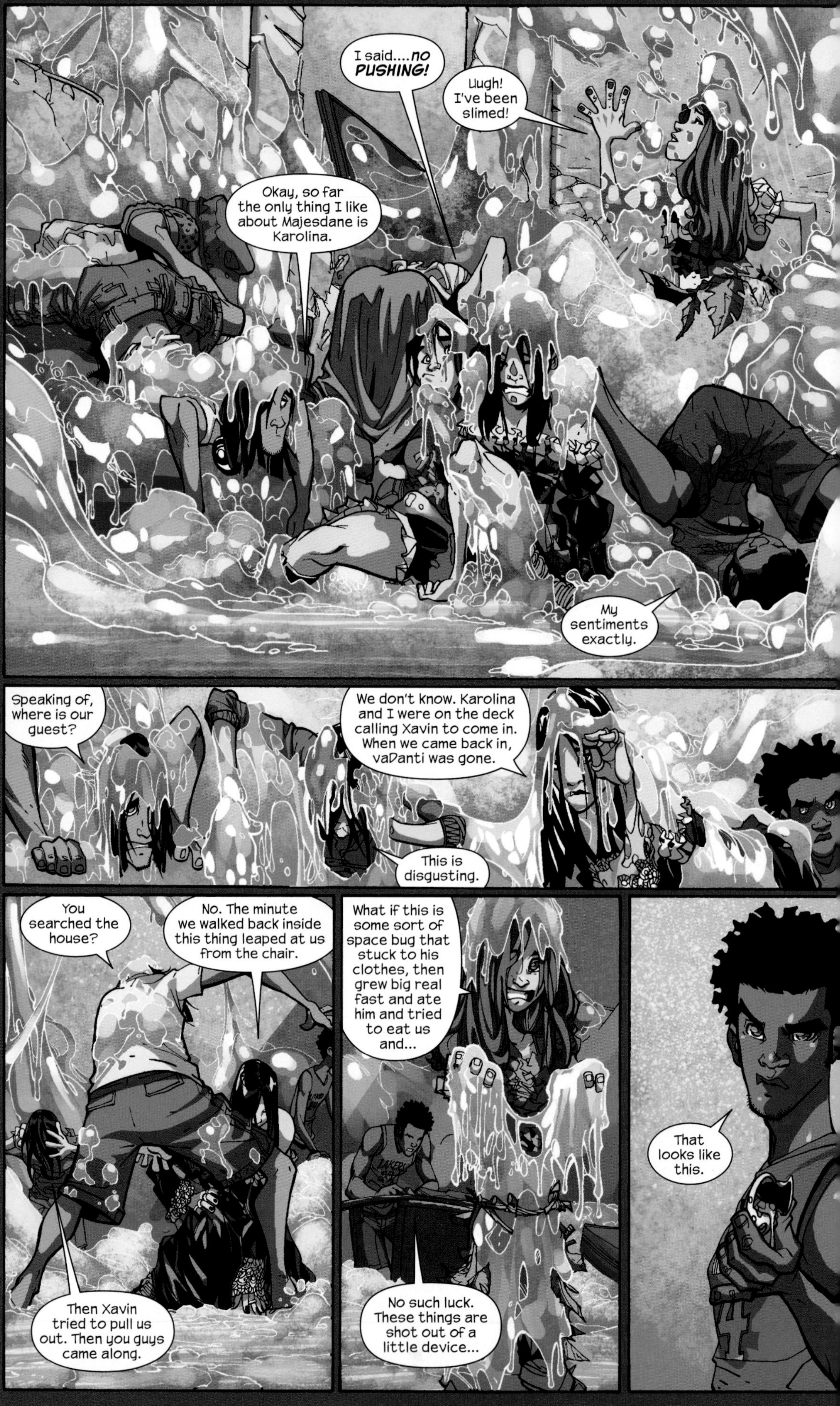
I said....no PUSHING!
Uugh! I've been slimed!
Okay, so far the only thing I like about Majesdane is Karolina.
My sentiments exactly.
Speaking of, where is our guest?
We don't know. Karolina and I were on the deck calling Xavin to come in. When we came back in, vaDanti was gone.
This is disgusting.
You searched the house?
No. The minute we walked back inside this thing leaped at us from the chair.
Then Xavin tried to pull us out. Then you guys came along.
What if this is some sort of space bug that stuck to his clothes, then grew big real fast and ate him and tried to eat us and...
No such luck. These things are shot out of a little device...
That looks like this.

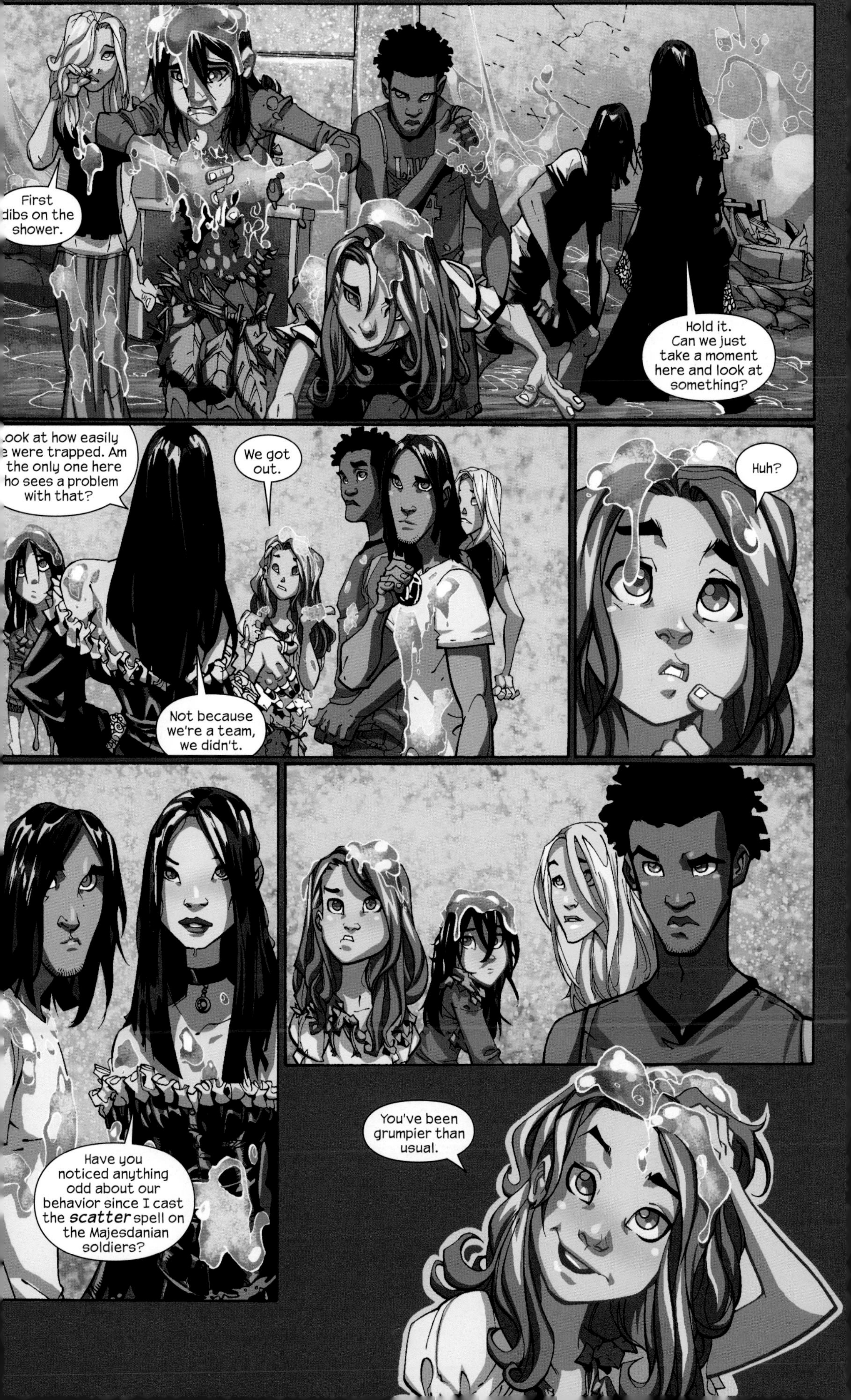
First dibs on the shower.
Hold it. Can we just take a moment here and look at something?
Look at how easily we were trapped. Am I the only one here who sees a problem with that?
We got out.
Not because we're a team, we didn't.
Huh?
Have you noticed anything odd about our behavior since I cast the *scatter* spell on the Majesdanian soldiers?
You've been grumpier than usual.

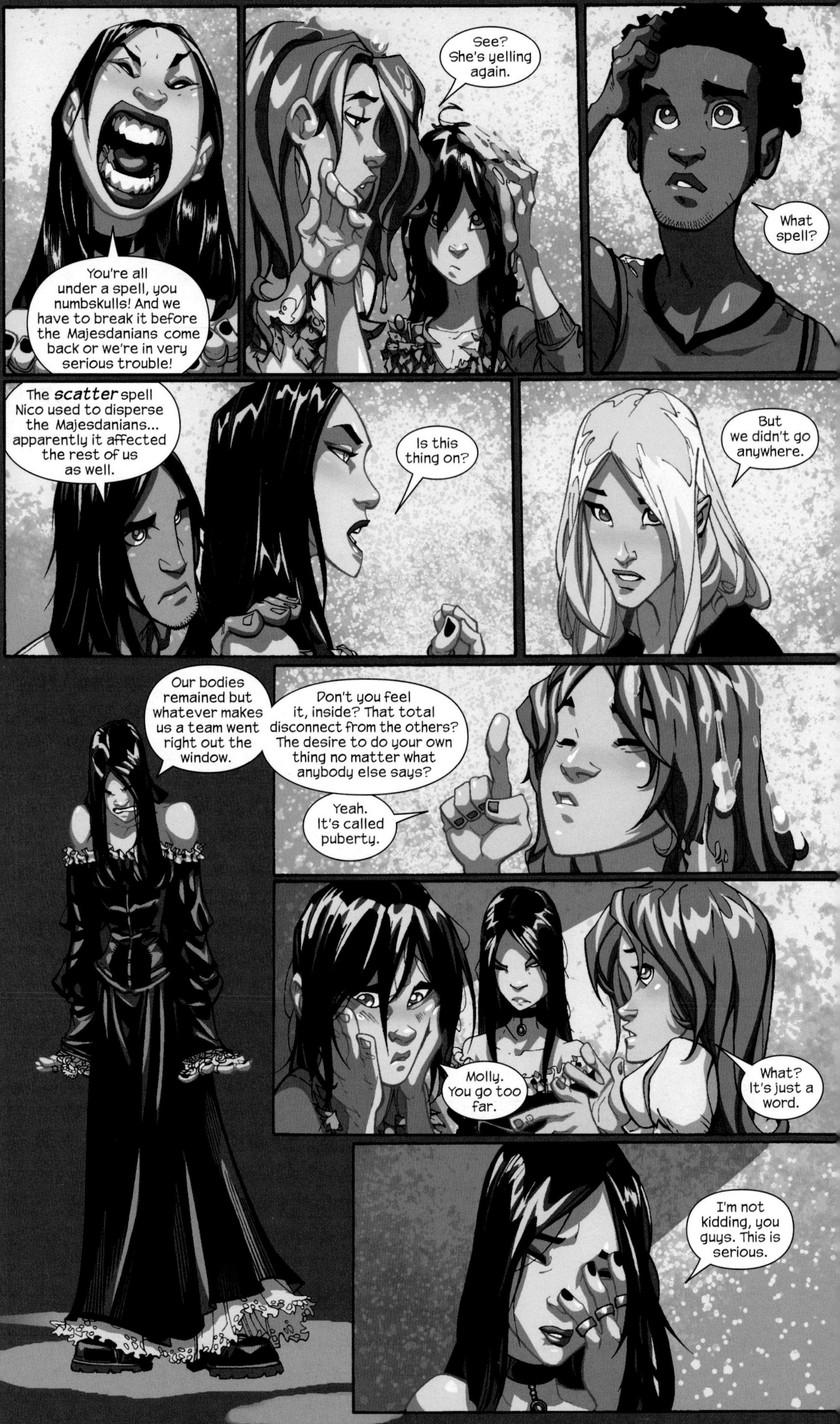
You're all under a spell, you numbskulls! And we have to break it before the Majesdanians come back or we're in very serious trouble!
See? She's yelling again.
What spell?
The scatter spell Nico used to disperse the Majesdanians... apparently it affected the rest of us as well.
Is this thing on?
But we didn't go anywhere.
Our bodies remained but whatever makes us a team went right out the window.
Don't you feel it, inside? That total disconnect from the others? The desire to do your own thing no matter what anybody else says?
Yeah. It's called puberty.
Molly. You go too far.
What? It's just a word.
I'm not kidding, you guys. This is serious.

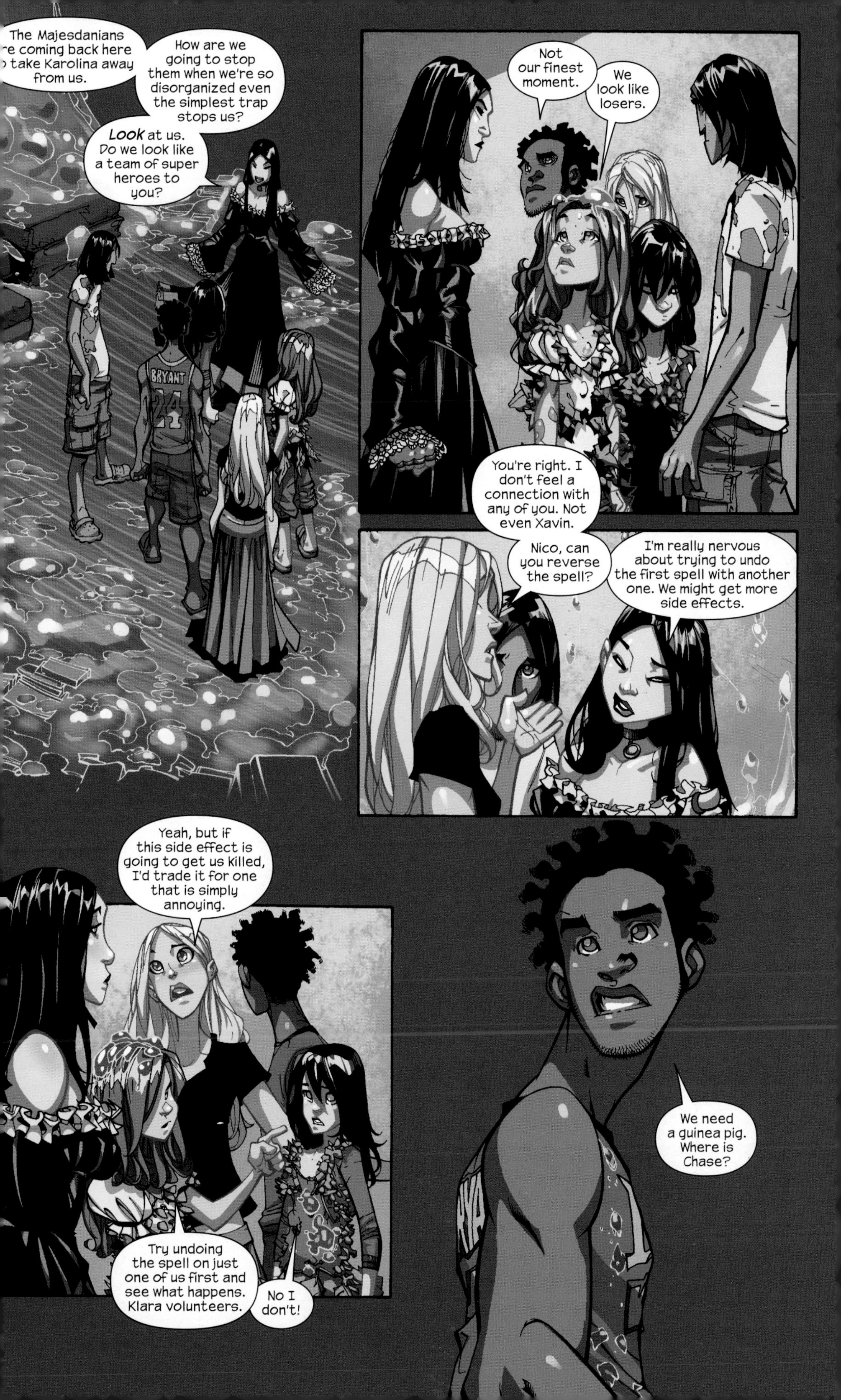
The Majesdanians
re coming back here
o take Karolina away
from us.
How are we going to stop them when we're so disorganized even the simplest trap stops us?
LOOK at us. Do we look like a team of super heroes to you?
BRYANT
24
Not our finest moment.
We look like losers.
You're right. I don't feel a connection with any of you. Not even Xavin.
Nico, can you reverse the spell?
I'm really nervous about trying to undo the first spell with another one. We might get more side effects.
Yeah, but if this side effect is going to get us killed, I'd trade it for one that is simply annoying.
Try undoing the spell on just one of us first and see what happens. Klara volunteers.
No I don't!
We need a guinea pig. Where is Chase?

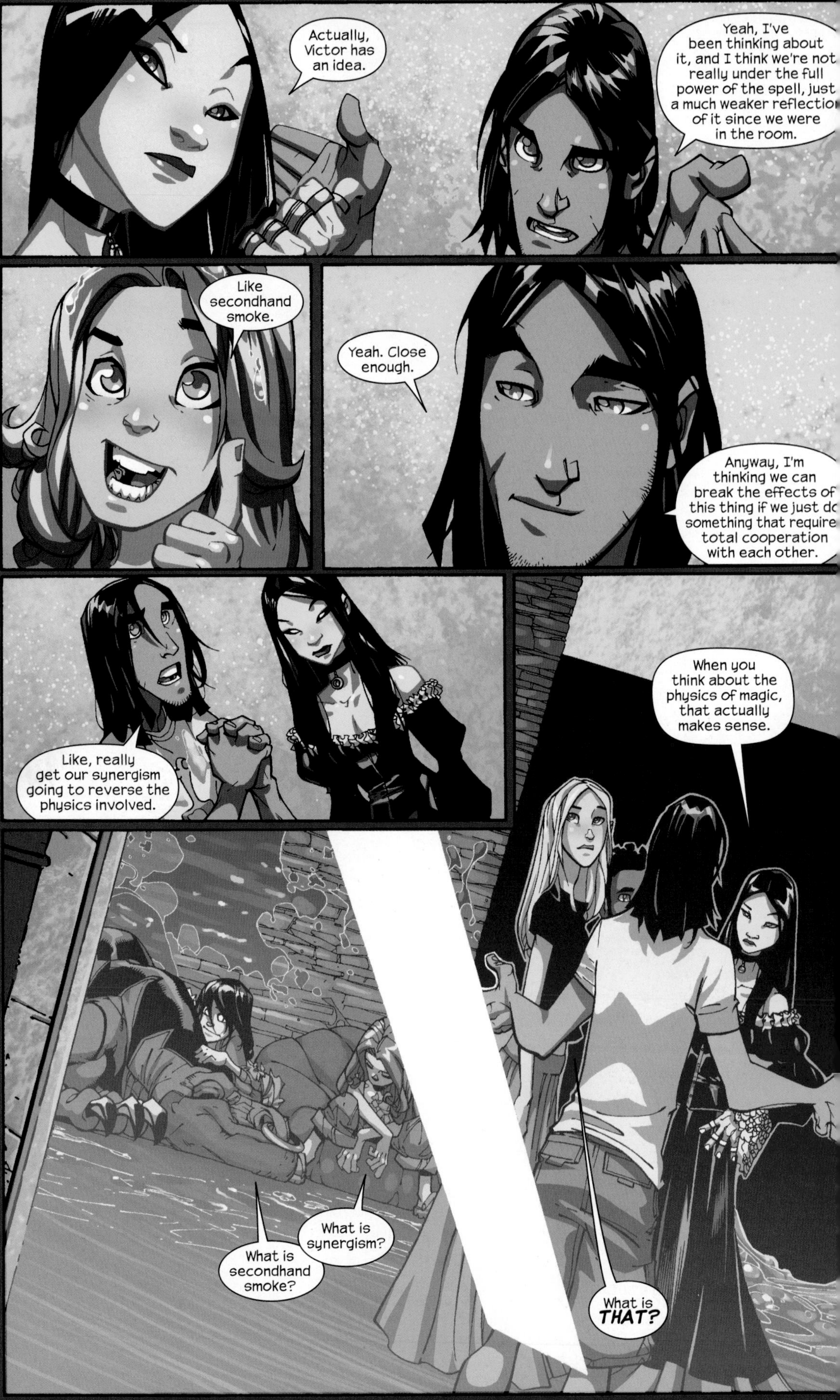

Actually, Victor has an idea.
Yeah, I've been thinking about it, and I think we're not really under the full power of the spell, just a much weaker reflectio of it since we were in the room.
Like secondhand smoke.
Yeah. Close enough.
Anyway, I'm thinking we can break the effects of this thing if we just do something that require total cooperation with each other.
Like, really get our synergism going to reverse the physics involved.
When you think about the physics of magic, that actually makes sense.
What is secondhand smoke?
What is synergism?
What is THAT?

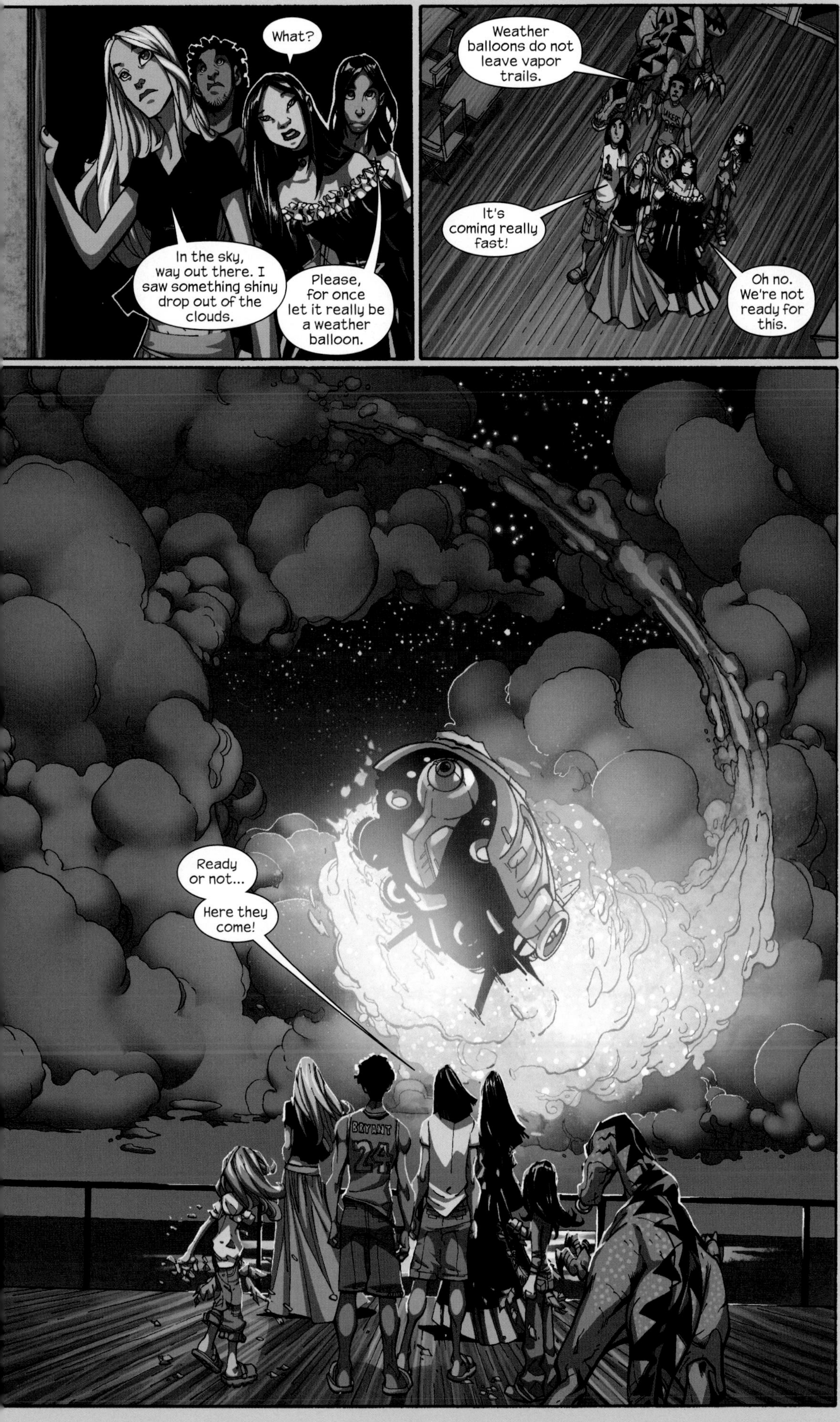
What?
In the sky, way out there. I saw something shiny drop out of the clouds.
Please, for once let it really be a weather balloon.
Weather balloons do not leave vapor trails.
It's coming really fast!
Oh no. We're not ready for this.
Ready or not...
Here they come!
BRYANT
24

5

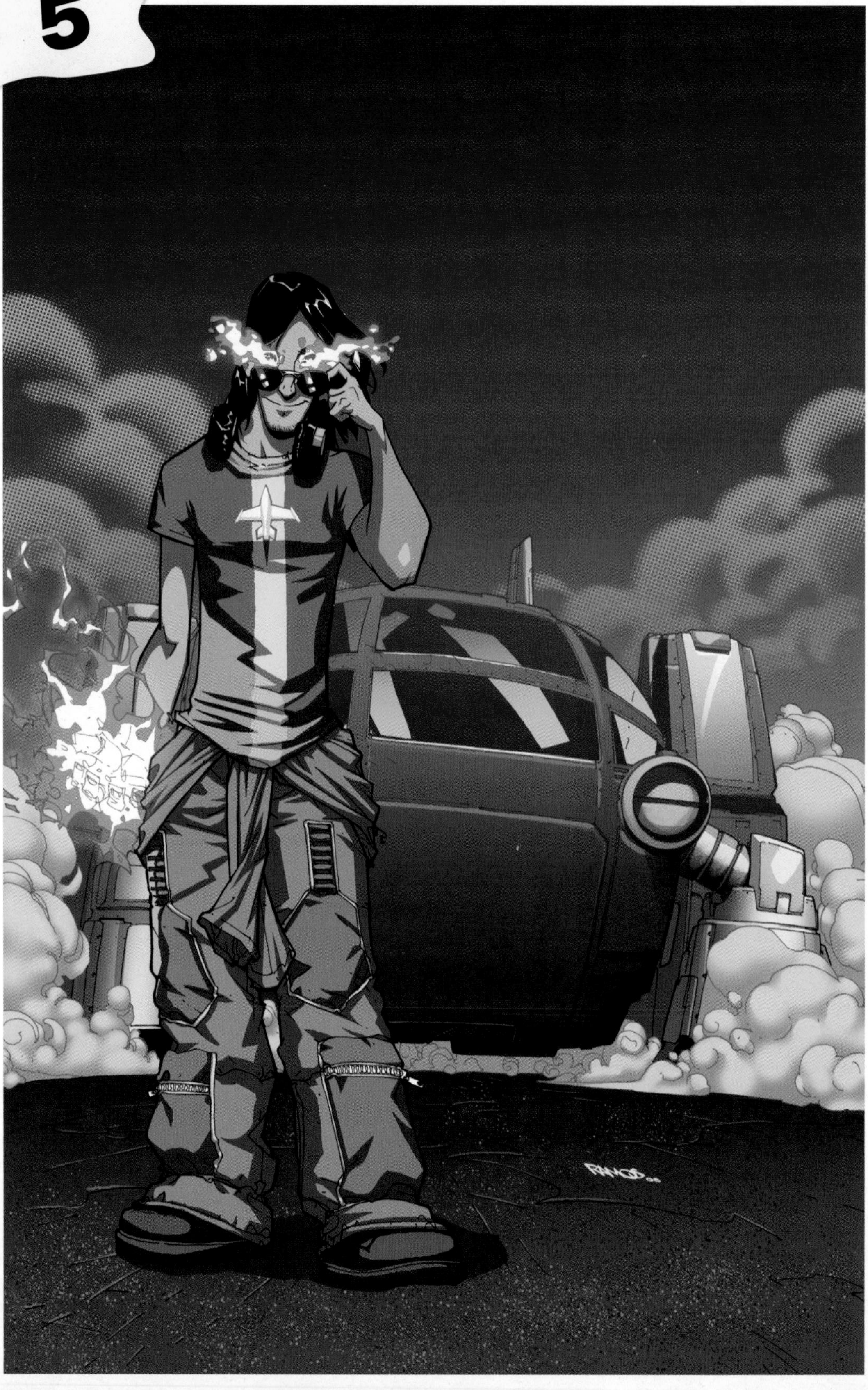

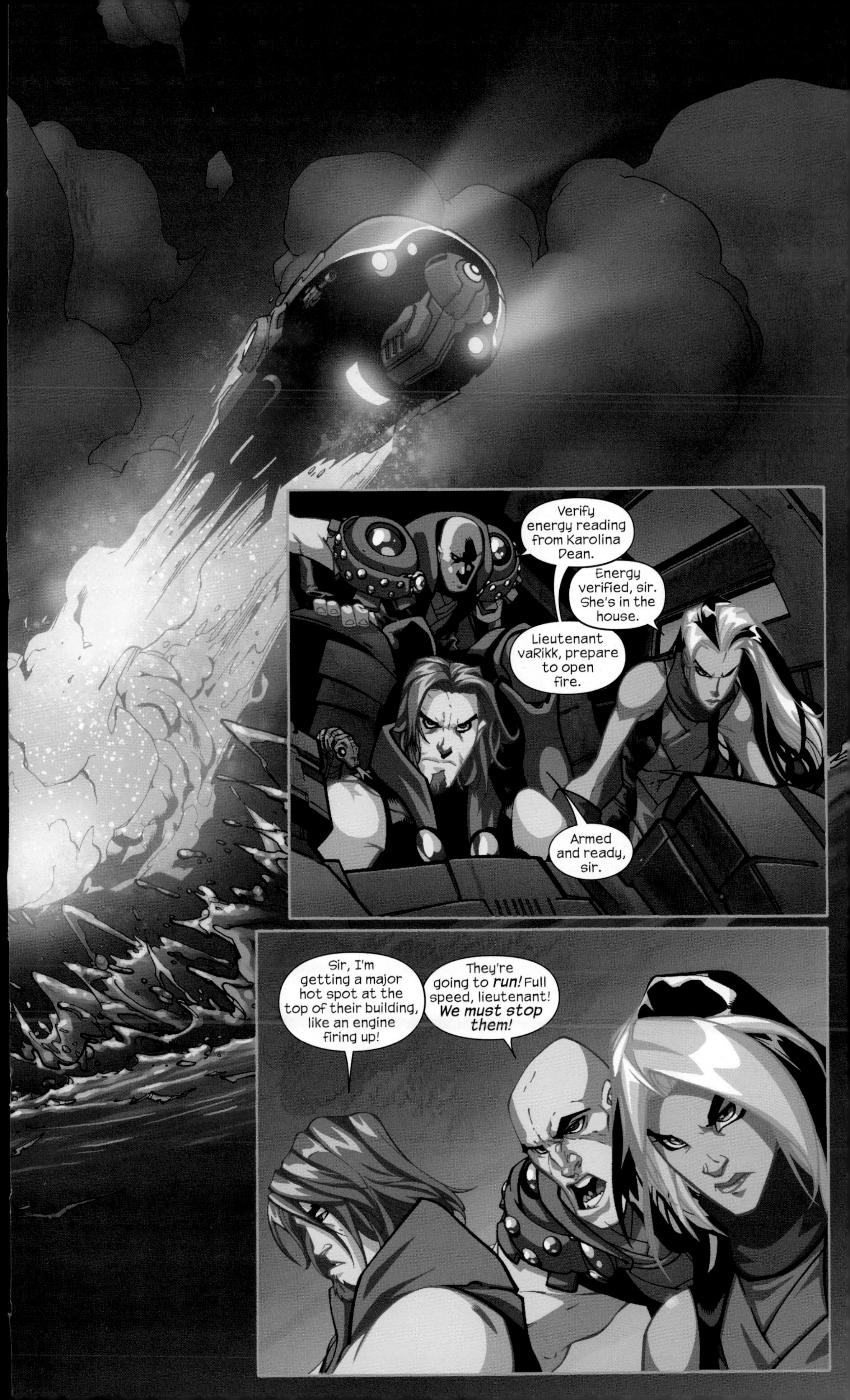
Verify energy reading from Karolina Dean.
Energy verified, sir. She's in the house.
Lieutenant vaRikk, prepare to open fire.
Armed and ready, sir.
Sir, I'm getting a major hot spot at the top of their building, like an engine firing up!
They're going to *run!* Full speed, lieutenant! ***We must stop them!***

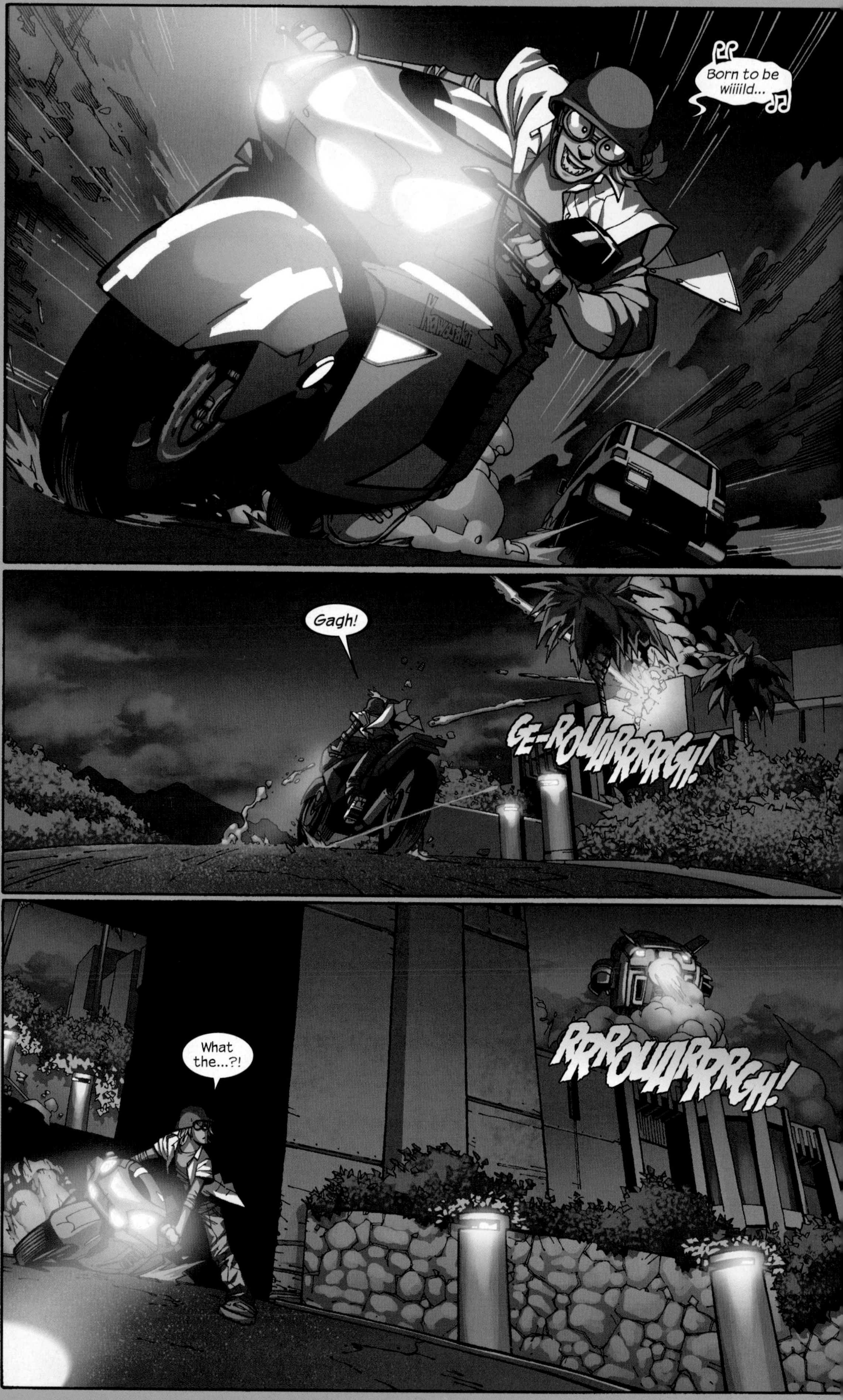
Born to be wiiiild...
Gagh!
GE-ROUUARRRRGH!
What the...?!
RRROUUARRRGH!

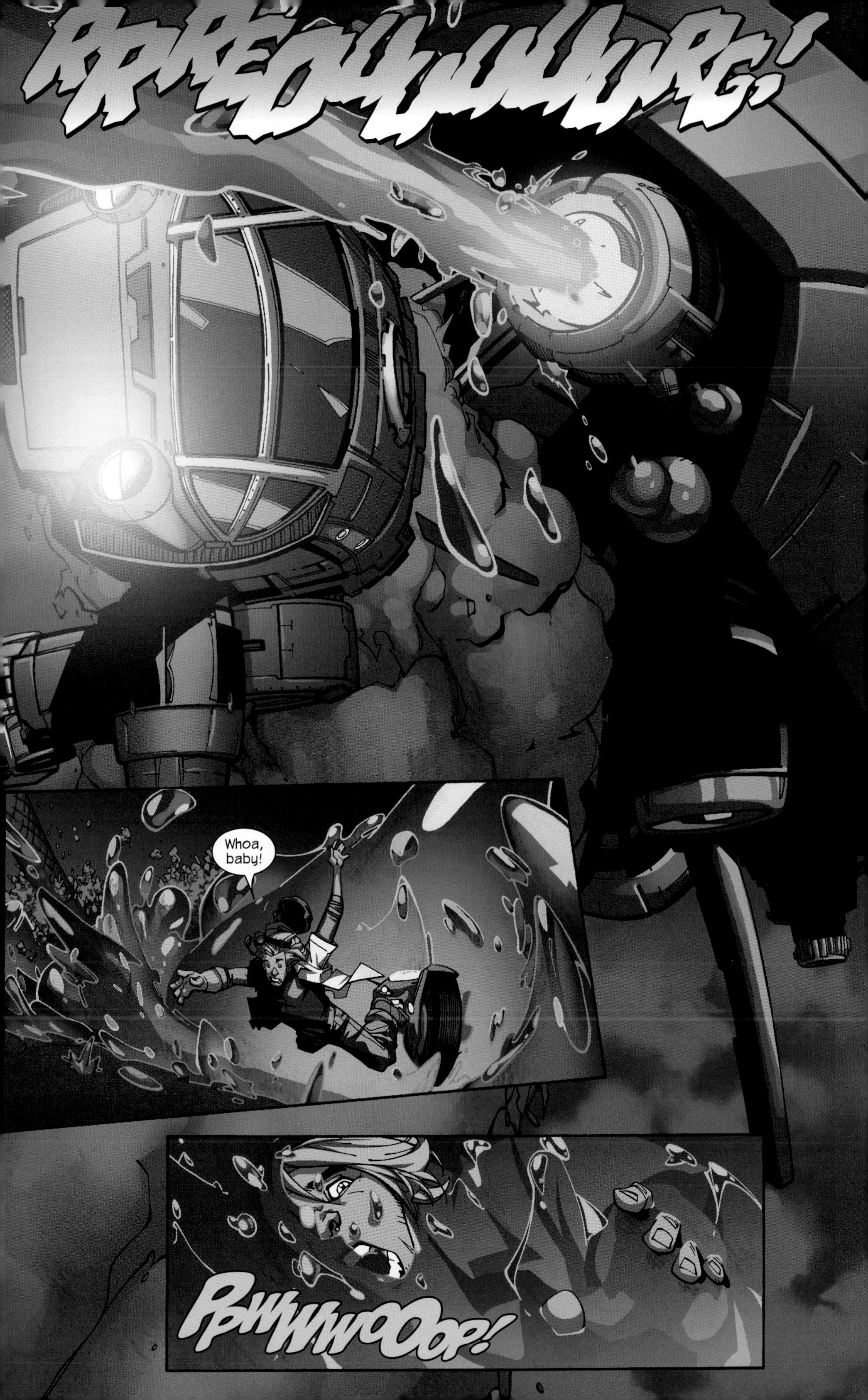
RRREOUUUURG!
Whoa, baby!
PBWWOOOP!

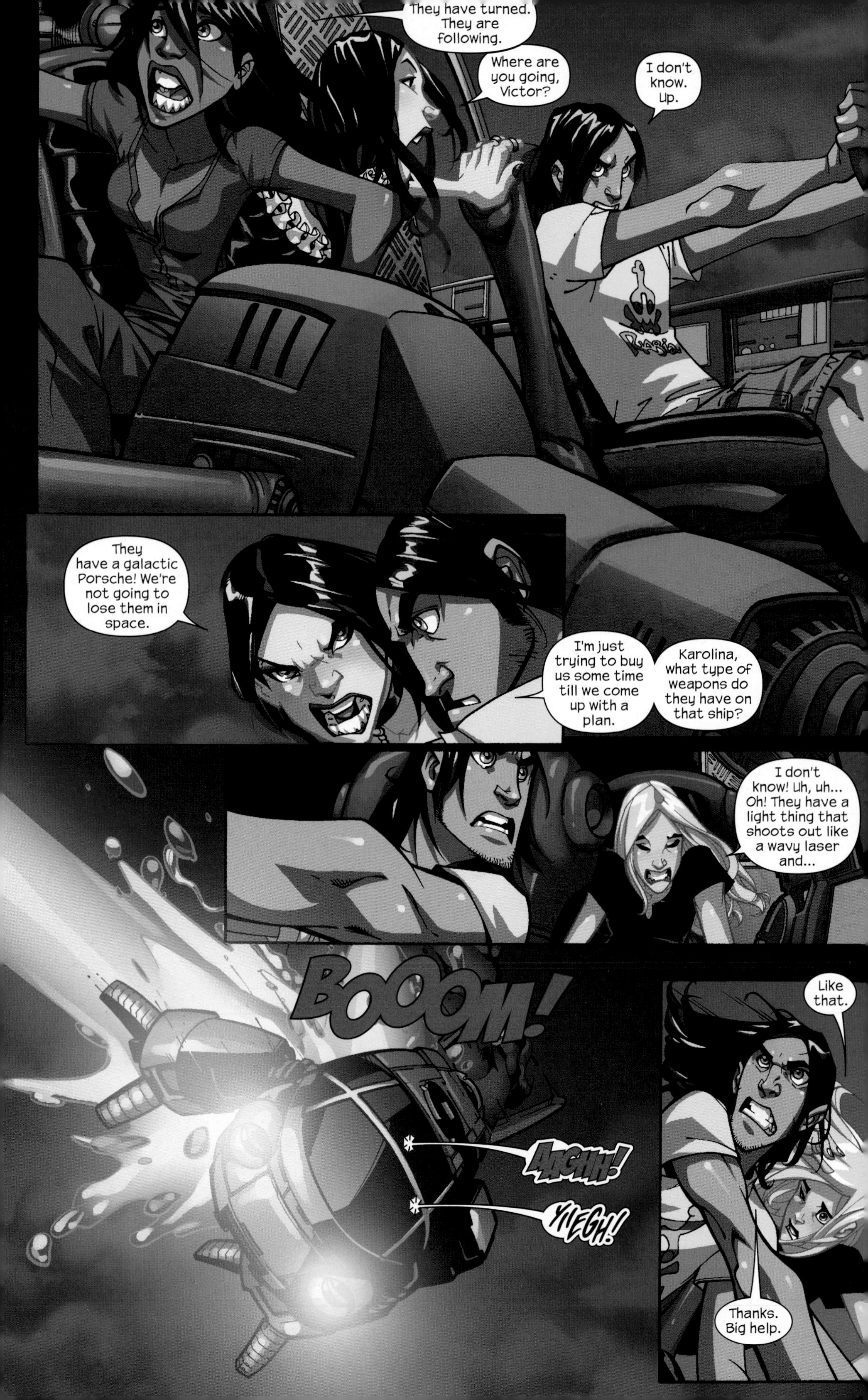
They have turned. They are following.
Where are you going, Victor?
I don't know. Up.
They have a galactic Porsche! We're not going to lose them in space.
I'm just trying to buy us some time till we come up with a plan.
Karolina, what type of weapons do they have on that ship?
I don't know! Uh, uh... Oh! They have a light thing that shoots out like a wavy laser and...
BOOOM!
AAGHH!
YNEGH!
Like that.
Thanks. Big help.

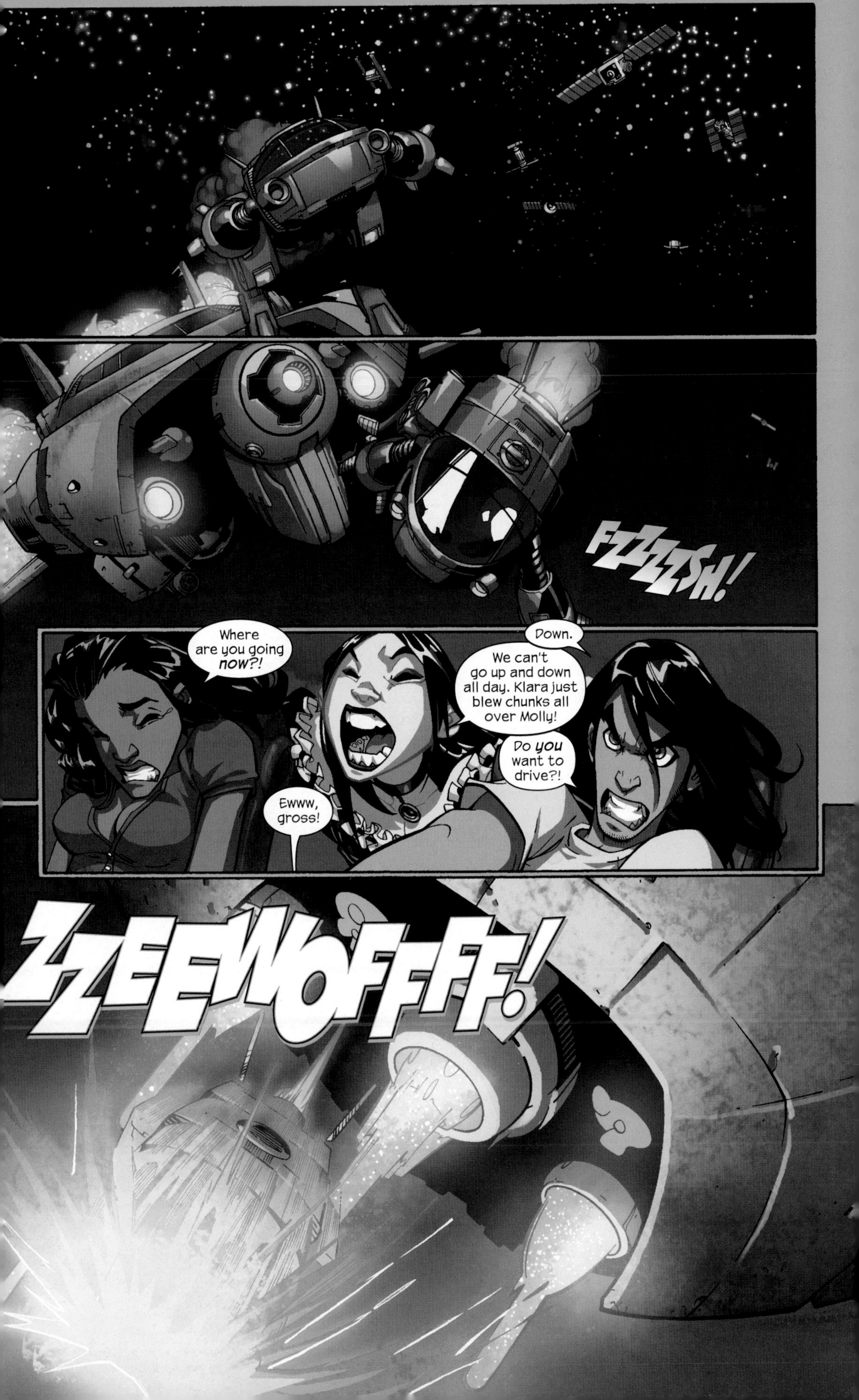
FZZZZSH!
Where are you going now?!
Down.
We can't go up and down all day. Klara just blew chunks all over Molly!
Do you want to drive?!
Ewww, gross!
ZZEEWOFFFF!

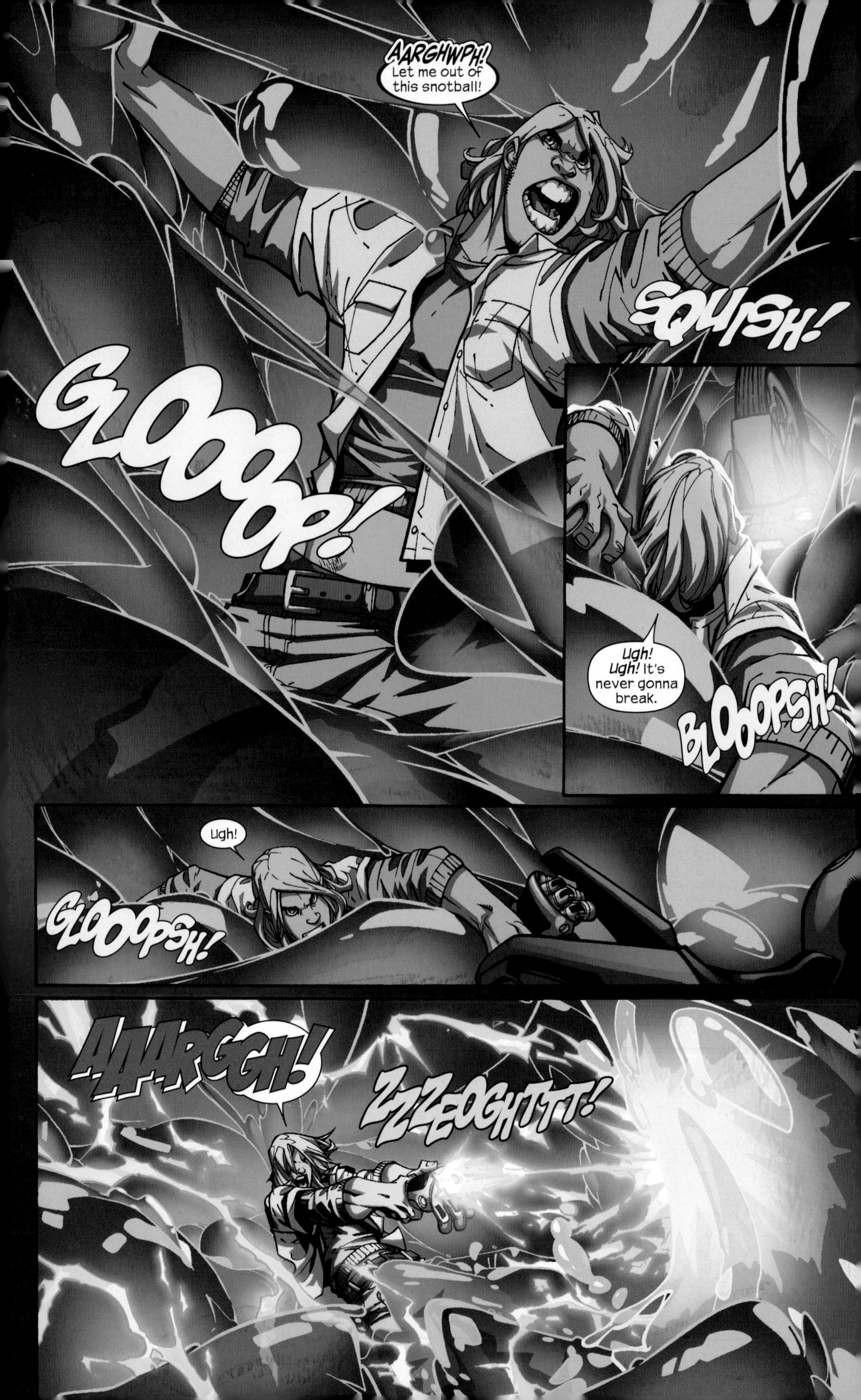
AARGHWPH! Let me out of this snotball!
SQUISH!
GLOOOOP!
Ugh! Ugh! It's never gonna break.
BLOOOPSH!
Ugh!
GLOOOPSH!
AAARGGH!
ZZZEOGHTTT!

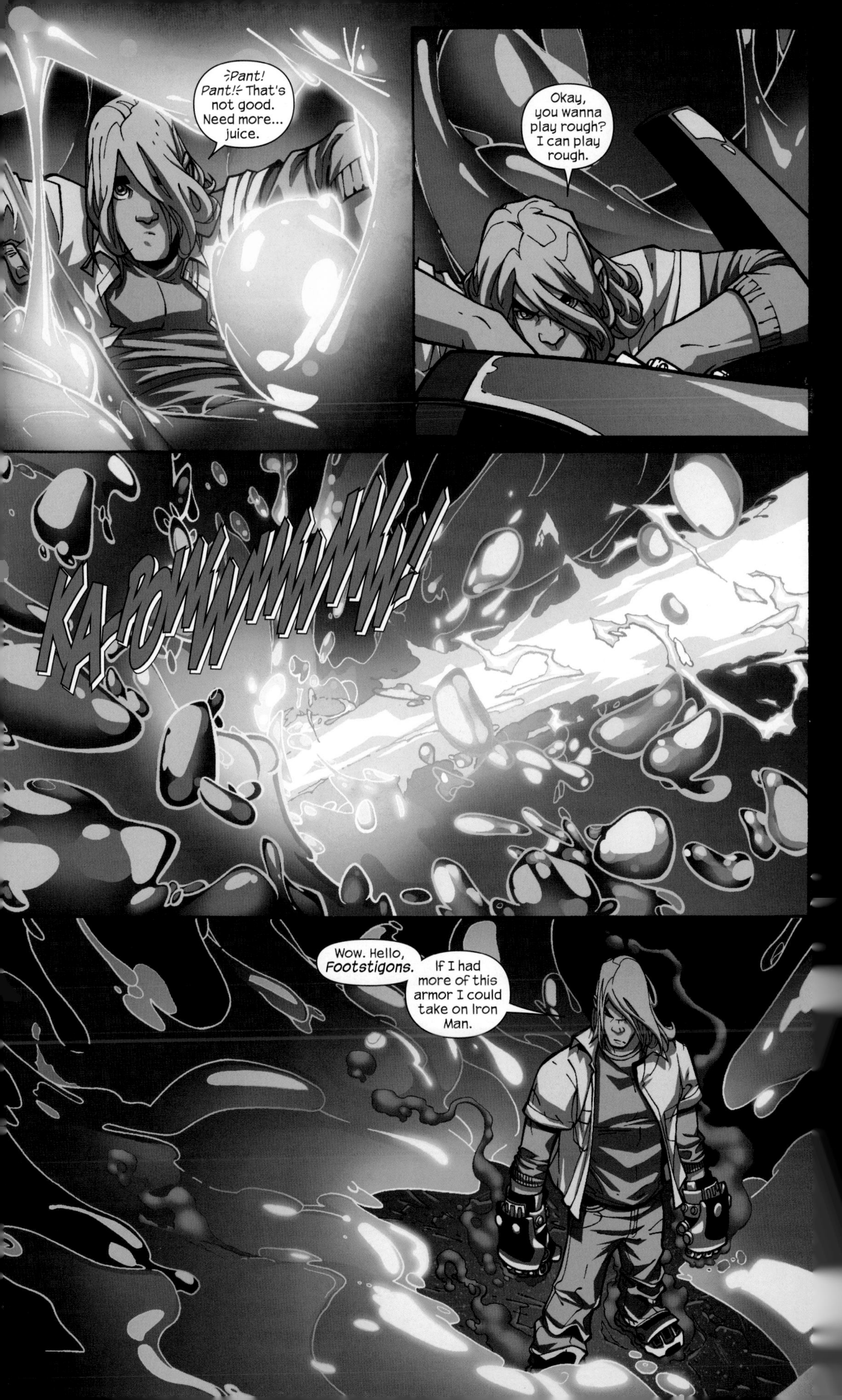

-Pant! Pant!- That's not good. Need more... juice.
Okay, you wanna play rough? I can play rough.
KA-POWWWWWWW!
Wow. Hello, Footstigons.
If I had more of this armor I could take on Iron Man.

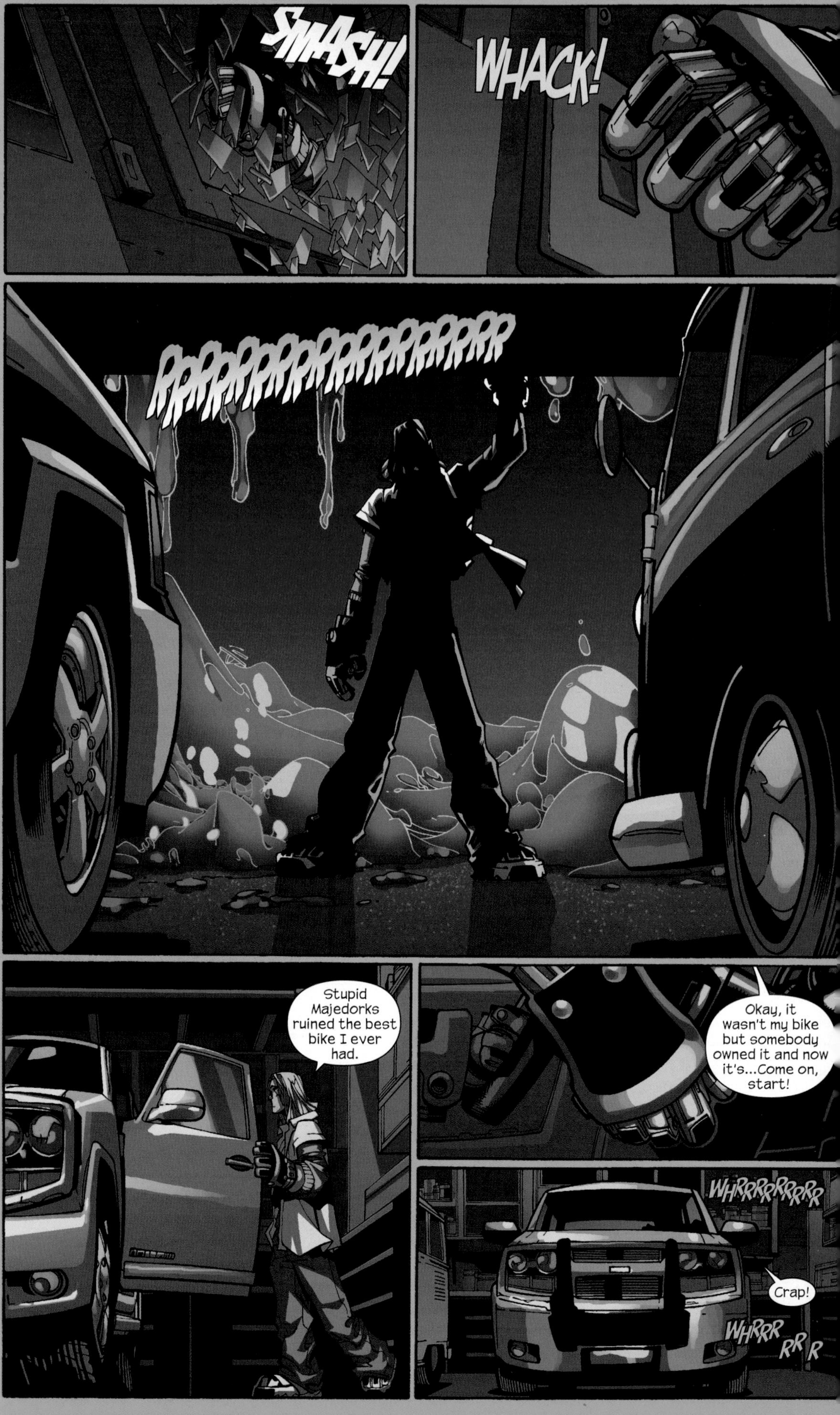
SMASH!
WHACK!
RRRRRRRRRRRRRRRRRRRRRRR
Stupid Majedorks ruined the best bike I ever had.
Okay, it wasn't my bike but somebody owned it and now it's...Come on, start!
WHRRRRRRRR
Crap!
WHRRR RRR

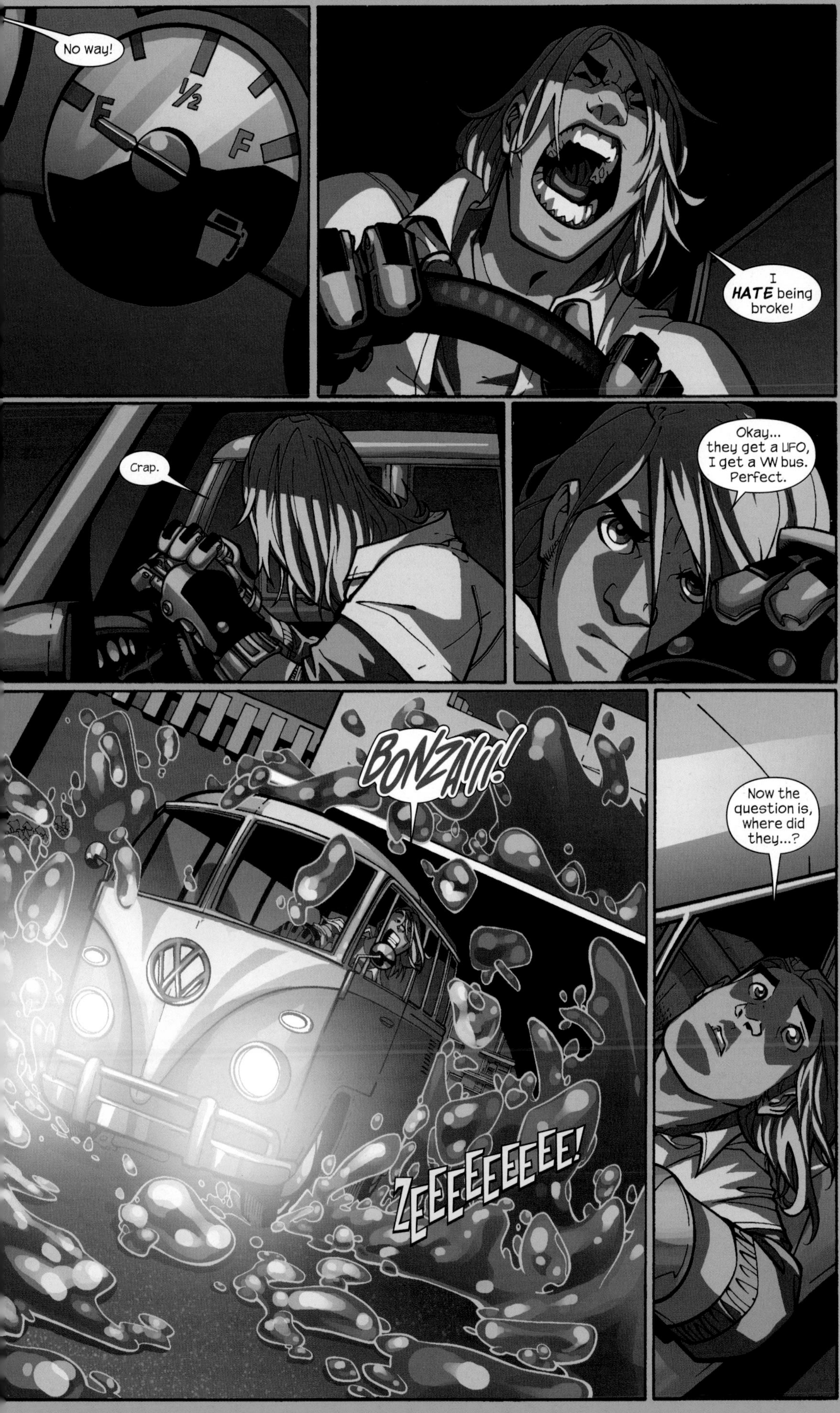
No way!
I HATE being broke!
Crap.
Okay... they get a UFO, I get a VW bus. Perfect.
BONZAI!!
ZEEEEEEEEE!
Now the question is, where did they...?

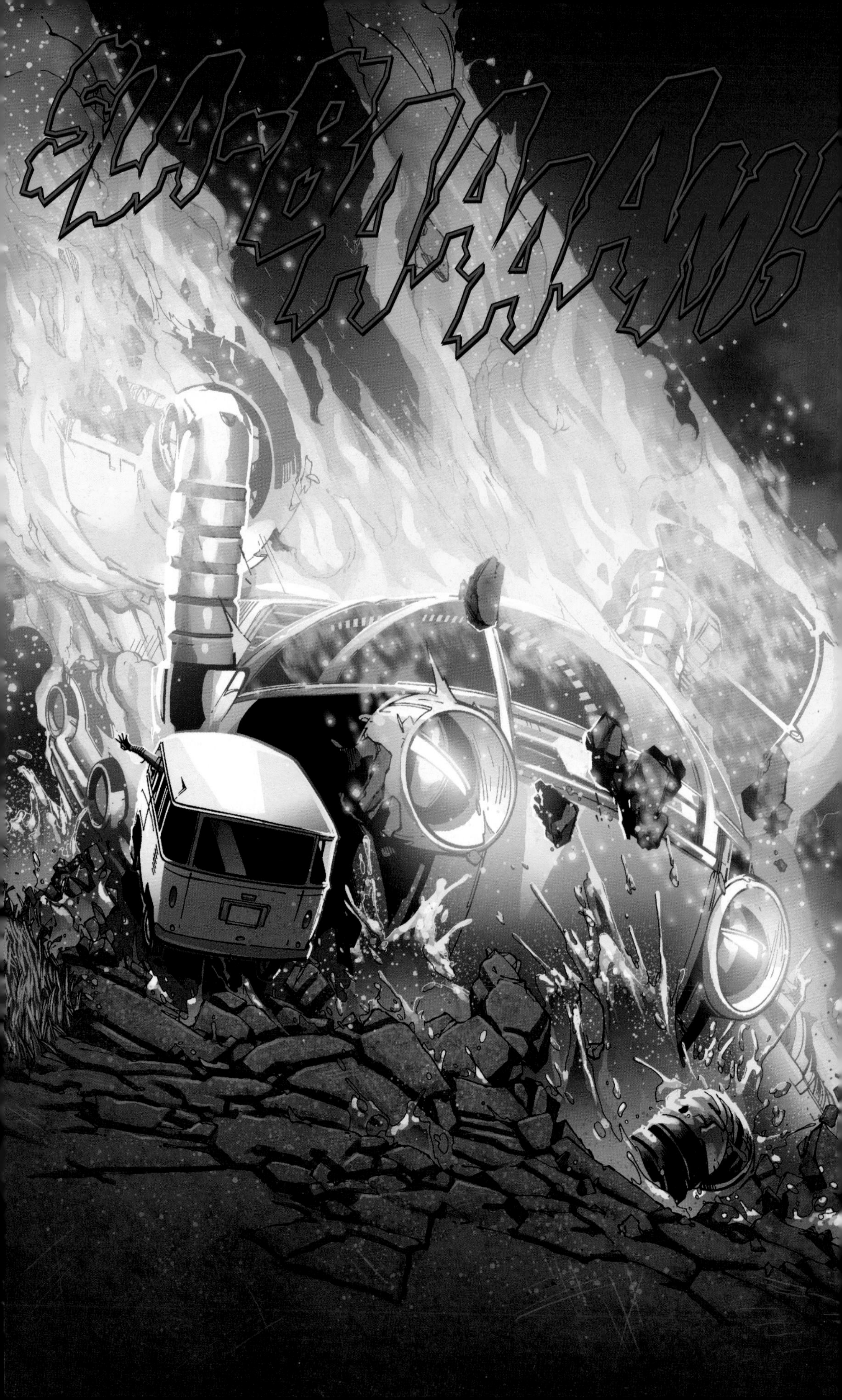

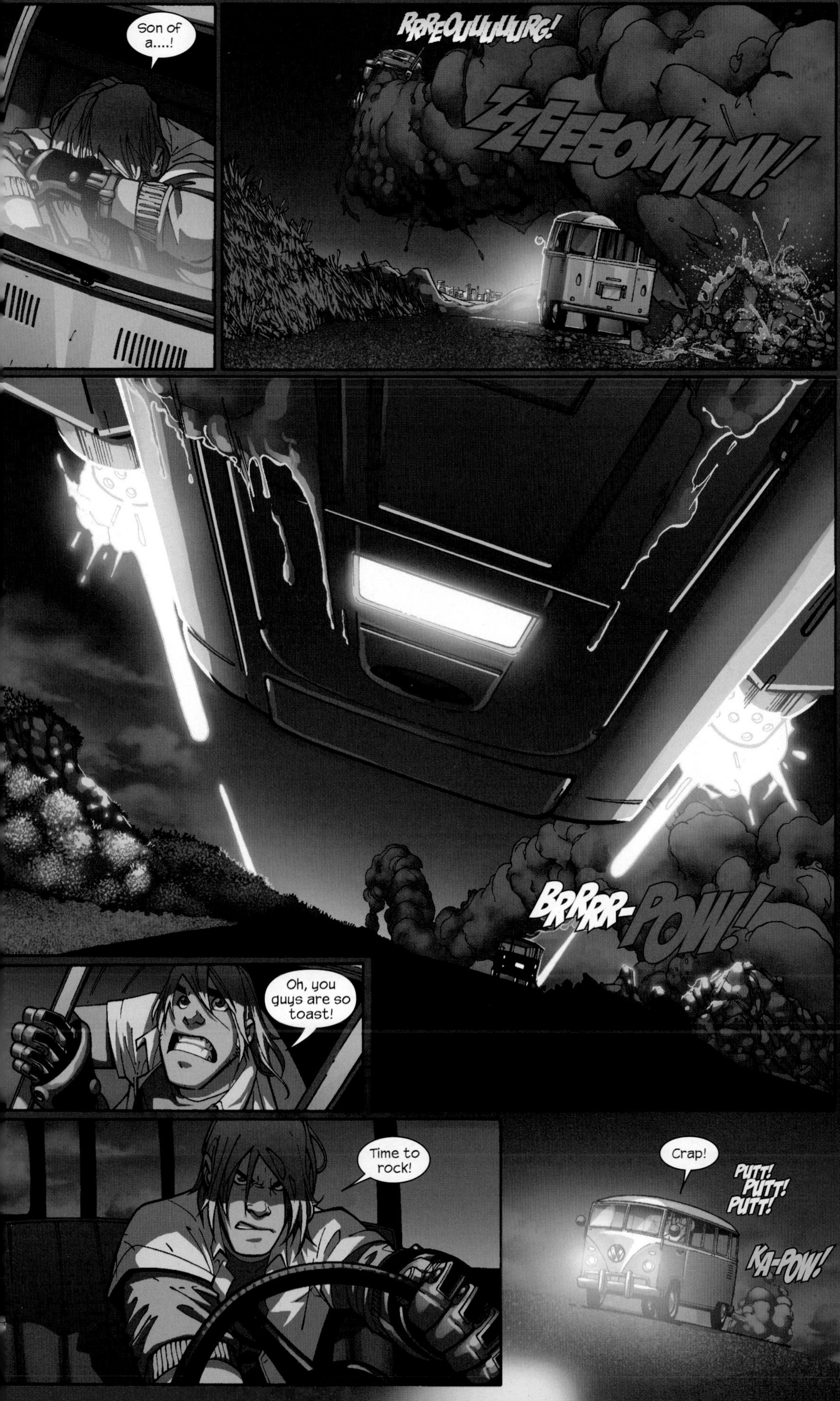
Son of a....!
RRREOUUUUURG!
ZZEEEOWWW!
BRRRR-POW!
Oh, you guys are so toast!
Time to rock!
Crap!
PUTT! PUTT! PUTT!
KA-POW!

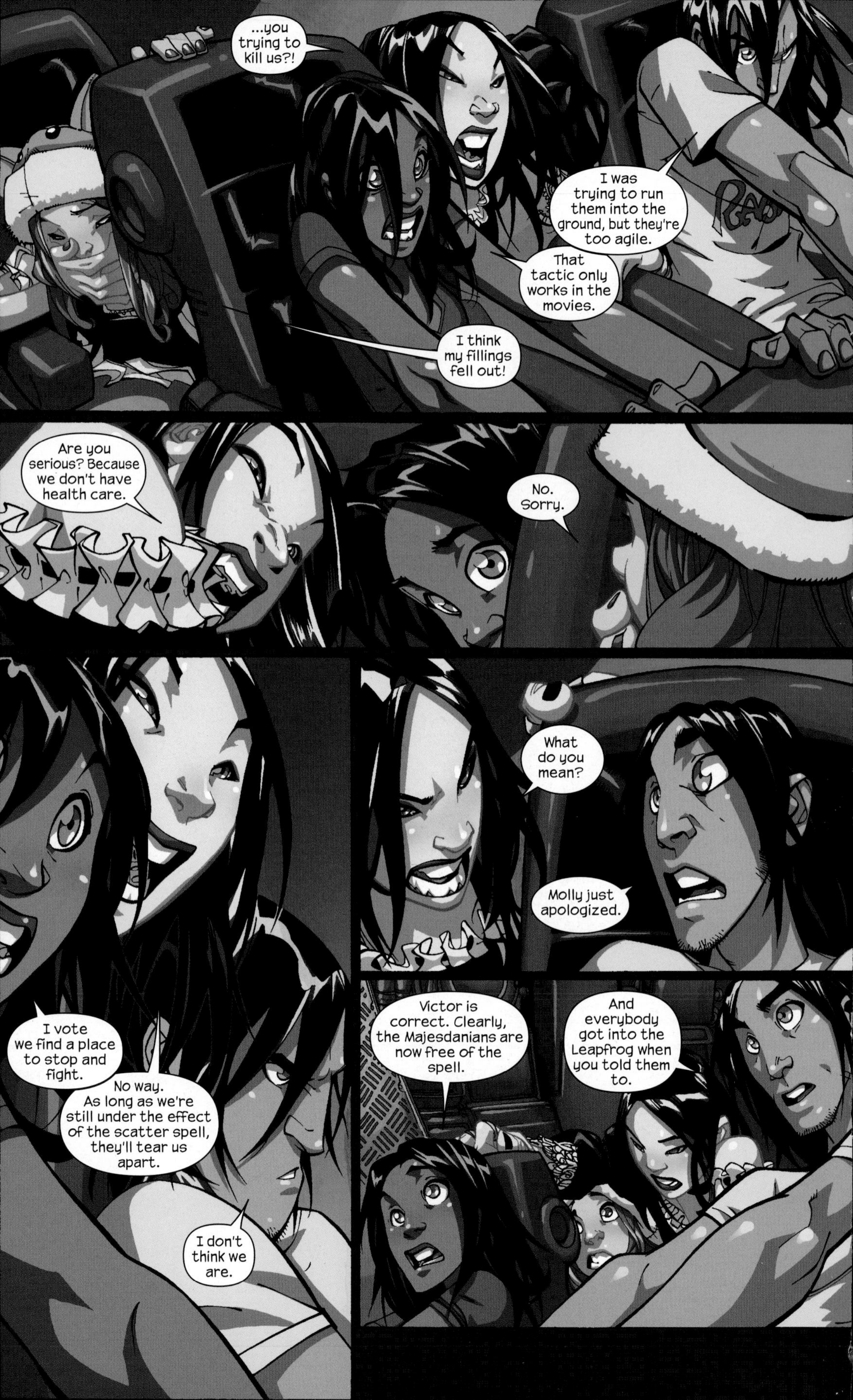
...you trying to kill us?!
I was trying to run them into the ground, but they're too agile.
That tactic only works in the movies.
I think my fillings fell out!
Are you serious? Because we don't have health care.
No. Sorry.
I vote we find a place to stop and fight.
No way. As long as we're still under the effect of the scatter spell, they'll tear us apart.
I don't think we are.
What do you mean?
Molly just apologized.
Victor is correct. Clearly, the Majesdanians are now free of the spell.
And everybody got into the Leapfrog when you told them to.

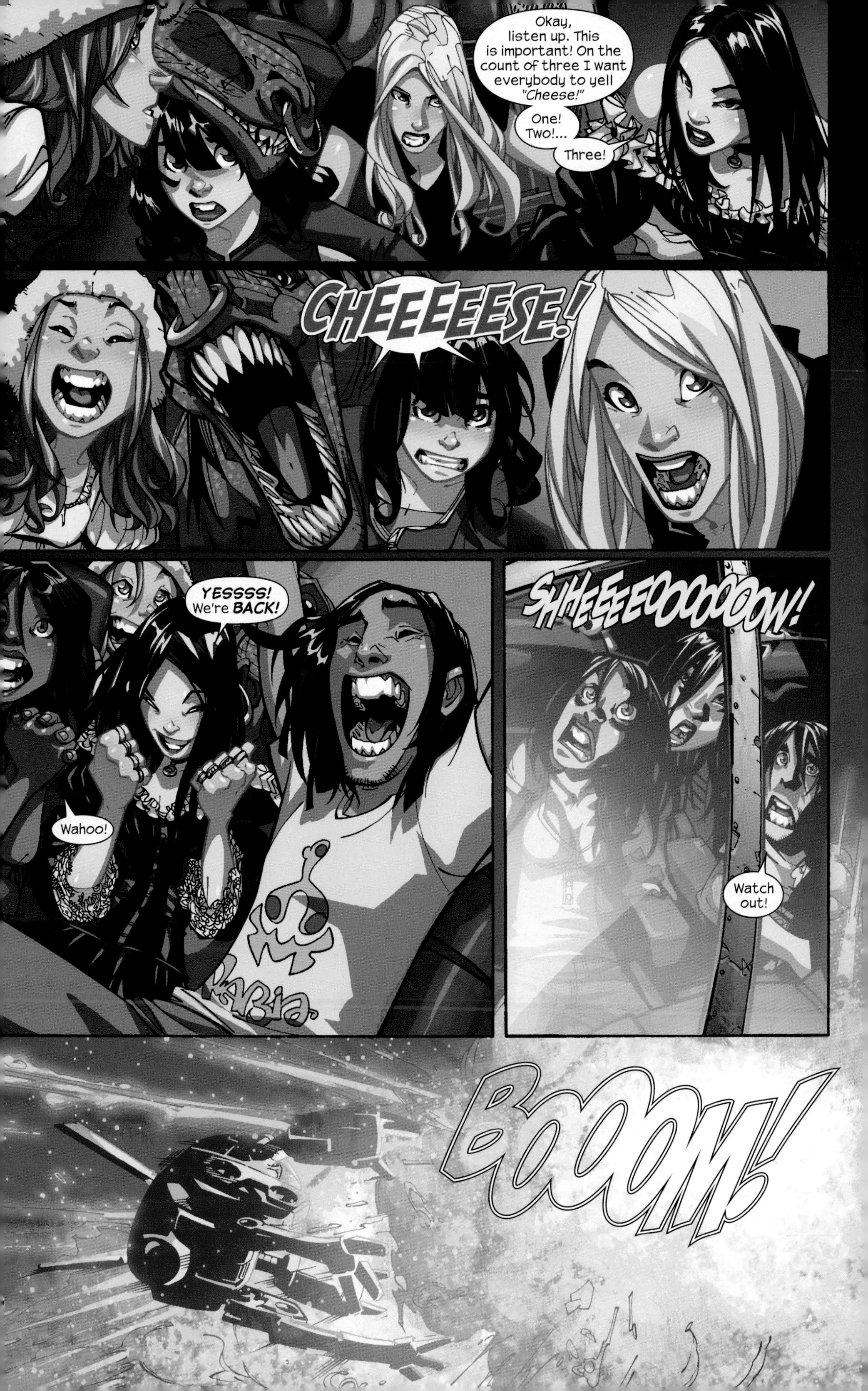
Okay, listen up. This is important! On the count of three I want everybody to yell "Cheese!"
One! Two!...
Three!
CHEEEEESE!
YESSSS! We're BACK!
Wahoo!
SHHEEEEOOOOOOW!
Watch out!
BOOOM!

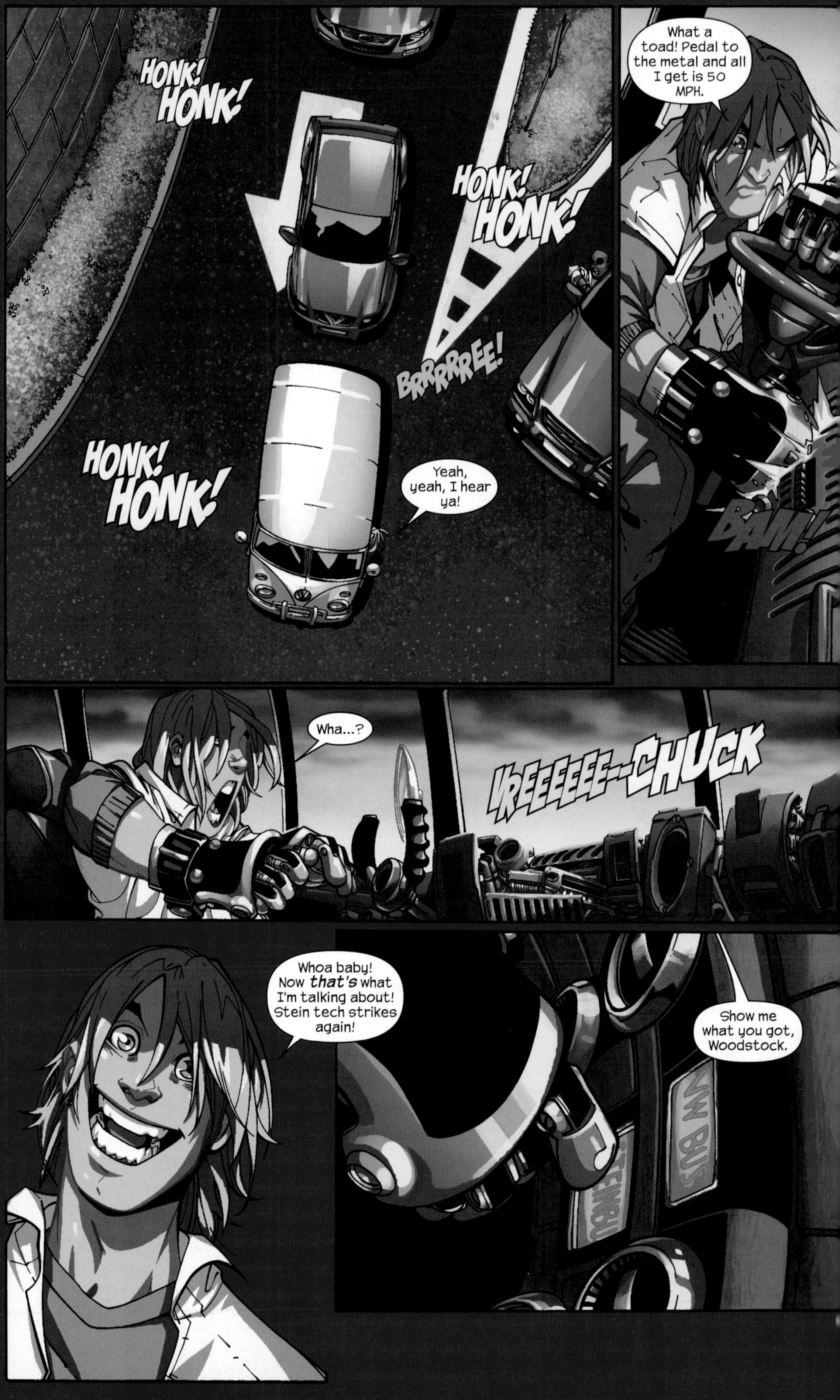
HONK! HONK!
HONK! HONK!
BRRRRREE!
HONK! HONK!
Yeah, yeah, I hear ya!
What a toad! Pedal to the metal and all I get is 50 MPH.
BAM!
Wha...?
VREEEEEE-CHUCK
Whoa baby! Now *that's* what I'm talking about! Stein tech strikes again!
Show me what you got, Woodstock.
VW BUS

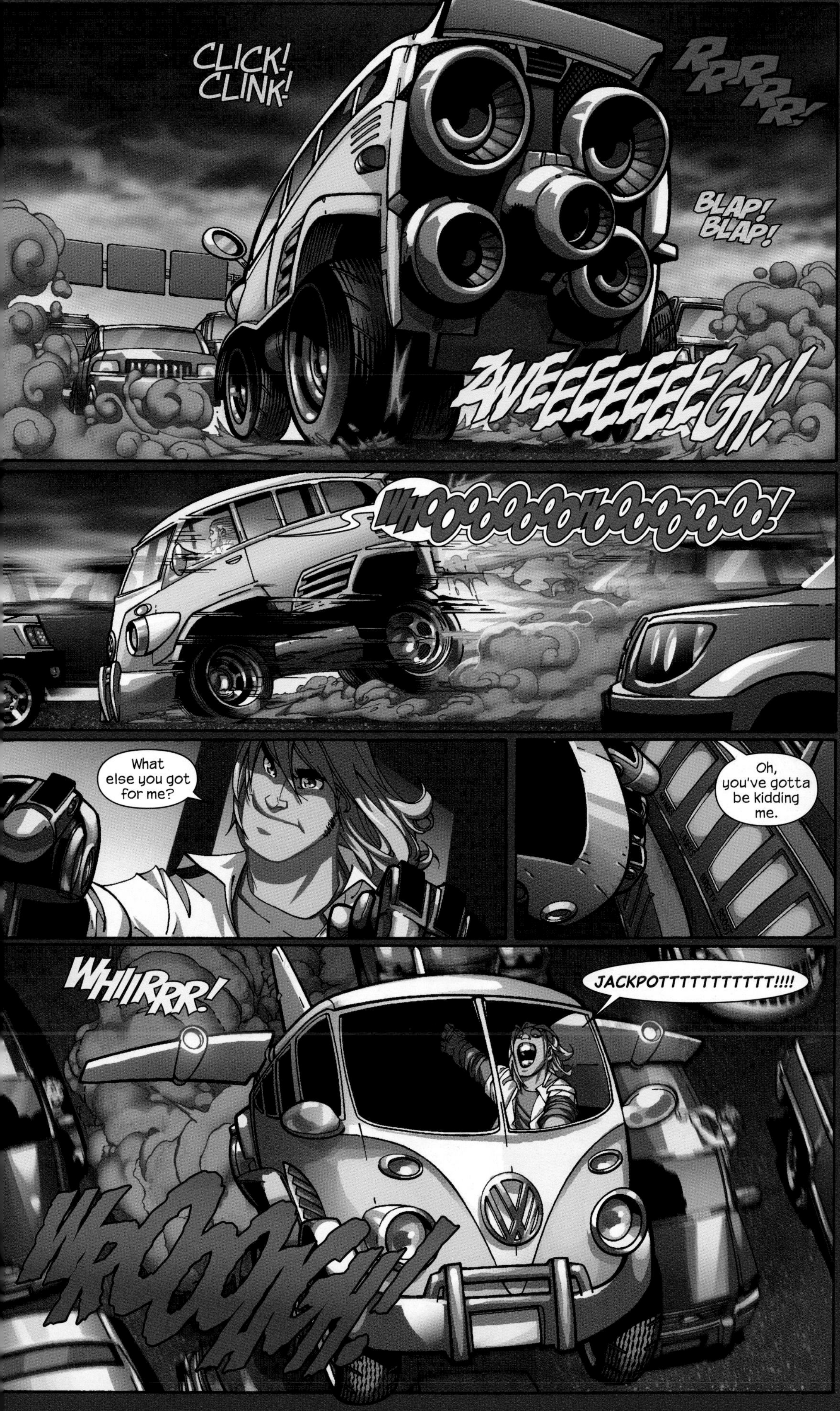

CLICK! CLINK!
RRRRR!
BLAP! BLAP!
ZWEEEEEEEEGH!
WHOOOOOOOHOOOOOOO!
What else you got for me?
Oh, you've gotta be kidding me.
WHIIRRR!
JACKPOTTTTTTTTTTT!!!!
VROOONGH!

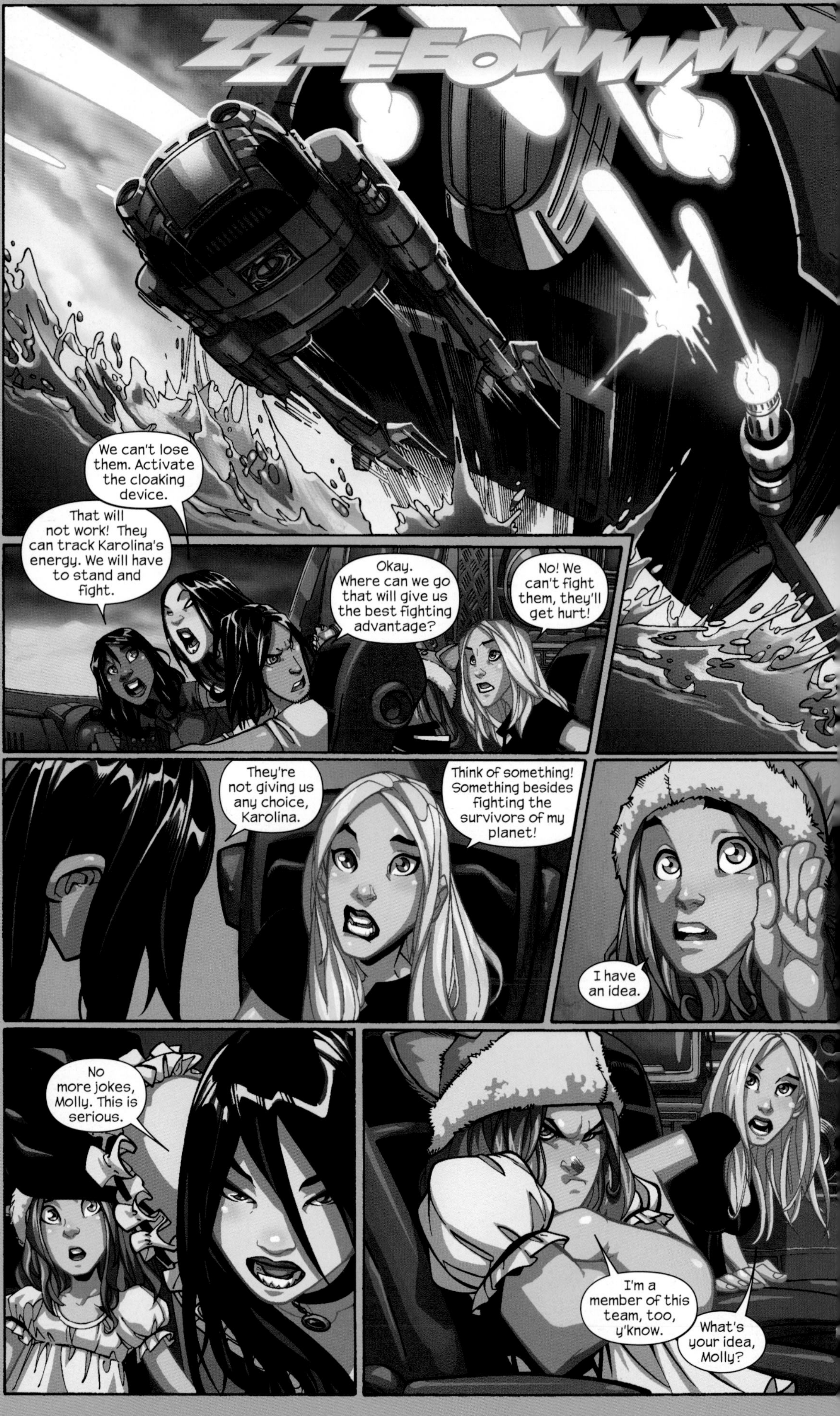
ZZEEEBOWWWW!
We can't lose them. Activate the cloaking device.
That will not work! They can track Karolina's energy. We will have to stand and fight.
Okay. Where can we go that will give us the best fighting advantage?
No! We can't fight them, they'll get hurt!
They're not giving us any choice, Karolina.
Think of something! Something besides fighting the survivors of my planet!
I have an idea.
No more jokes, Molly. This is serious.
I'm a member of this team, too, y'know.
What's your idea, Molly?

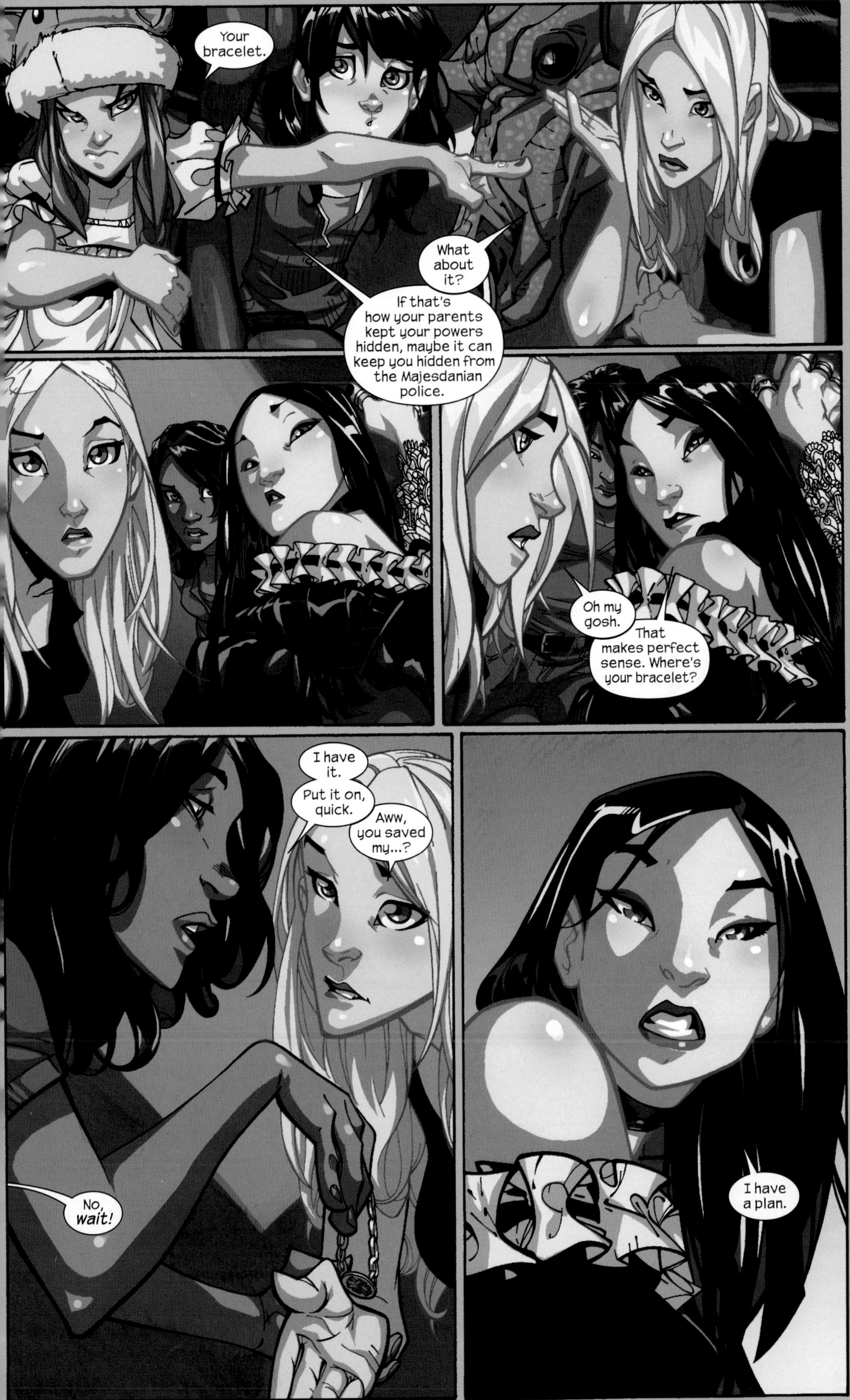

Your bracelet.
What about it?
If that's how your parents kept your powers hidden, maybe it can keep you hidden from the Majesdanian police.
Oh my gosh.
That makes perfect sense. Where's your bracelet?
I have it.
Put it on, quick.
Aww, you saved my...?
No, wait!
I have a plan.

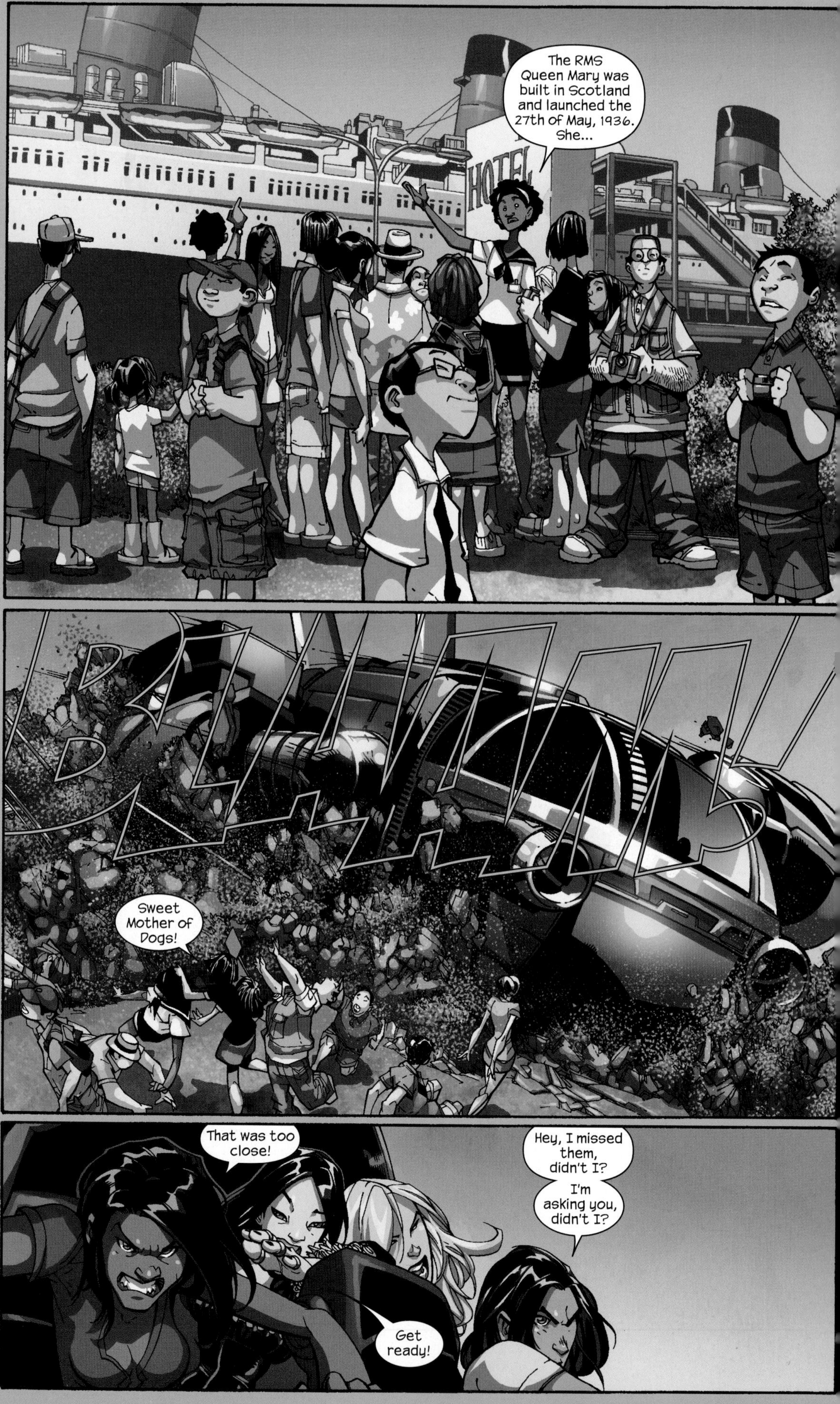
The RMS Queen Mary was built in Scotland and launched the 27th of May, 1936. She...
HOTEL
Sweet Mother of Dogs!
That was too close!
Hey, I missed them, didn't I?
I'm asking you, didn't I?
Get ready!

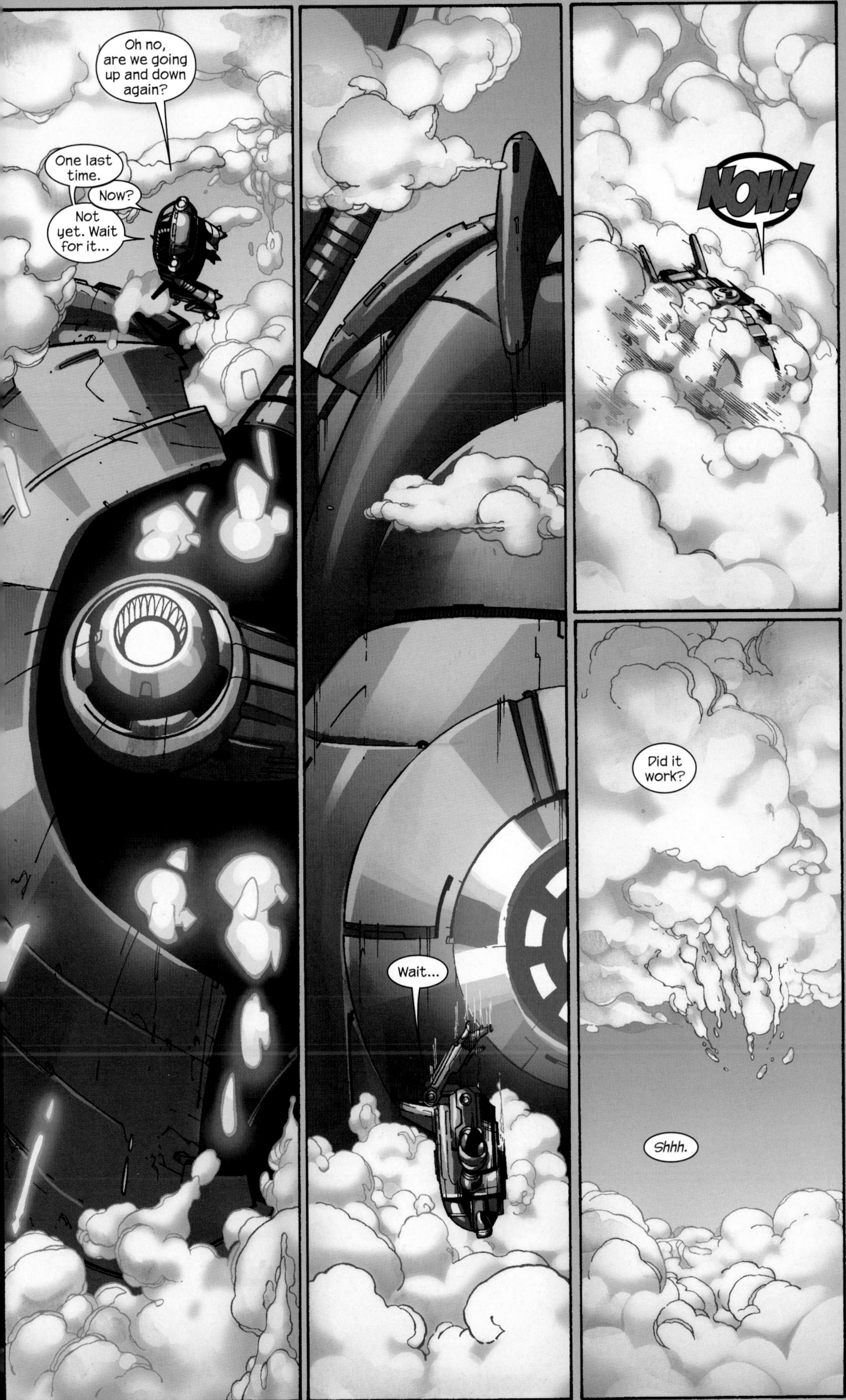

Oh no, are we going up and down again?
One last time.
Now?
Not yet. Wait for it...
Wait...
NOW!
Did it work?
Shhh.

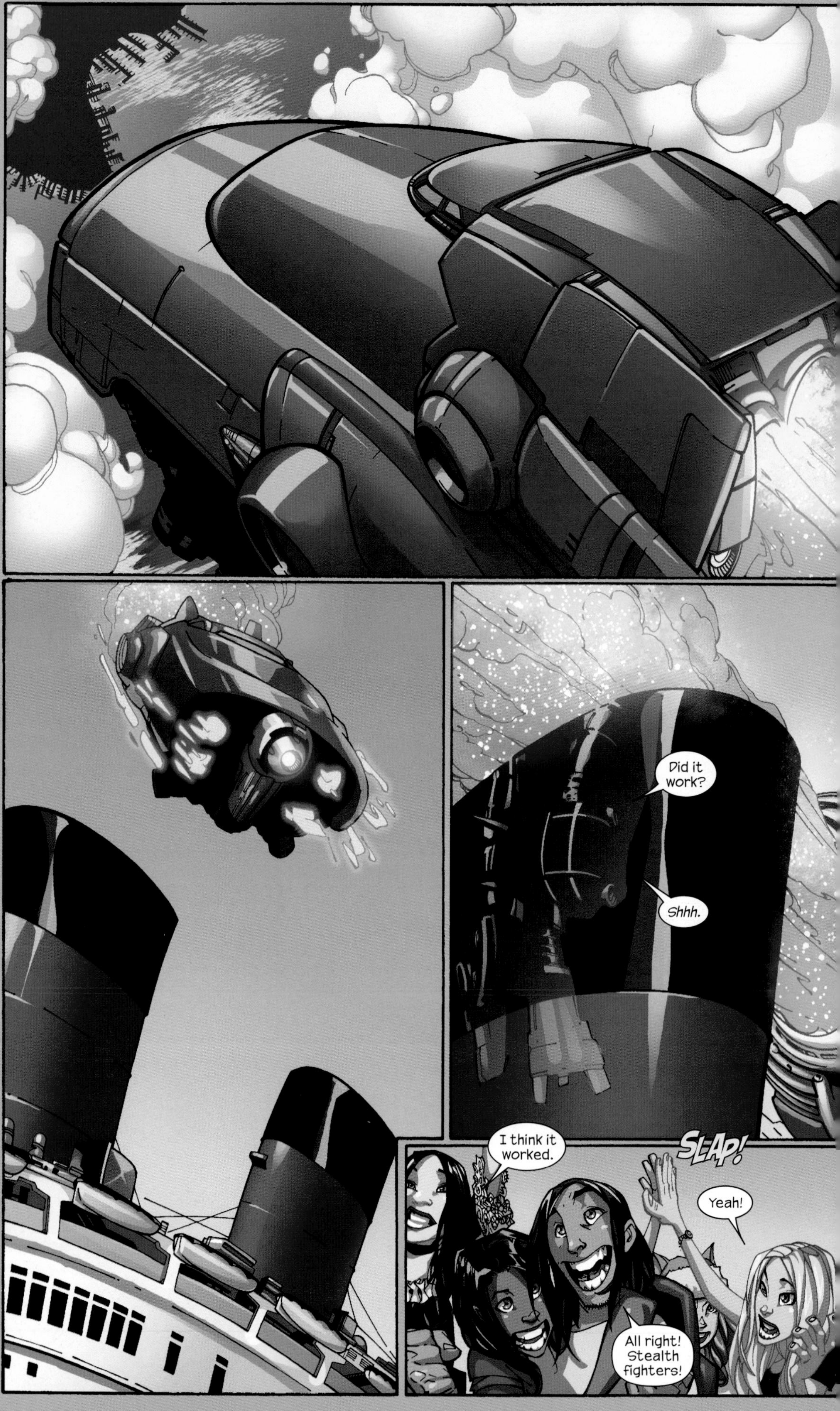
Did it work?
Shhh.
I think it worked.
SLAP!
Yeah!
All right! Stealth fighters!

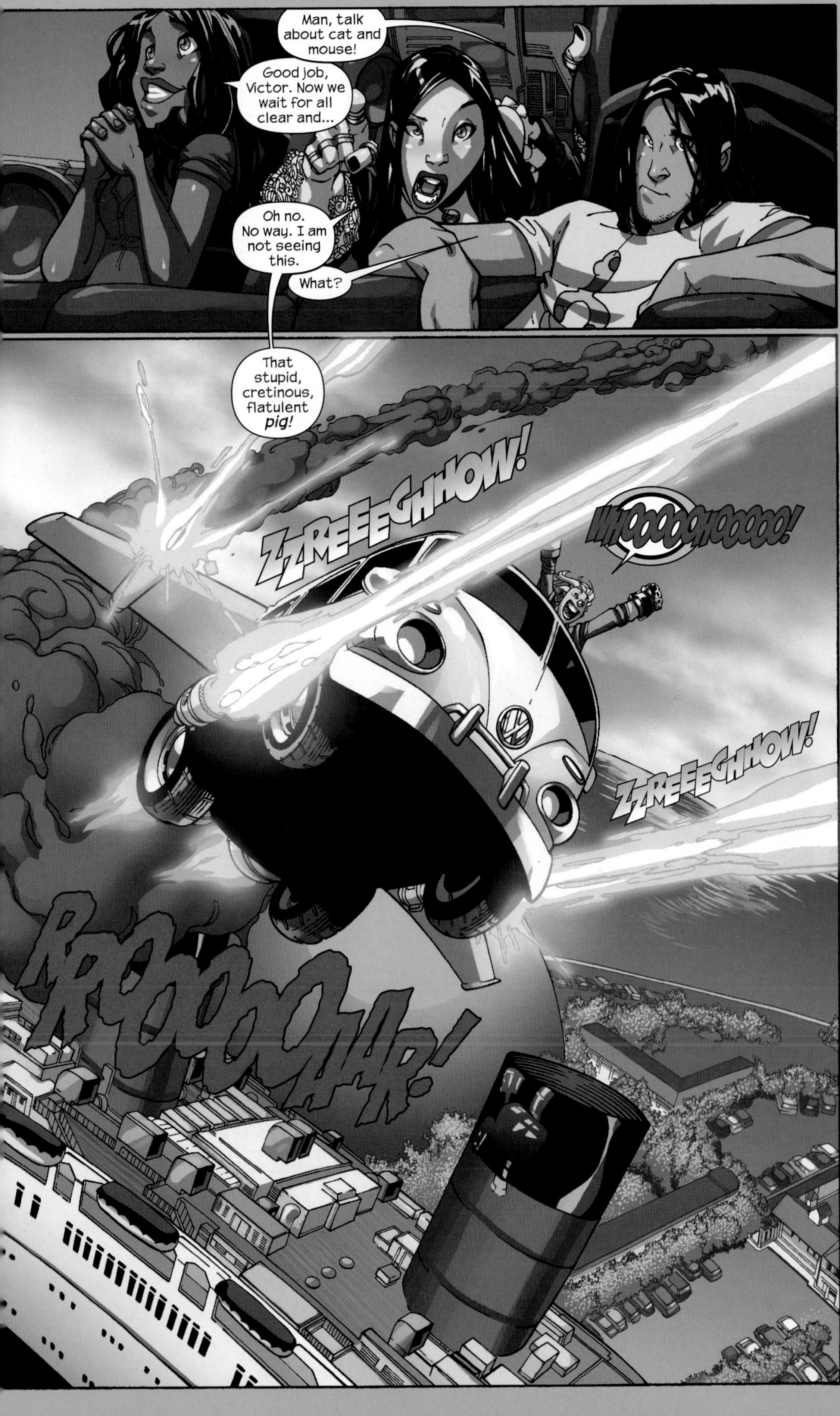
Man, talk about cat and mouse!
Good job, Victor. Now we wait for all clear and...
Oh no. No way. I am not seeing this.
What?
That stupid, cretinous, flatulent *pig!*
ZZREEEEGHHOW!
WHOOOOOHOOOOO!
ZZREEEEGHHOW!
RROOOOAR!

6

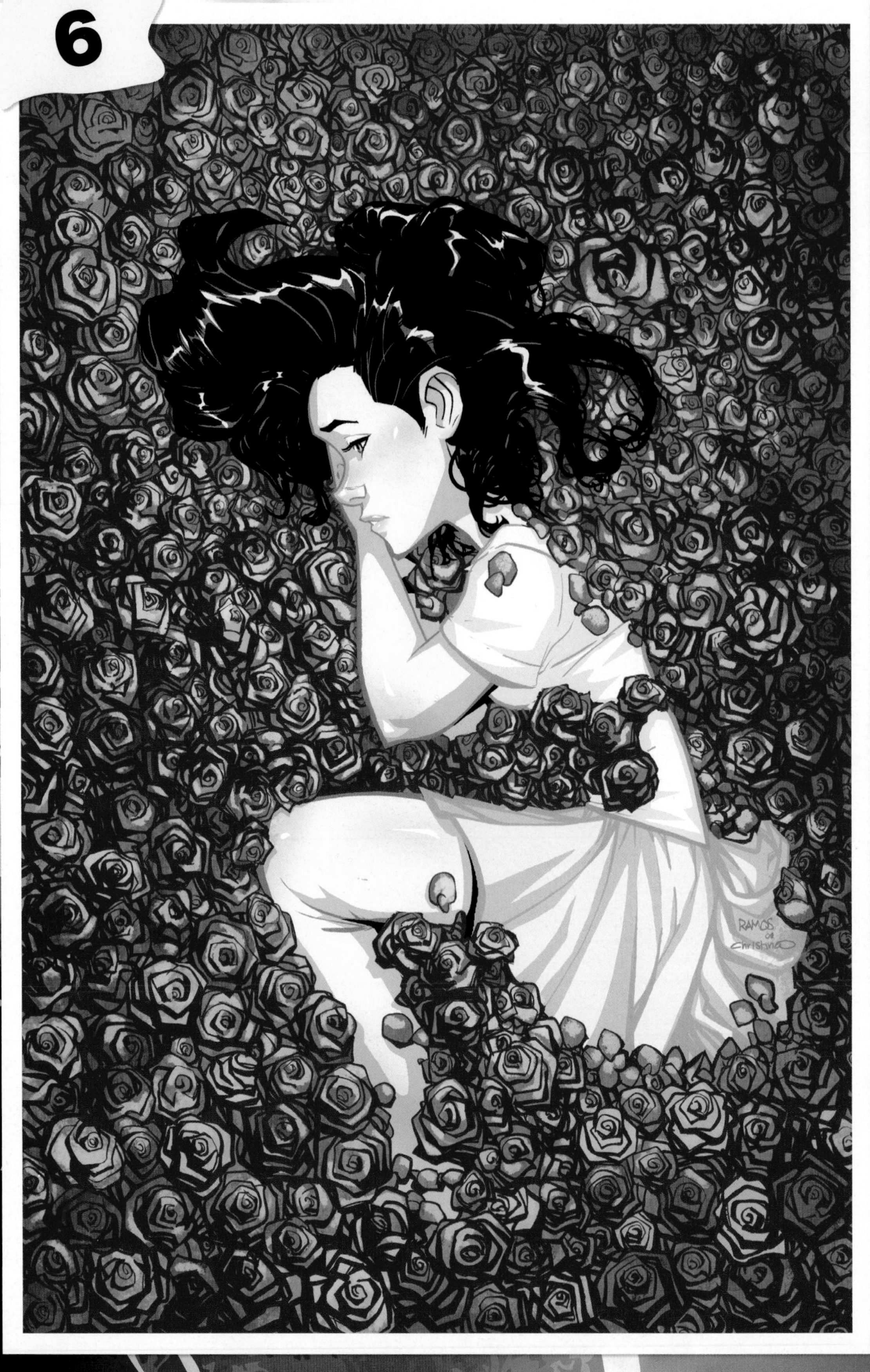
RAMOS 08 Christina

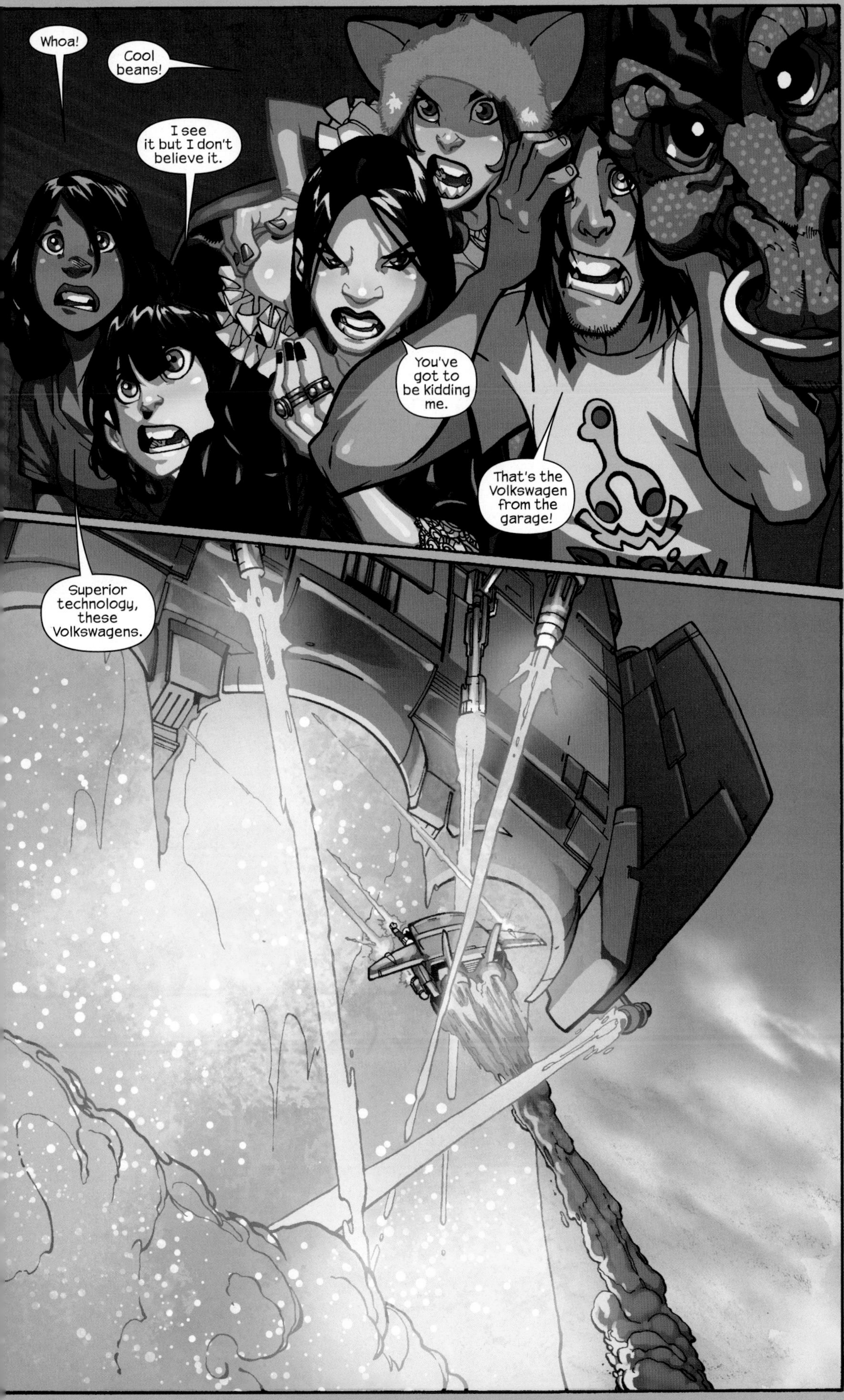
Whoa!
Cool beans!
I see it but I don't believe it.
You've got to be kidding me.
That's the Volkswagen from the garage!
Superior technology, these Volkswagens.

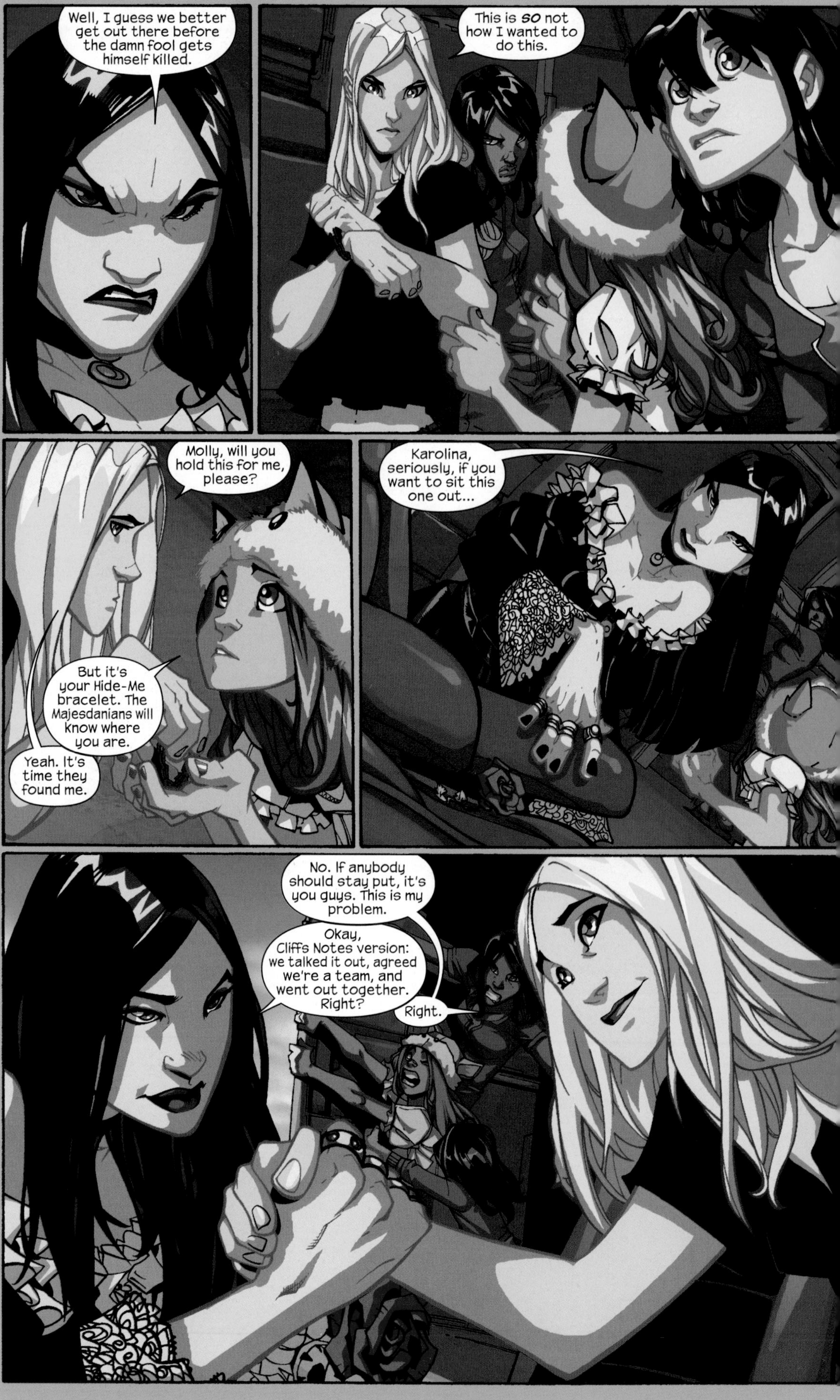
Well, I guess we better get out there before the damn fool gets himself killed.
This is SO not how I wanted to do this.
Molly, will you hold this for me, please?
But it's your Hide-Me bracelet. The Majesdanians will know where you are.
Yeah. It's time they found me.
Karolina, seriously, if you want to sit this one out...
No. If anybody should stay put, it's you guys. This is my problem.
Okay, Cliffs Notes version: we talked it out, agreed we're a team, and went out together. Right?
Right.

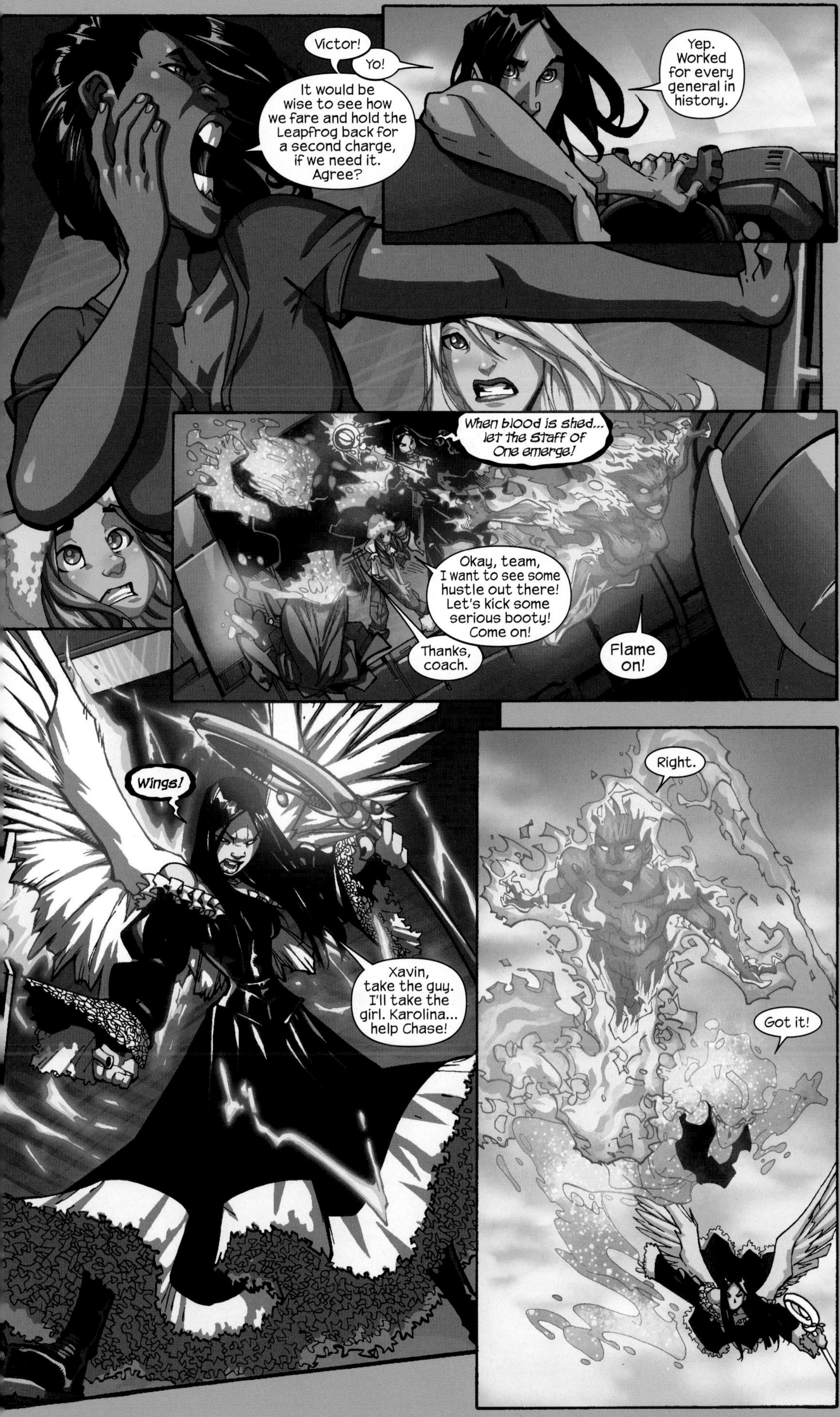

Victor!
Yo!
It would be wise to see how we fare and hold the Leapfrog back for a second charge, if we need it. Agree?
Yep. Worked for every general in history.
When blood is shed... let the Staff of One emerge!
Okay, team, I want to see some hustle out there! Let's kick some serious booty! Come on!
Thanks, coach.
Flame on!
Wings!
Xavin, take the guy. I'll take the girl. Karolina... help Chase!
Right.
Got it!

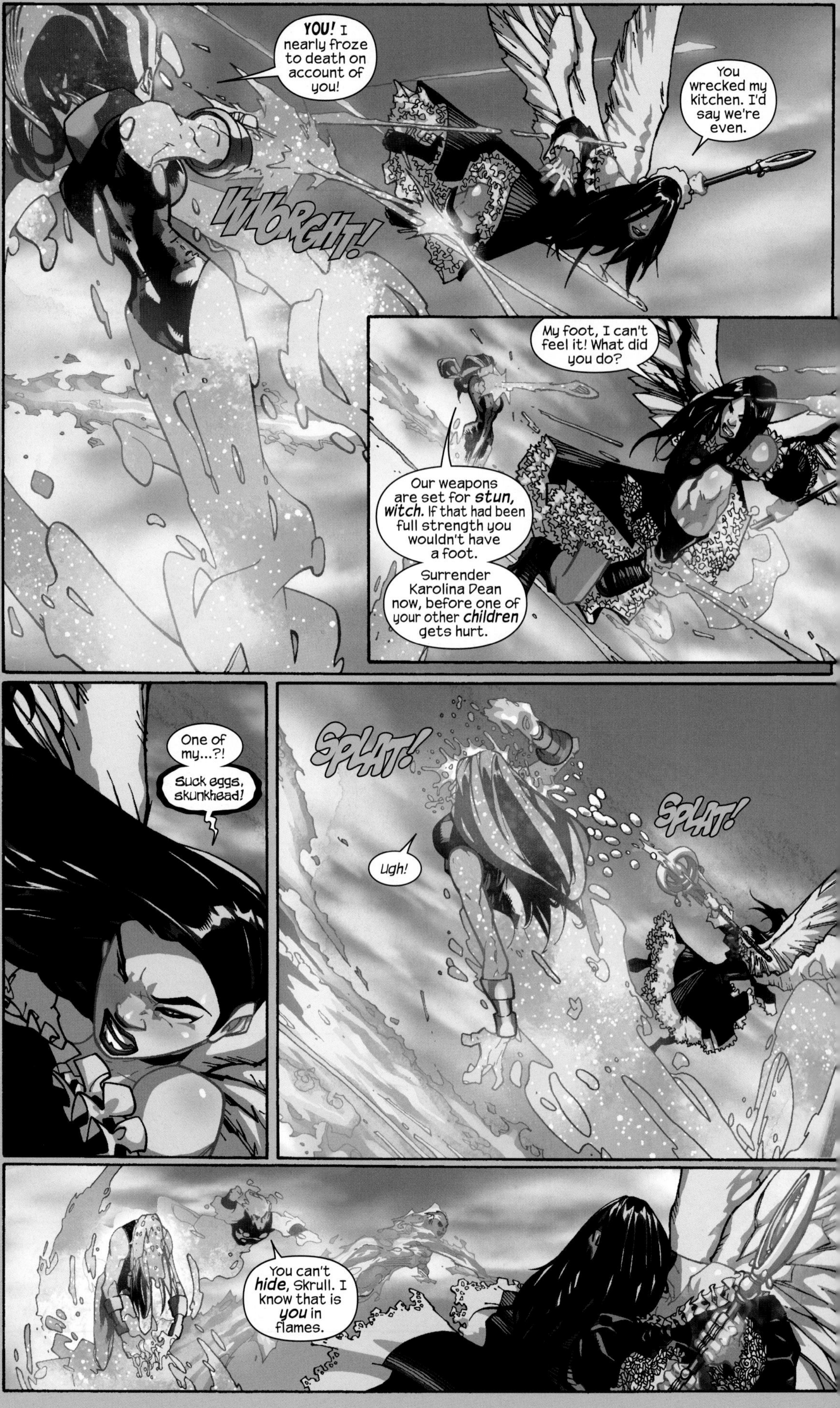

YOU! I nearly froze to death on account of you!
You wrecked my kitchen. I'd say we're even.
WHORGHT!
My foot, I can't feel it! What did you do?
Our weapons are set for stun, witch. If that had been full strength you wouldn't have a foot.
Surrender Karolina Dean now, before one of your other children gets hurt.
One of my...?!
Suck eggs, skunkhead!
SPLAT!
SPLAT!
Ugh!
You can't hide, Skrull. I know that is you in flames.

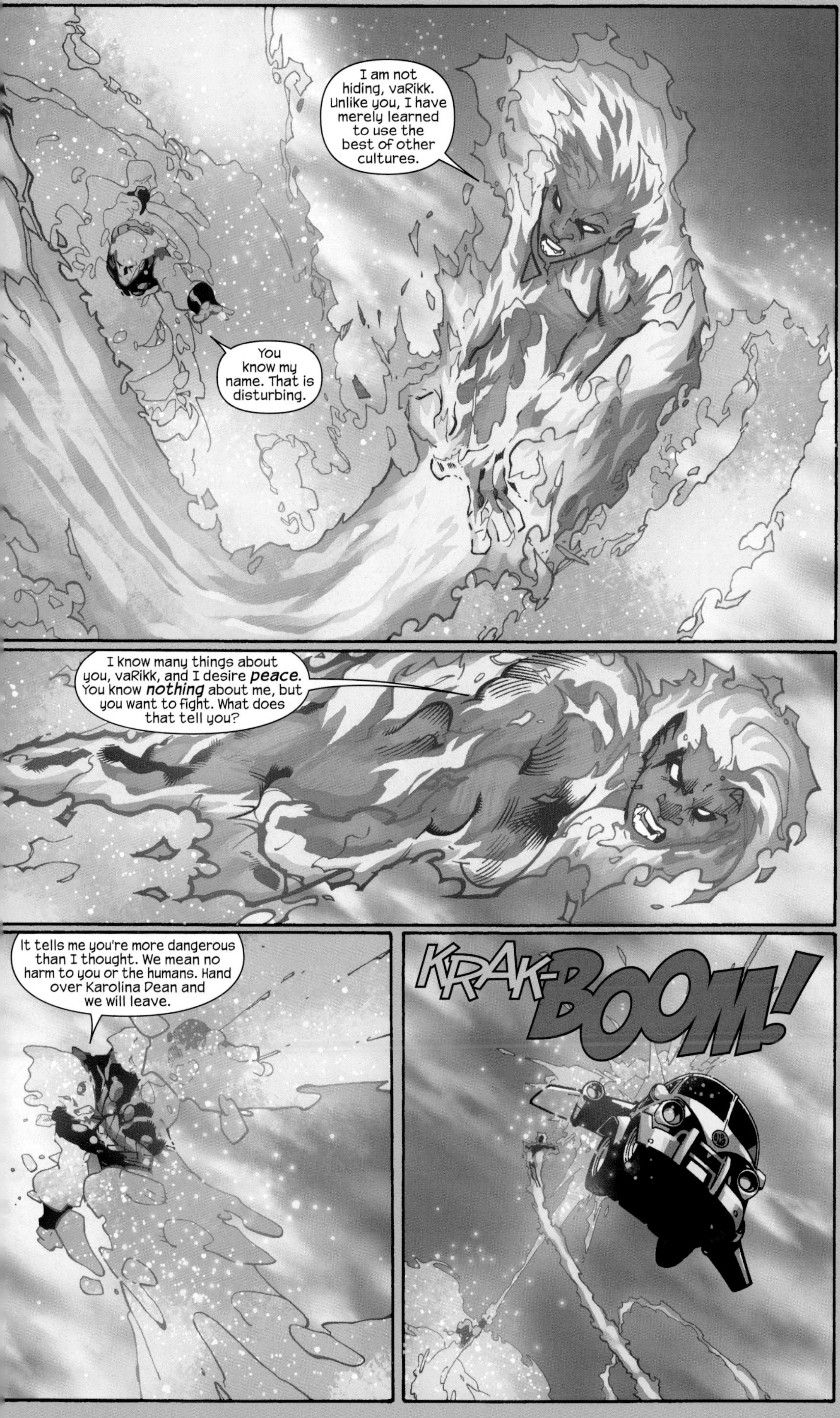
I am not hiding, vaRikk. Unlike you, I have merely learned to use the best of other cultures.
You know my name. That is disturbing.
I know many things about you, vaRikk, and I desire *peace*. You know *nothing* about me, but you want to fight. What does that tell you?
It tells me you're more dangerous than I thought. We mean no harm to you or the humans. Hand over Karolina Dean and we will leave.
KRAK-BOOM!

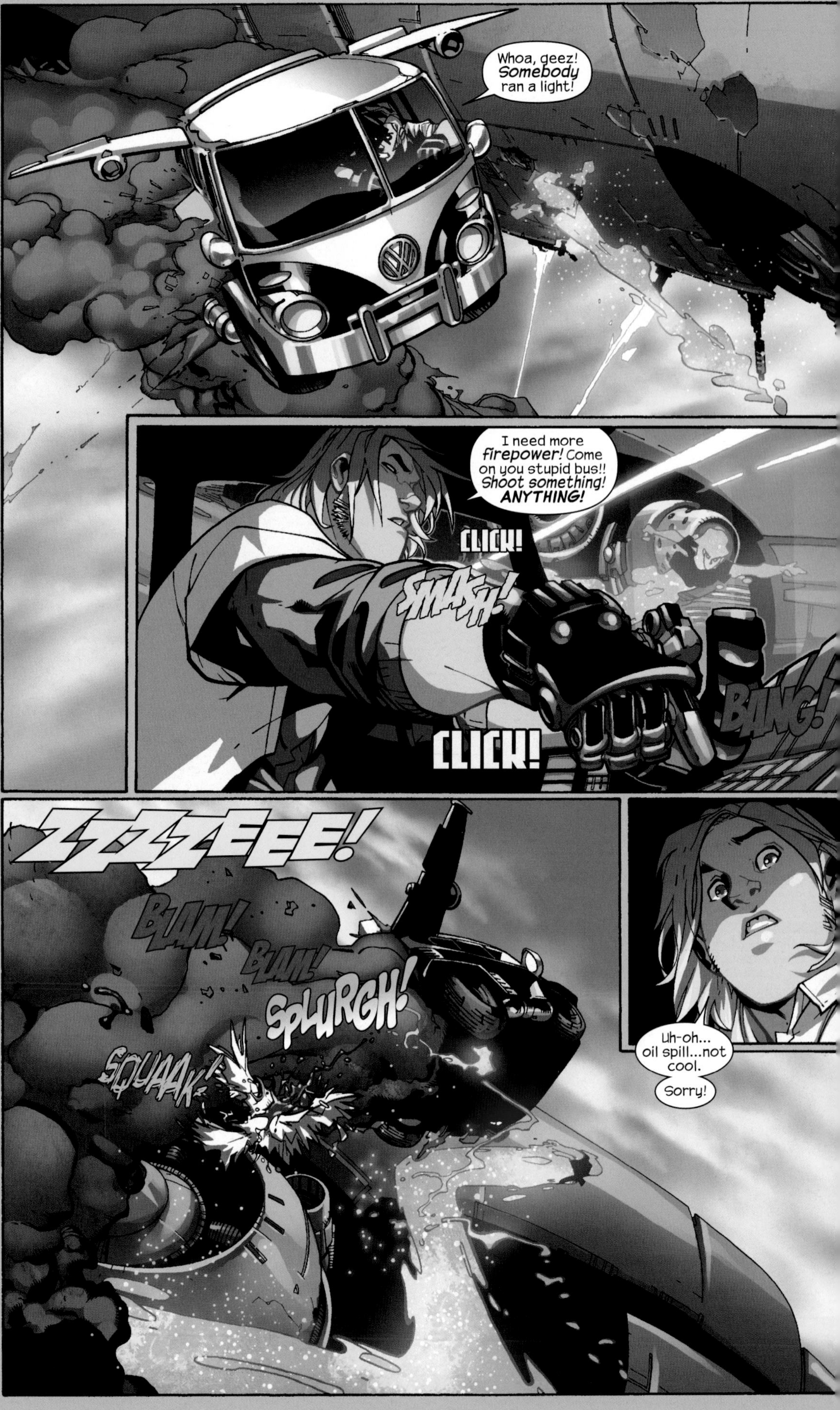
Whoa, geez! Somebody ran a light!
I need more firepower! Come on you stupid bus!! Shoot something! ANYTHING!
CLICK!
SMASH!
CLICK!
BANG!
ZZZZEEEE!
BLAM!
BLAM!
SPLURGH!
SQUAAK!
Uh-oh... oil spill...not cool.
Sorry!

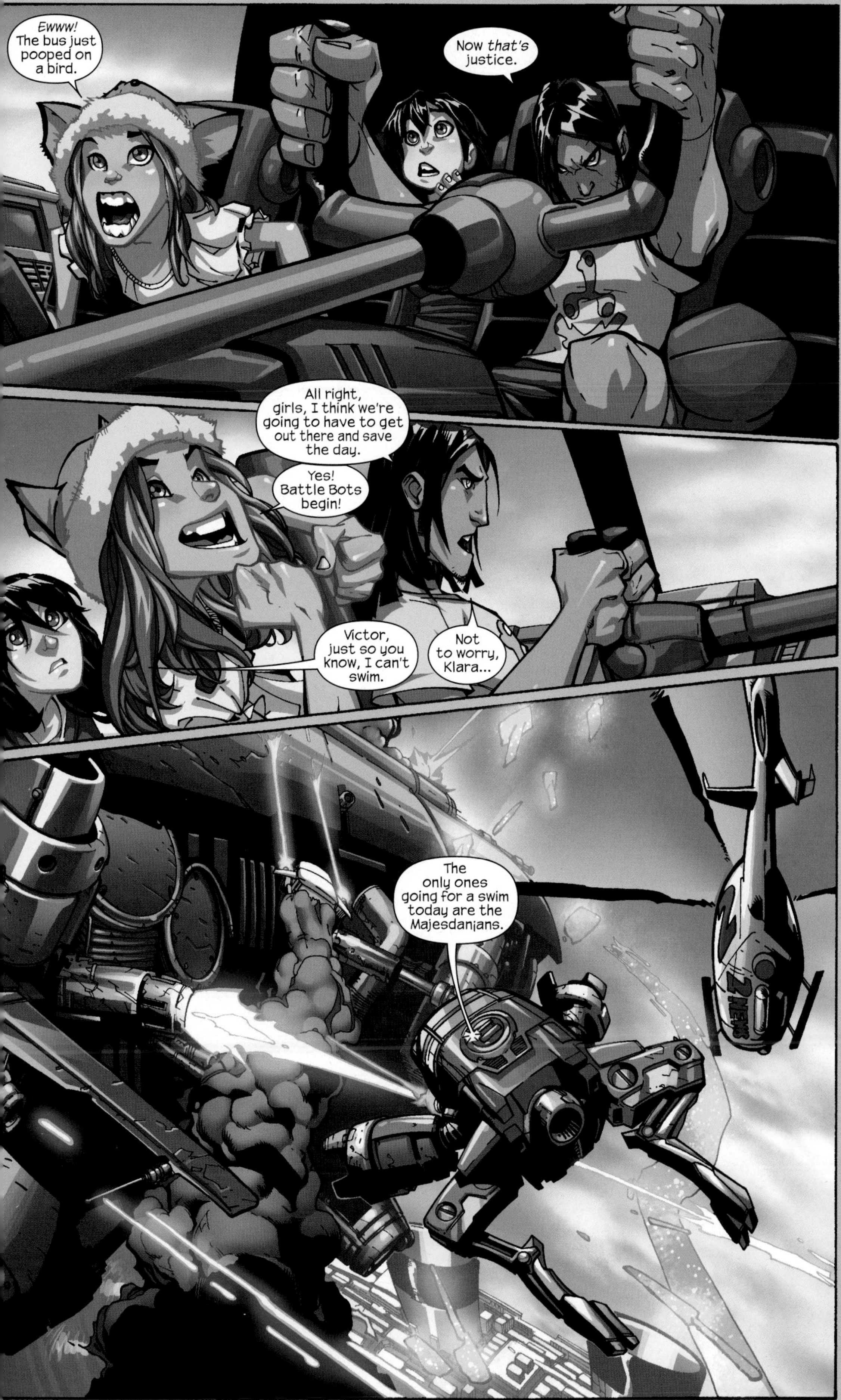

Ewww! The bus just pooped on a bird.
Now *that's* justice.
All right, girls, I think we're going to have to get out there and save the day.
Yes! Battle Bots begin!
Victor, just so you know, I can't swim.
Not to worry, Klara...
The only ones going for a swim today are the Majesdanians.
2 NEWS

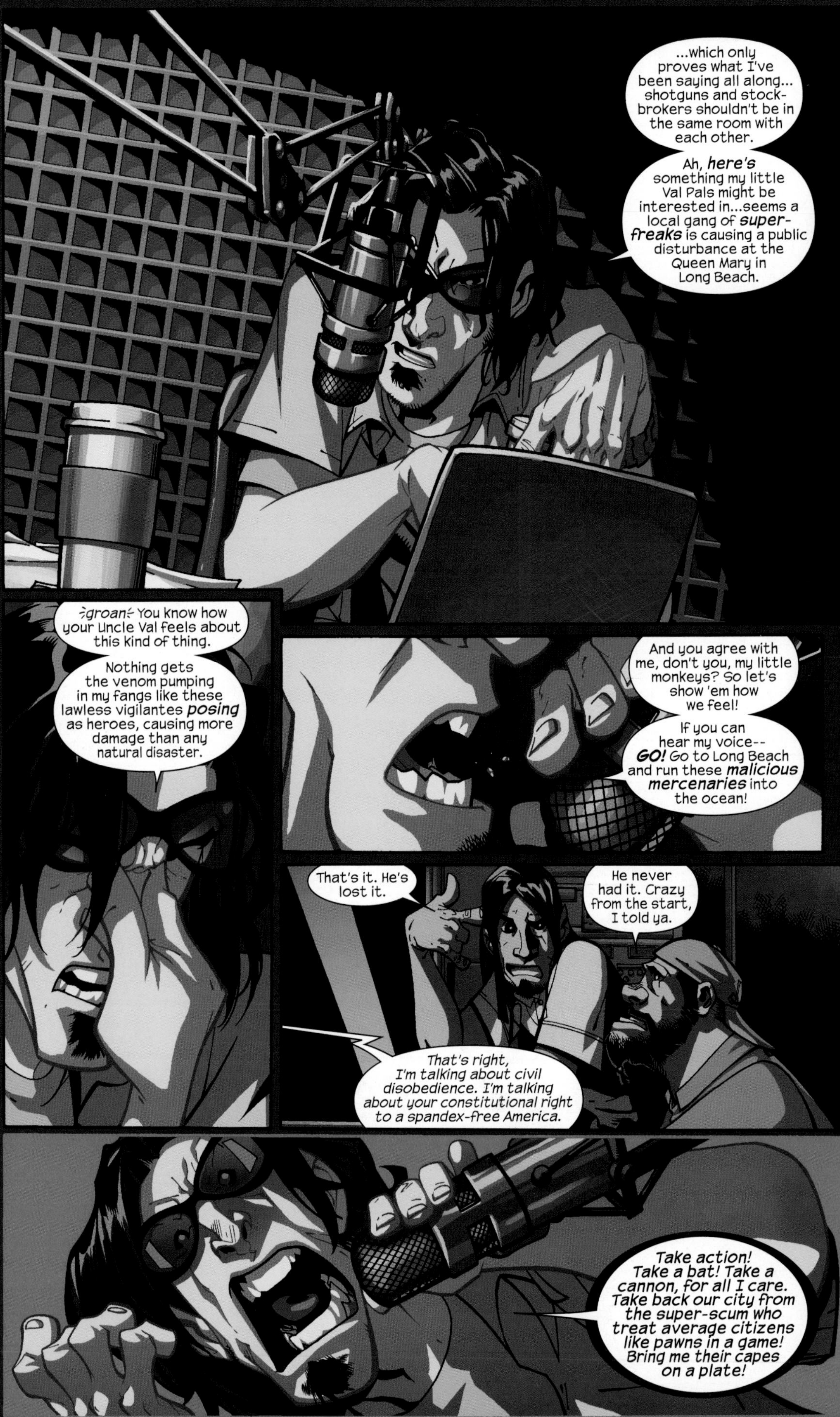

...which only proves what I've been saying all along... shotguns and stock-brokers shouldn't be in the same room with each other.
Ah, here's something my little Val Pals might be interested in...seems a local gang of super-freaks is causing a public disturbance at the Queen Mary in Long Beach.
-groan- You know how your Uncle Val feels about this kind of thing.
Nothing gets the venom pumping in my fangs like these lawless vigilantes posing as heroes, causing more damage than any natural disaster.
And you agree with me, don't you, my little monkeys? So let's show 'em how we feel!
If you can hear my voice-- GO! Go to Long Beach and run these malicious mercenaries into the ocean!
That's it. He's lost it.
He never had it. Crazy from the start, I told ya.
That's right, I'm talking about civil disobedience. I'm talking about your constitutional right to a spandex-free America.
Take action! Take a bat! Take a cannon, for all I care. Take back our city from the super-scum who treat average citizens like pawns in a game! Bring me their capes on a plate!

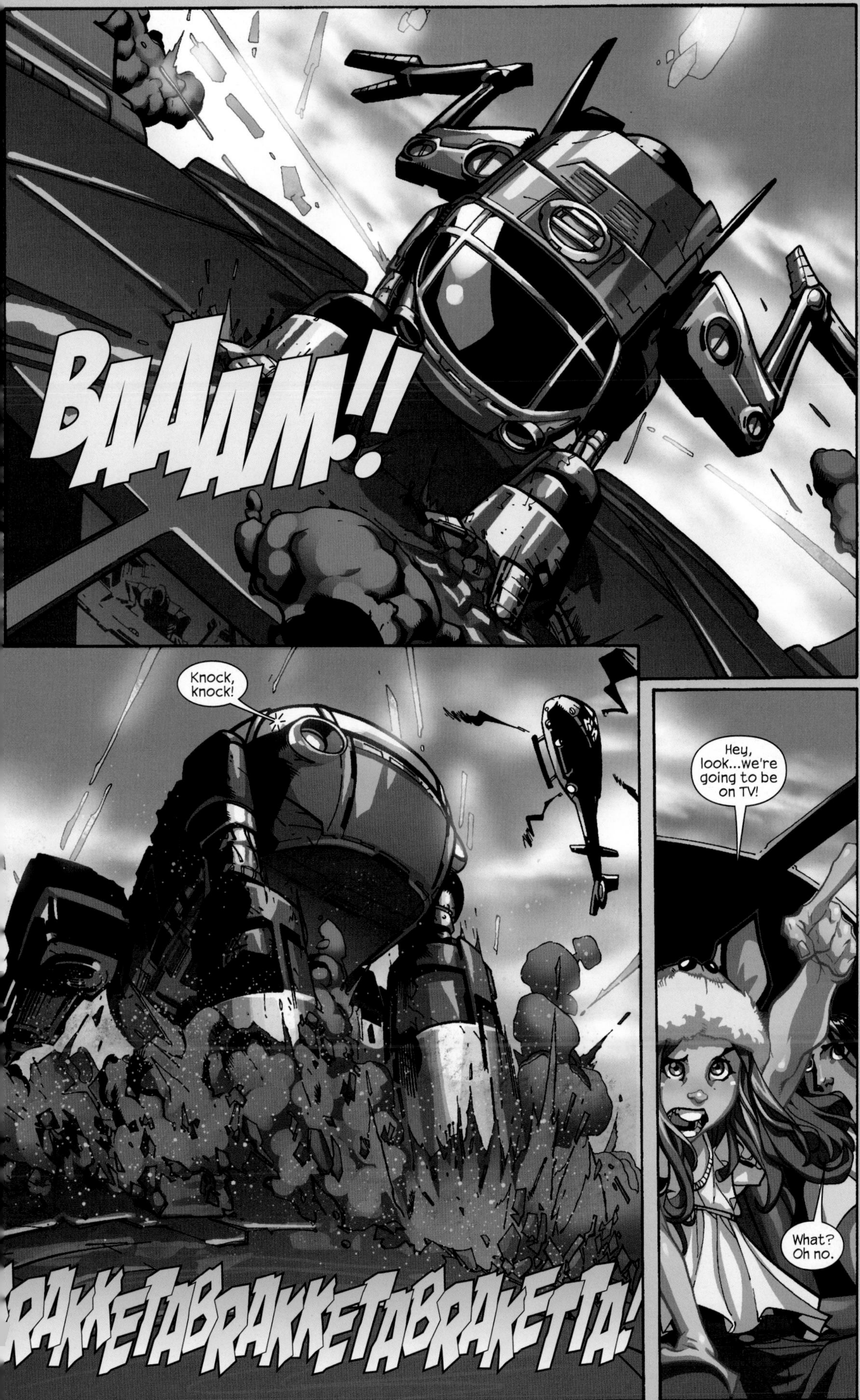
BAAAM!!
Knock, knock!
BRAKKETABRAKKETABRAKETTA!
Hey, look...we're going to be on TV!
What? Oh no.

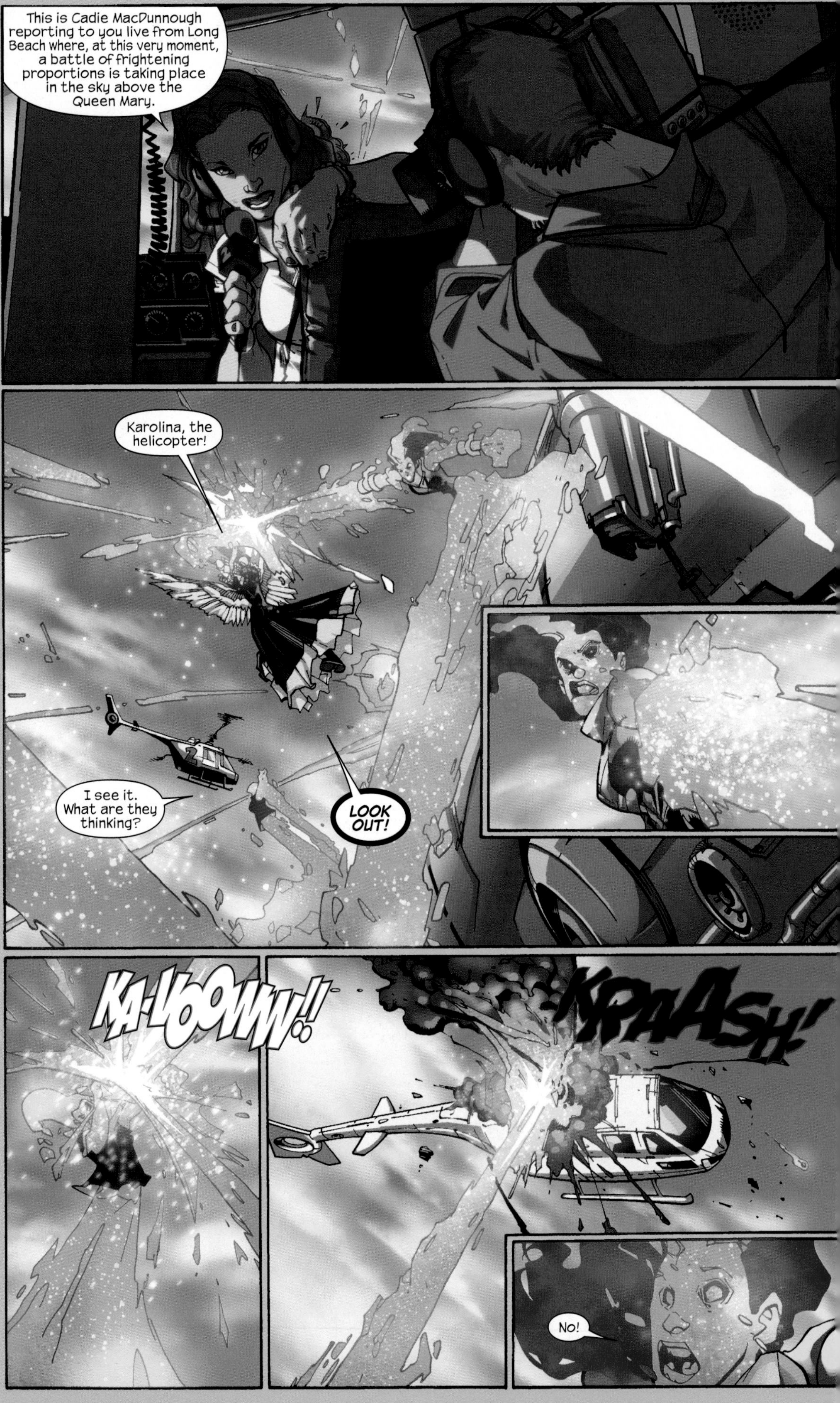
This is Cadie MacDunnough reporting to you live from Long Beach where, at this very moment, a battle of frightening proportions is taking place in the sky above the Queen Mary.
Karolina, the helicopter!
I see it. What are they thinking?
LOOK OUT!
KA-VOOMM!!
KRAASH!
No!

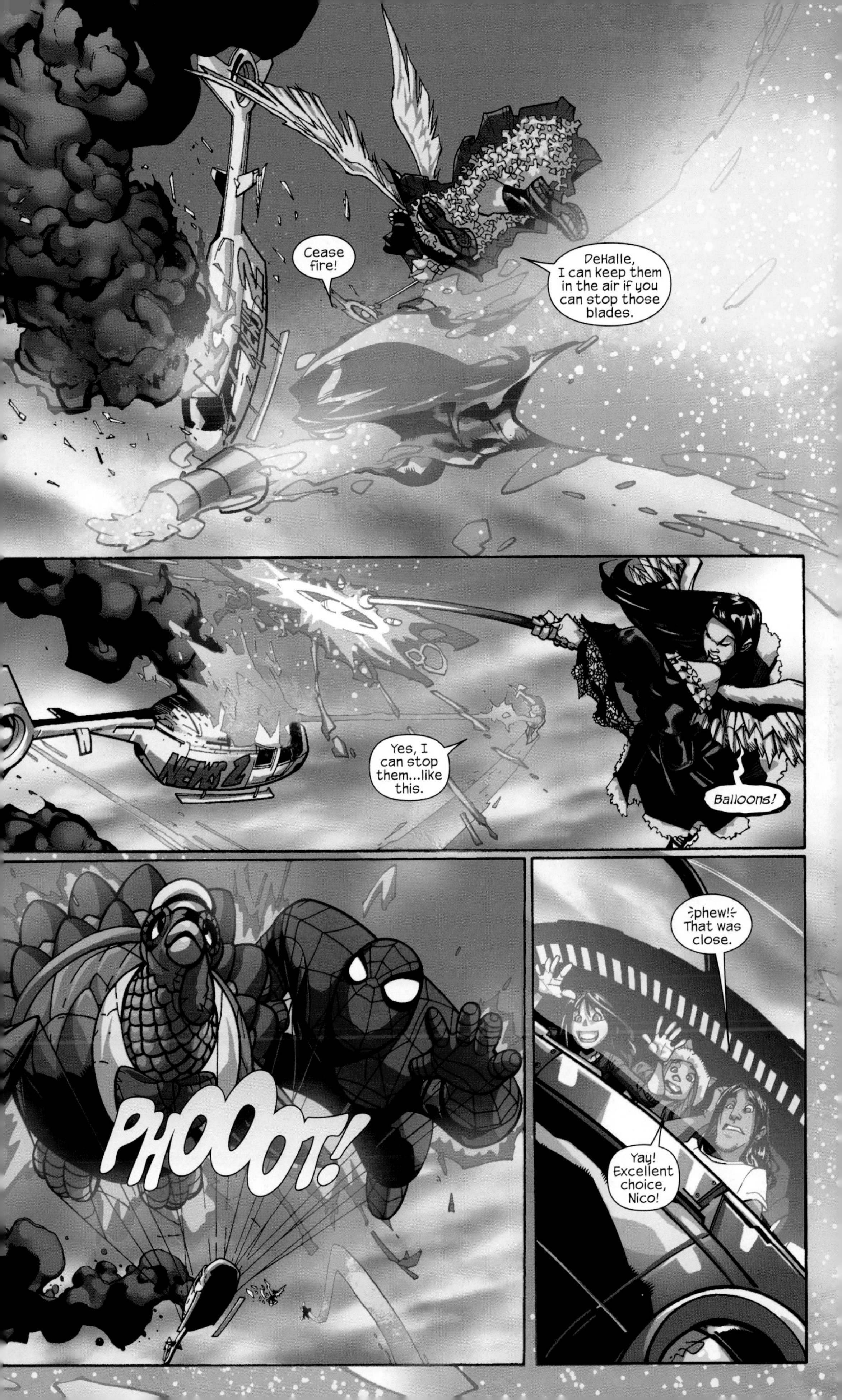

Cease fire!
DeHalle, I can keep them in the air if you can stop those blades.
NEWS 2
Yes, I can stop them...like this.
Balloons!
PHOOOT!
phew! That was close.
Yay! Excellent choice, Nico!

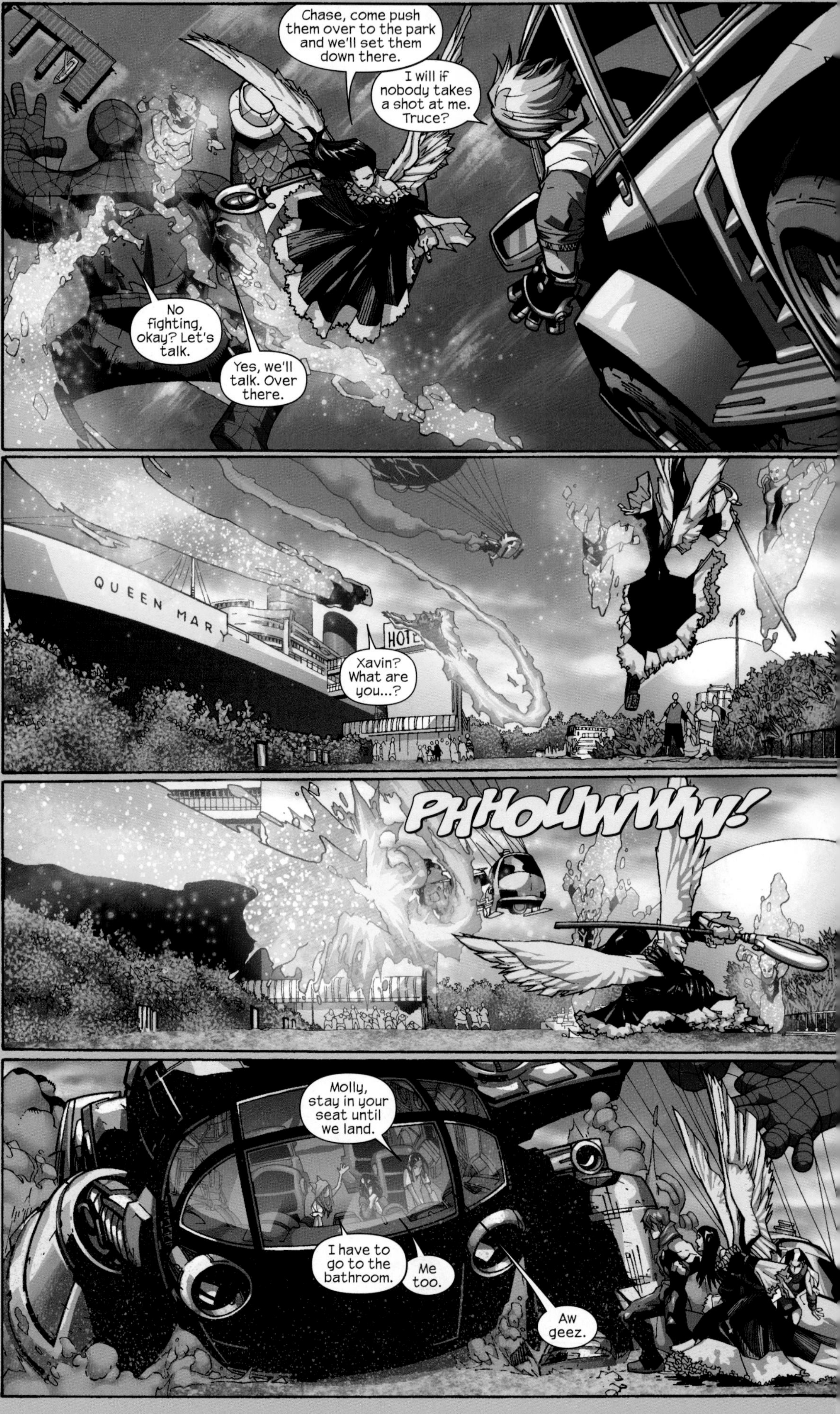
Chase, come push them over to the park and we'll set them down there.
I will if nobody takes a shot at me. Truce?
No fighting, okay? Let's talk.
Yes, we'll talk. Over there.
QUEEN MARY
HOTE
Xavin? What are you...?
PHHOUWWW!
Molly, stay in your seat until we land.
I have to go to the bathroom.
Me too.
Aw geez.

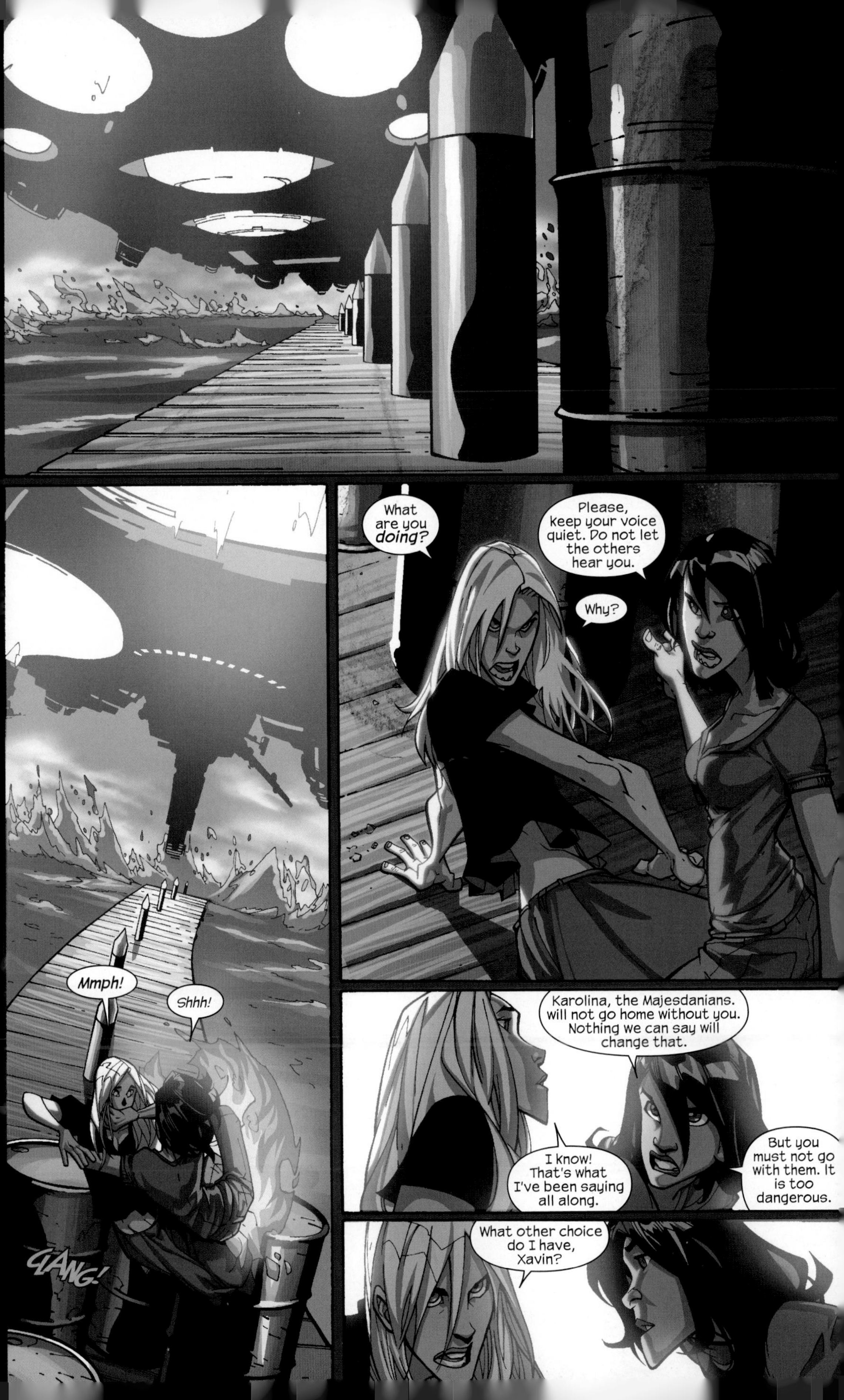
Mmph!
Shhh!
CLANG!
What are you *doing*?
Please, keep your voice quiet. Do not let the others hear you.
Why?
Karolina, the Majesdanians. will not go home without you. Nothing we can say will change that.
I know! That's what I've been saying all along.
But you must not go with them. It is too dangerous.
What other choice do I have, Xavin?

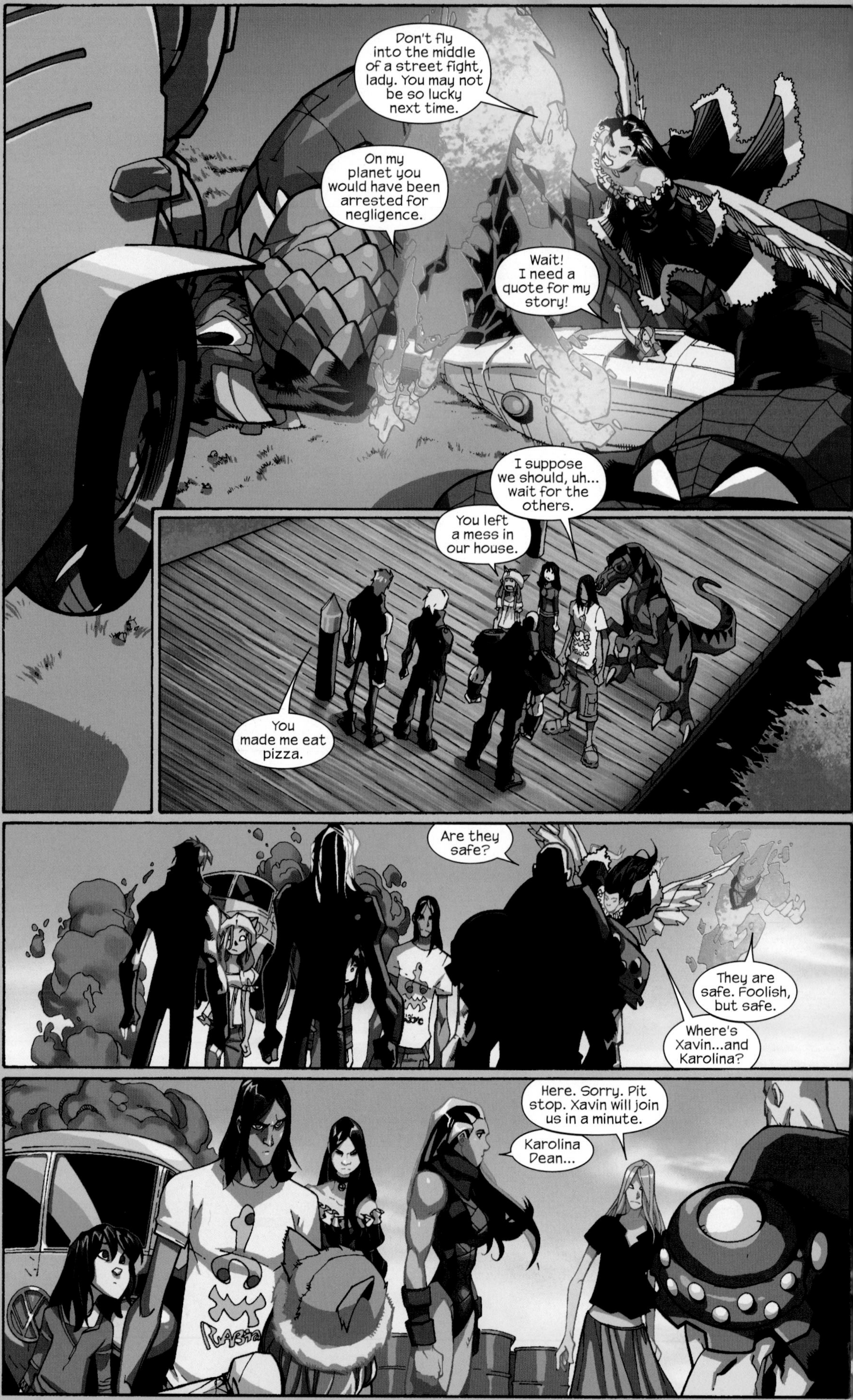
Don't fly into the middle of a street fight, lady. You may not be so lucky next time.
On my planet you would have been arrested for negligence.
Wait! I need a quote for my story!
I suppose we should, uh... wait for the others.
You left a mess in our house.
You made me eat pizza.
Are they safe?
They are safe. Foolish, but safe.
Where's Xavin...and Karolina?
Here. Sorry. Pit stop. Xavin will join us in a minute.
Karolina Dean...

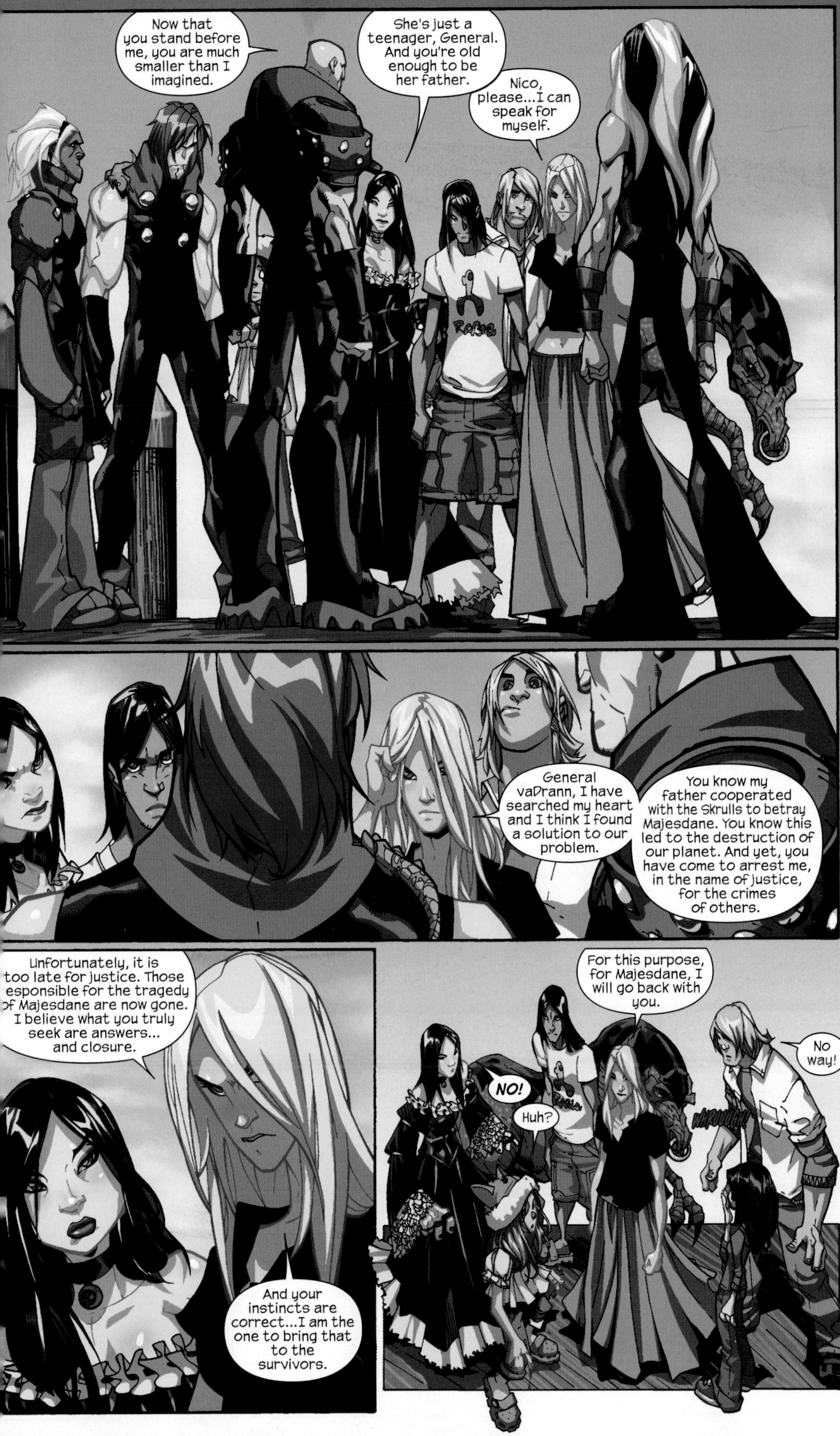
Now that you stand before me, you are much smaller than I imagined.
She's just a teenager, General. And you're old enough to be her father.
Nico, please...I can speak for myself.
General vaDrann, I have searched my heart and I think I found a solution to our problem.
You know my father cooperated with the Skrulls to betray Majesdane. You know this led to the destruction of our planet. And yet, you have come to arrest me, in the name of justice, for the crimes of others.
Unfortunately, it is too late for justice. Those esponsible for the tragedy of Majesdane are now gone. I believe what you truly seek are answers... and closure.
And your instincts are correct...I am the one to bring that to the survivors.
For this purpose, for Majesdane, I will go back with you.
NO!
Huh?
No way!

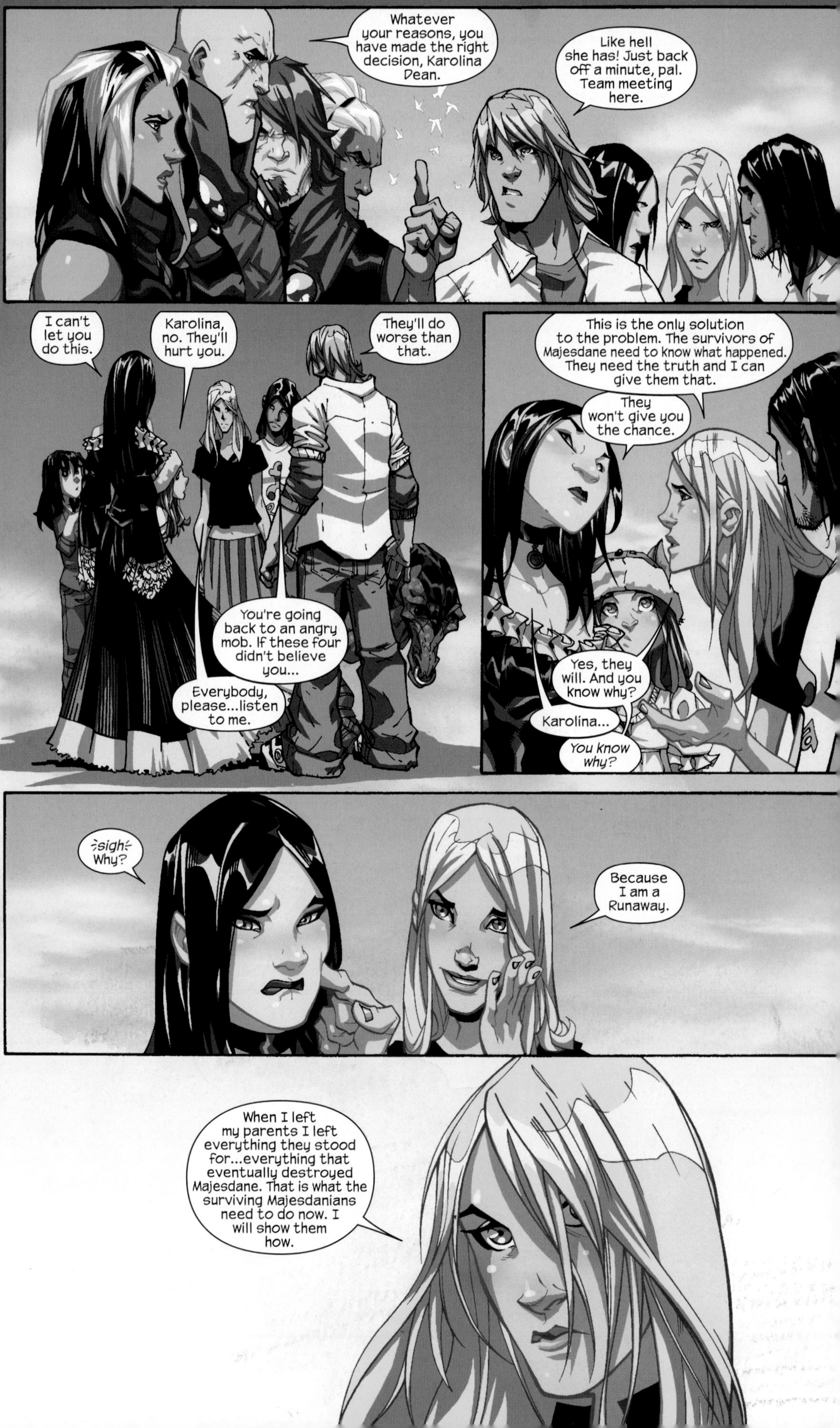
Whatever your reasons, you have made the right decision, Karolina Dean.
Like hell she has! Just back off a minute, pal. Team meeting here.
I can't let you do this.
Karolina, no. They'll hurt you.
They'll do worse than that.
You're going back to an angry mob. If these four didn't believe you...
Everybody, please...listen to me.
This is the only solution to the problem. The survivors of Majesdane need to know what happened. They need the truth and I can give them that.
They won't give you the chance.
Yes, they will. And you know why?
Karolina...
You know why?
sigh Why?
Because I am a Runaway.
When I left my parents I left everything they stood for...everything that eventually destroyed Majesdane. That is what the surviving Majesdanians need to do now. I will show them how.

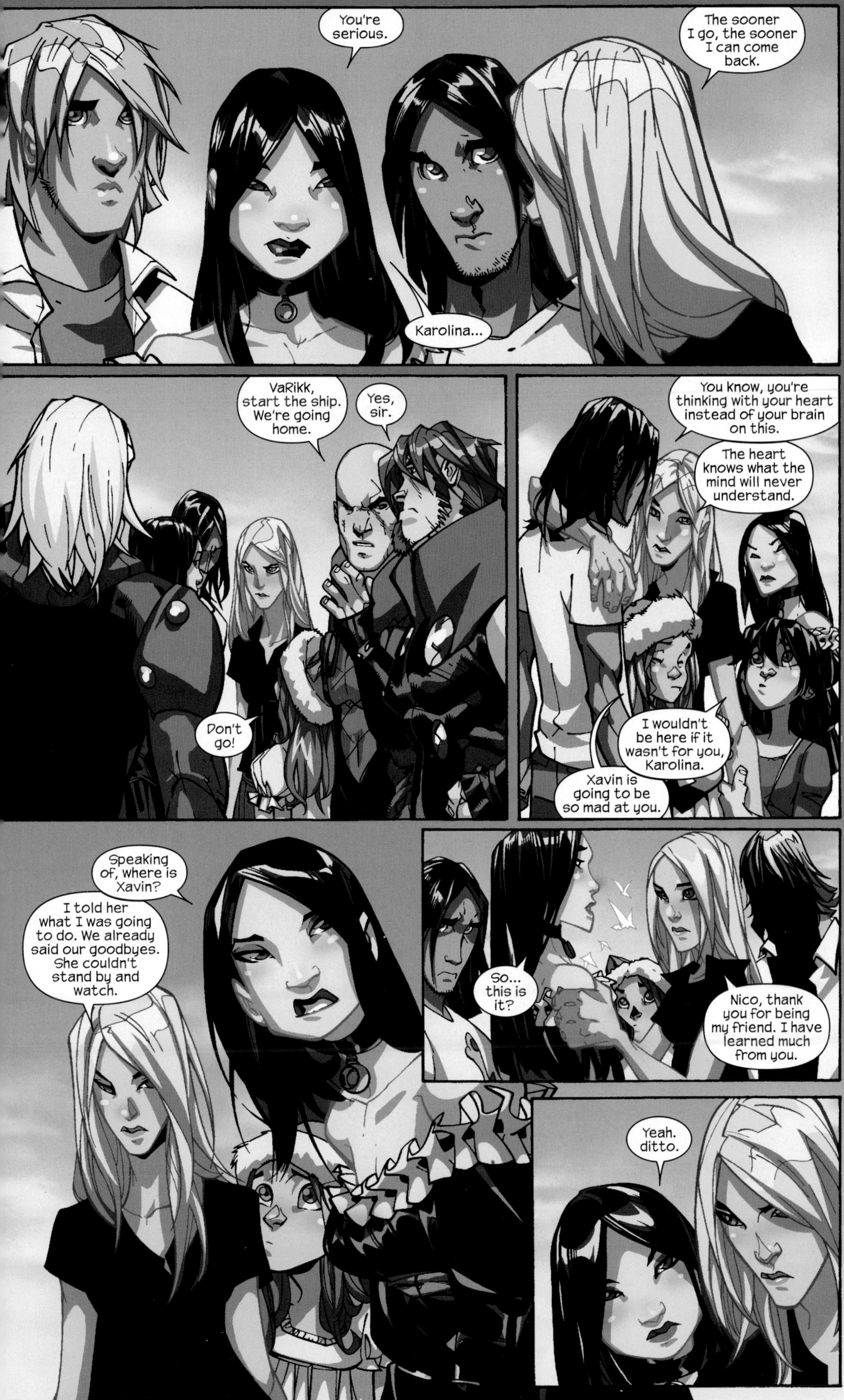
You're serious.
The sooner I go, the sooner I can come back.
Karolina...
VaRikk, start the ship. We're going home.
Yes, sir.
Don't go!
You know, you're thinking with your heart instead of your brain on this.
The heart knows what the mind will never understand.
I wouldn't be here if it wasn't for you, Karolina.
Xavin is going to be so mad at you.
Speaking of, where is Xavin?
I told her what I was going to do. We already said our goodbyes. She couldn't stand by and watch.
So... this is it?
Nico, thank you for being my friend. I have learned much from you.
Yeah. ditto.

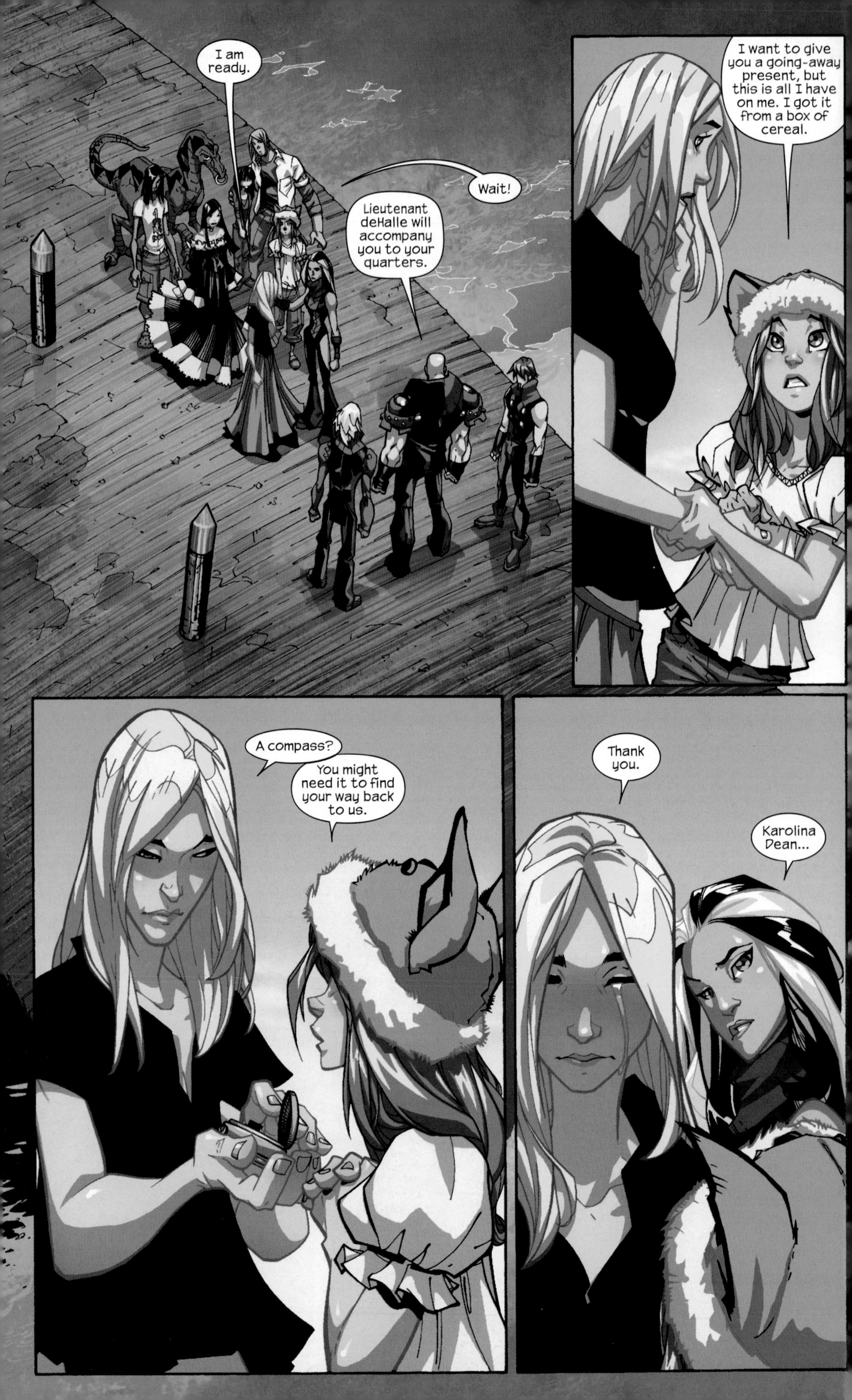
I am ready.
Wait!
Lieutenant deHalle will accompany you to your quarters.
I want to give you a going-away present, but this is all I have on me. I got it from a box of cereal.
A compass?
You might need it to find your way back to us.
Thank you.
Karolina Dean...

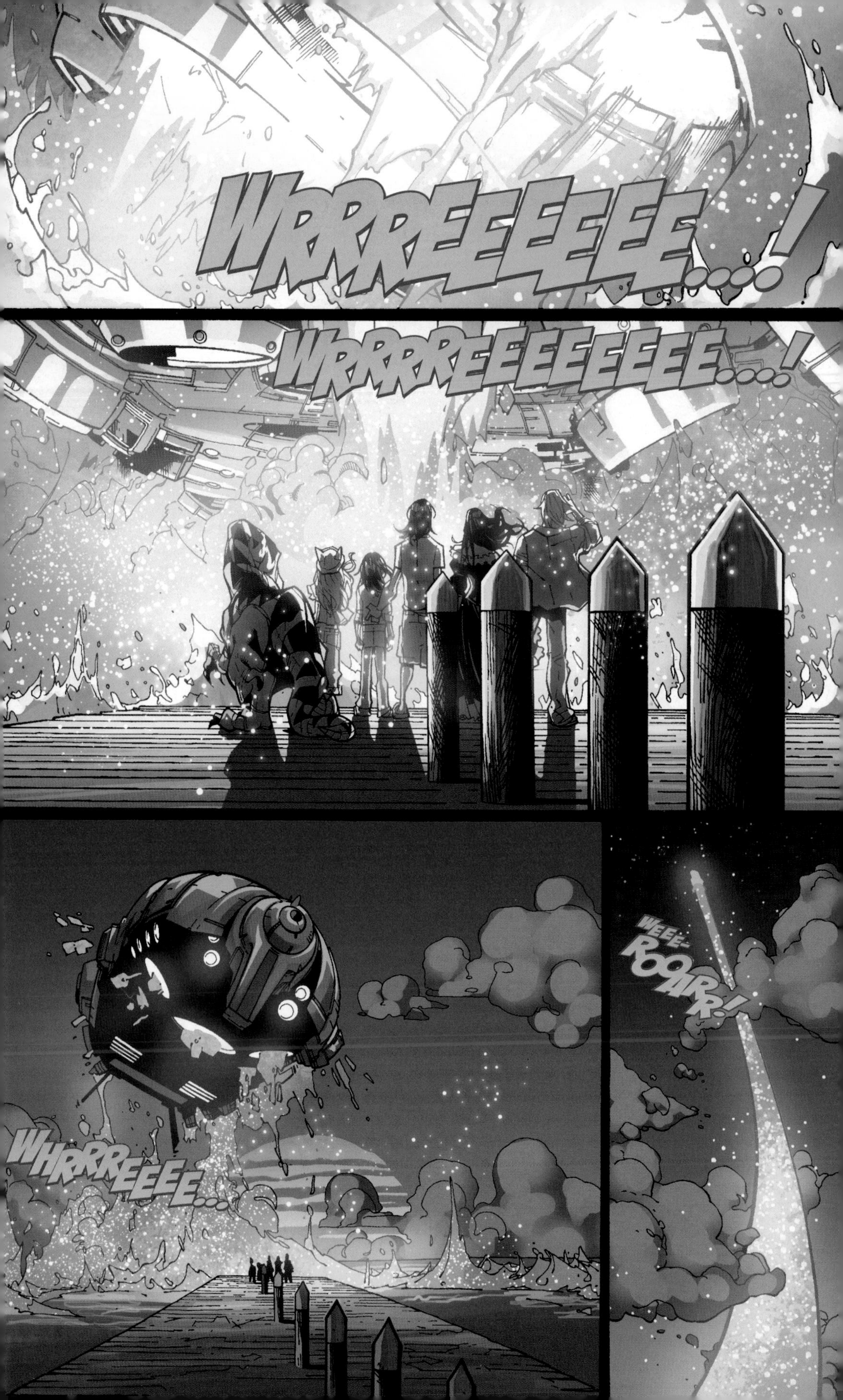
WRRREEEEEEE....!
WRRRRREEEEEEEEE....!
WHRRREEEE...
WEEE-ROOARR!

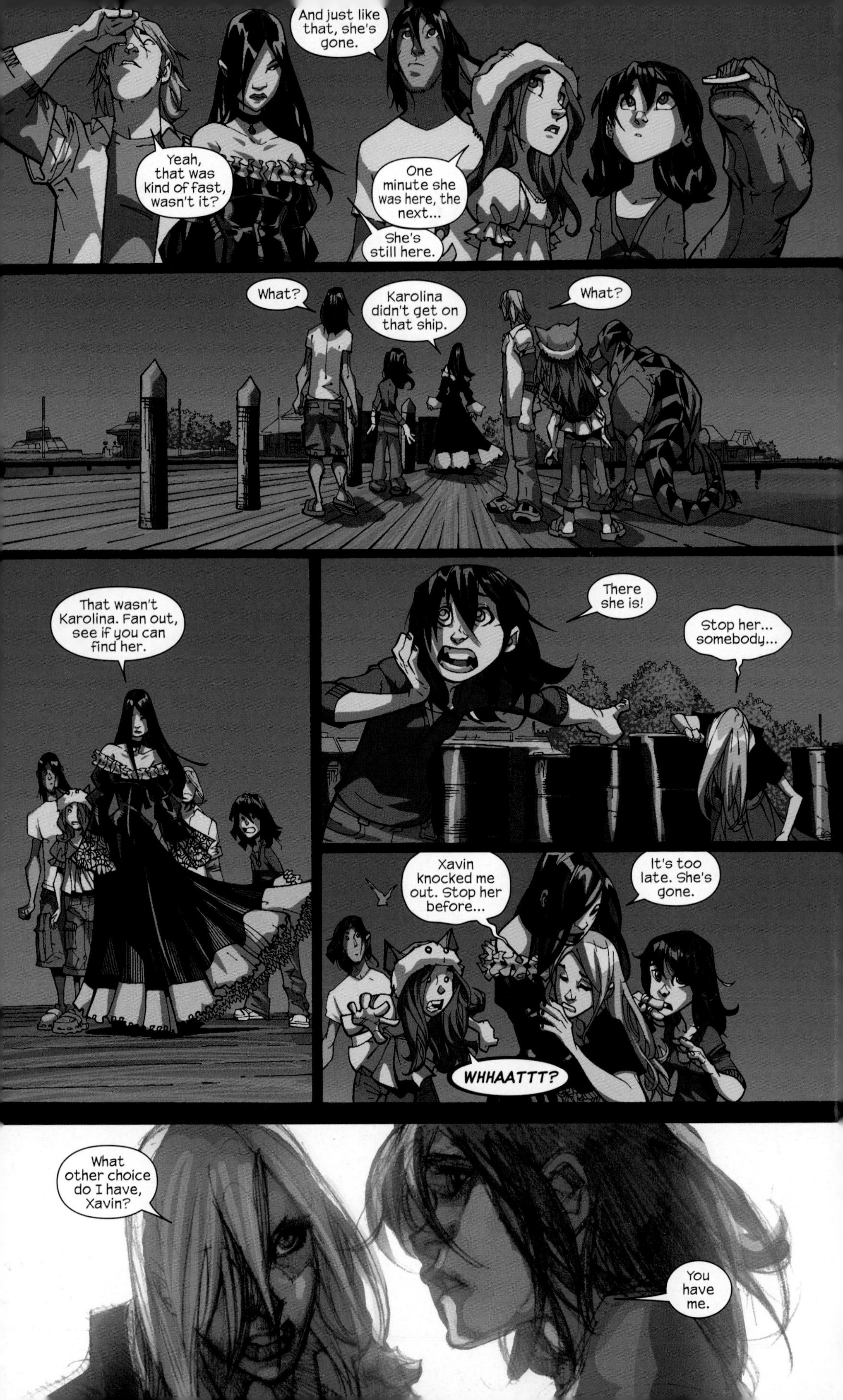
And just like that, she's gone.
Yeah, that was kind of fast, wasn't it?
One minute she was here, the next...
She's still here.
What?
Karolina didn't get on that ship.
What?
That wasn't Karolina. Fan out, see if you can find her.
There she is!
Stop her... somebody...
Xavin knocked me out. Stop her before...
It's too late. She's gone.
WHHAATTT?
What other choice do I have, Xavin?
You have me.

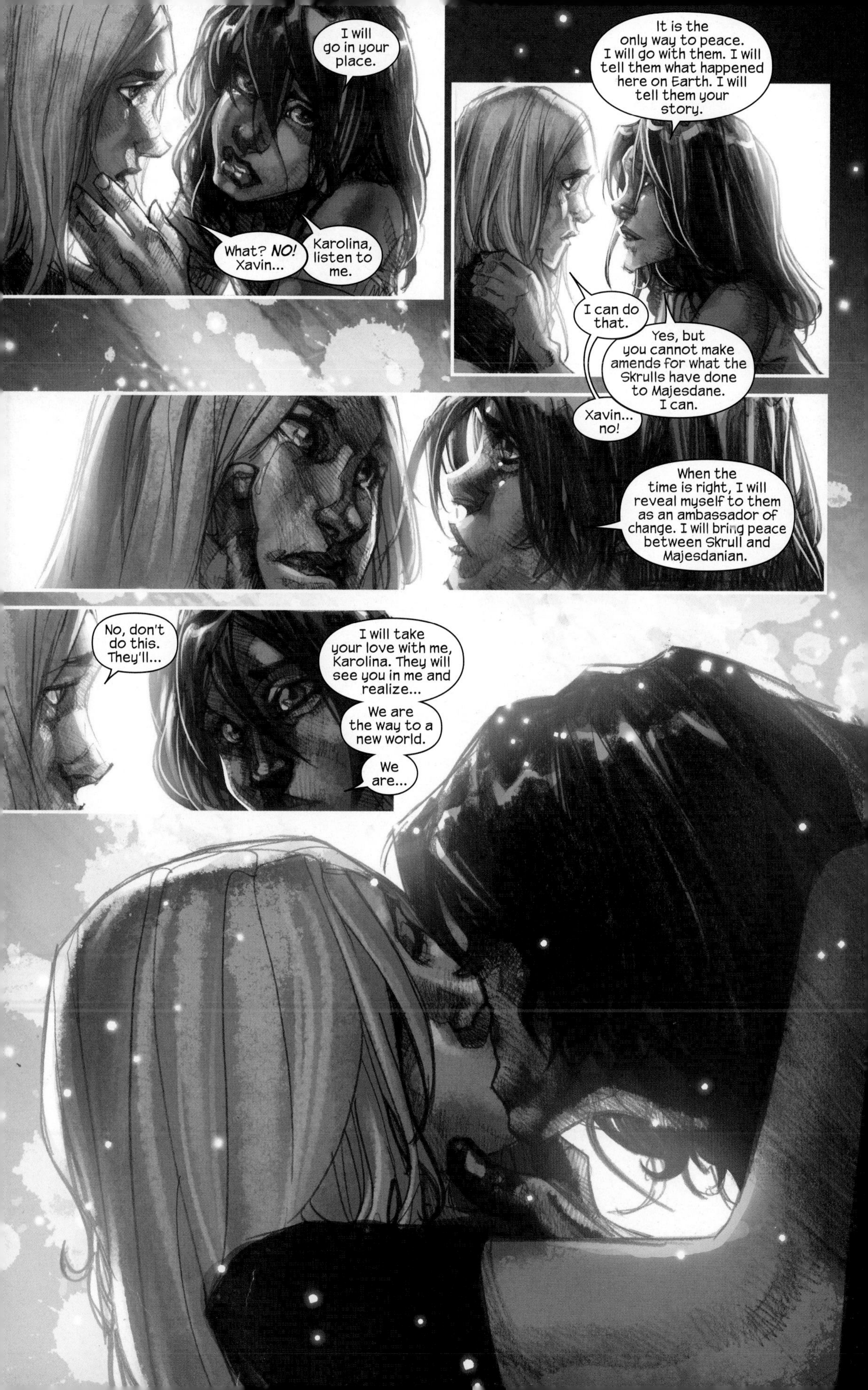

I will go in your place.
What? NO! Xavin...
Karolina, listen to me.
It is the only way to peace. I will go with them. I will tell them what happened here on Earth. I will tell them your story.
I can do that.
Yes, but you cannot make amends for what the Skrulls have done to Majesdane. I can.
Xavin... no!
When the time is right, I will reveal myself to them as an ambassador of change. I will bring peace between Skrull and Majesdanian.
No, don't do this. They'll...
I will take your love with me, Karolina. They will see you in me and realize...
We are the way to a new world.
We are...

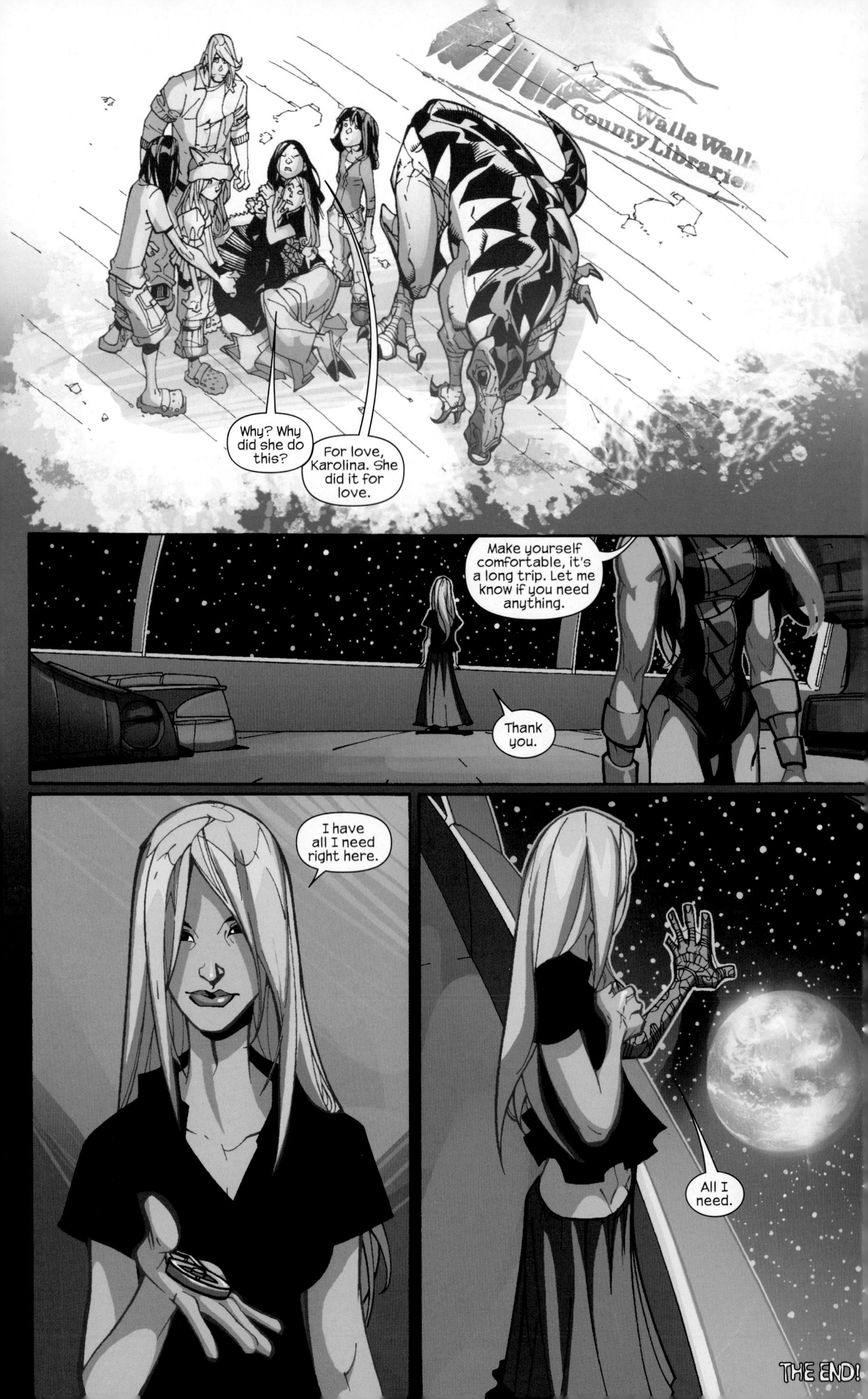
Why? Why did she do this?
For love, Karolina. She did it for love.
Make yourself comfortable, it's a long trip. Let me know if you need anything.
Thank you.
I have all I need right here.
All I need.
THE END!